Till He Come

[Communion Meditations]

By:

Ivan Herald

© 2023

Till He Come
[Communion Meditations]
Copyright © 2023.
Ivan Herald

 *FAME*

(Australian <u>F</u>amily <u>A</u>nd <u>M</u>arriage <u>E</u>ducation)

Revised Edition.
The original production of 'Till He Come' was available only on CD providing Ministers & Churches the ability to run off respective studies. The origins of this work go back to the mid-1970s. This edition has been fully reworked, re-edited and extended.

ISBN: 978-0-9585226-7-0

All rights reserved. No part of this publication, either text, diagrams, photographs or cover may be reproduced, stored in a retrieval system (except for e-book purchases) or transmitted in any form or by any means electronic, mechanical, photocopying, recording, or any other manner except for quotations in printed reviews, without the prior permission of the author, publisher, and/or the copyright holder.

2023 Cover design by: Nieva Cayabyab (Philippines)

INDEX

Preface To 'Till He Come'	6
Study/Meditation 1 – Adam's Table	10
Study/Meditation 2 – Cain And Abel's Table	15
Study/Meditation 3 – Noah's Table	20
Study/Meditation 4 – The Post-Flood Table	26
Study/Meditation 5 – Melchizedek's Table – Part 1 A Table Provided	32
Study/Meditation 6 – Melchizedek's Table – Part 2 A Table For The Righteous	38
Study/Meditation 7 – Abraham's Altar Table	43
Study/Meditation 8 – The Wilderness Table	50
Study/Meditation 9 – Tabernacle Table – Part 1 The Table Of Shewbread	56
Study/Meditation 10 – Tabernacle Table – Part 2 The Position Of The Table	63
Study/Meditation 11 – Tabernacle Table – Part 3 Service And Servants Of The Table	69
Study/Meditation 12 – Table Of Recompense	76
Study/Meditation 13 – Ruth's Table	83
Study/Meditation 14 – The Table Of Saul	90
Study/Meditation 15 – Psalm 23 Table – Part 1 What A Preparation	95
Study/Meditation 16 – Psalm 23 Table – Part 2 What A Victory	102
Study/Meditation 17 – The Table Of David For Mephibosheth	107
Study/Meditation 18 – Solomon's Temple Table	114
Study/Meditation 19 – The Table Of Solomon – Part 1 The Magnitude Of The Table	120
Study/Meditation 20 – The Table Of Solomon – Part 2 The Incomparable Table	126
Study/Meditation 21 – The Table Of Solomon – Part 3 The Standing Of His Servants	132

Study/Meditation 22 – The Table Of Solomon – Part 4 Descending From The Throne To The Table	138
Study/Meditation 23 – The Table Of Solomon – Part 5 The Table Of The Beloved	144
Study/Meditation 24 – The Shulamite's Table – Part 1 The Circular Table	150
Study/Meditation 25 – The Shulamite's Table – Part 2 The Response That Flowed	158
Study/Meditation 26 – Jezebel's Table	167
Study/Meditation 27 – The Table Of Elijah	173
Study/Meditation 28 – The Restored Table Of Hezekiah	178
Study/Meditation 29 – The Table Of Nehemiah	185
Study/Meditation 30 – Malachi's Table	191
Study/Meditation 31 – The Christmas Table	198
Study/Meditation 32 – The Table – A Place Of Manners	203
Study/Meditation 33 – The Table Of Crumbs	208
Study/Meditation 34 – The Garments Of The Table	214
Study/Meditation 35 – The Last Supper – Part 1 A Table Prepared	224
Study/Meditation 36 – The Last Supper – Part 2 A Table Instituted	230
Study/Meditation 37 – The Last Supper – Part 3 Table Of Service	236
Study/Meditation 38 – The Last Supper – Part 4 Betrayal At The Table	242
Study/Meditation 39 – The Table Of Emmaus	248
Study/Meditation 40 – The Table Of The Early Church	254
Study/Meditation 41 – Tables Of The Heart	260
Study/Meditation 42 – The Lord's Table	265
Study/Meditation 43 – Communion Of The Body And Blood Of Christ	270
Study/Meditation 44 – The Cup Of Blessing	275
Study/Meditation 45 – A Table Of Comparisons	281

Study/Meditation 46 – Paul's Table Teaching – Part 1 A Table Received	287
Study/Meditation 47 – Paul's Table Teaching – Part 2 The Proof Of The Table	291
Study/Meditation 48 – Paul's Table Teaching – Part 3 The Warning	297
Study/Meditation 49 – The Table Of The Marriage Supper Of The Lamb – Part 1 The Table And Its Surroundings	304
Study/Meditation 50 – The Table Of The Marriage Supper Of The Lamb – Part 2 The Bride Of The Table	310
Study/Meditation 51 – The Great Table Of God's Wrath	316
Study/Meditation 52 – The Millennial Table	321
Conclusion To The Studies & Meditations	326

PREFACE

There are several parts of the liturgy of the church that are common across most Christian denominations, but special to each is 'Communion.' It survives by many names: Holy Communion; The Lord's Table; The Eucharist; The Lord's Supper; Breaking of Bread; The Last Supper; The Sacrament – on the names and personal preferences go.

I Corinthians 11: 26 refers to the fact that we are encouraged to participate in 'Communion,' *'Till He Come.'* Jesus is coming back and the sacrament of 'Communion' not only reminds us again of the potency of the work of salvation in our daily life but the glorious hope and reality that Jesus is coming back again. Interesting that this church practice of 'Communion,' reminding us of our glorious salvation, is interconnected with the concept and reality of the Second Coming of Christ.

Some churches celebrate 'Communion' every week, others once a month. Various other patterns prevail according to local church preferences. One ought not to be critical of the pattern of how other churches celebrate 'Communion,' but appreciate that each church has to develop its own culture, with good reason, which will include the acceptance of when and how often 'Communion' is celebrated.

One of the primary reasons this work was originally written was to broaden the minds of those presenting 'Communion' to their local congregation. I wanted them to think outside of the tradition of repetitively using the famed and oft-quoted, though beautiful I Corinthians 11: 23 to 34 passage as their sole centrality of thought for the church's 'Communion' service.

There is nothing wrong with using this I Corinthian 11 passage, but to have it read fifty-two times in the church's yearly pattern of services is a bit much. It doesn't show originality in presenting the great 'Communion' message.

Allow one caution about this work. Obviously, when reading each of the Studies and/or Meditations you will see there is far more information than can be transmitted in a single 'Communion' service. The studies are not written for you to fully read out. I am just presenting an environment for you to think more broadly about the 'Communion' service. I want you to become excited about a 'Communion' message, so that such an atmosphere of excitement may transmit to those in the church 'Communion' service.

Certainly use what is presented. But, temper how much you use. Condense it. Keep it tight, short and impactful. Possibly break up a single Study/Meditation perhaps into two communion messages. Use the central theme of the study/meditation, but always watch time. It is not your moment of glory to present communion, it is your honour. Don't spoil it.

Churches **don't** need or want a second sermon around the Communion Table. No one wants another message in the service with a second speaker different from the preacher for that day. I've seen people lasting ten to fifteen minutes just sharing his/her communion message and comments, let alone dispersing the elements of communion.

Often, and sadly, I have seen individuals, who are presenting 'Communion,' engrossed in their own mini-sermon, wandering from one Scripture to another. The texts are often interconnecting in their thinking, but the congregation can't see the connection at all. They wonder where it's all heading.

'Communion' should be an inspired moment redirecting us back to the wondrous work of salvation. Take the central thought of each Study/Meditation and inspire people with a fresh approach to celebrating 'Communion.'

In concluding this Preface let us consider six quick comparisons of what 'Communion' is and what it is not, or more correctly should not become.

Ritual Vs Reality

It is so easy to let 'Communion' become a ritual within our church and life individually, instead of it being a personal reality, where the wonder and grace of salvation flood over us afresh. Always opt for reality.

Personal Vs Predictable

'Communion' should be something very personal to each of us, rather than a predictable part of the church service. Certainly, it may predictably be in the church service, but we choose for this time for us to have a personal and intimate encounter with our Saviour and the wonder of the salvation He has purchased for us.

The only thing predictable is we're going to have true personal time and experience with the Lord.

Life Vs Liturgy

There is nothing wrong with church liturgy – the way a church 'does church,' and conducts its service. However, don't let 'Communion' become so formalised, enshrined and institutionalised, becoming set in stone in a ritualistic performance, like other aspects of the service. Instead, it should be injecting life into the service for each participant, 'Communion' is more than liturgy – the way we do things, it is life and a fresh encounter with the giver of life.

Inspirational Vs Indoctrination

'Communion' should be inspirational leaving individuals feeling like they have touched the Lord in a fresh way during the service. Though it embraces doctrine, it is not merely an indoctrination moment. It is an inspirational moment.

Renewal Vs Religious

The time of 'Communion' should not merely be a religious act, though it embraces religion. It should be a time of renewal of our faith. It may embrace repentance as we consider the great work of the cross to be everyday practical and potent in our life. It is more than a religious moment it is the renewal of our faith.

Encounter Vs Evading

'Communion' brings us again to an encounter with our God and the work of salvation. People can evade this truth through religious adherence and ceremony. But we are merely using religion to mask relationships. With such an attitude we are evading an encounter with God. Communion should be an opportunity to meet God again through an encounter yet again with salvation's principles.

The origins of this work go back to the mid-1970s when I laboriously typed sections of the studies and meditations out on a non-electric typewriter.

Well, do I remember hiking into the bush on a friend's property with my tent, water, bible and my trusty typewriter, which basically weighed more than the rest of what I was carrying put together. I was on a four-day prayer, and fasting retreat. I recall typing out a few of these studies as a form of personal meditation during that time away.

When I started with what is now this work, I had absolutely no intention of creating fifty-two chapters or studies, equal to the weeks of the year. Truly it just happened. Since their origins, I have revised and revisited the studies and meditations several times to renew them and update their approach, but this is the first time they have appeared in book format.

Trusting these fifty-two studies will inspire you and cause you to celebrate every time you participate in 'Communion,' *Till He Come.*

Ivan Herald
Sydney
© 2023

(Australian **F**amily **A**nd **M**arriage **E**ducation)

Study/Meditation 1

ADAM'S TABLE

Take your mind back to that glorious beginning when mankind was at peace with God and themselves, in harmony with the very forces that created their existence. Man and animal alike lived in untold splendour in the exquisite beauty of the Garden of Eden. Allow your hearts to reflect upon this sense of utter tranquility and harmony that surpasses anything this world can presently see, or will see, 'Till He Come.'

Birds of a thousand colours swept in graceful arcs in the heavens glinting a shimmering display of beauty that left the earth bathed in the consciousness of: "Then God saw everything that He had made, and indeed *it was* very good." (Genesis 1: 31). Flowers burst upon the sight in an incredible array of perfumed beauty and skilful design.

Animals lounged in quiet resting repose in this atmosphere of peacefulness. No animal viewed another as food. Clear crystal streams flowed from the mountains through the garden. Lambs, gazelles and squirrels muzzled for forage beside the blissful lion. This was Eden. Tranquility and beauty became kissing cousins and joy was spread everywhere.

It seemed that in the late afternoon, the entire creative realm shifted with warm expectancy. They were stirred with a consciousness that the creator, through His voice, was soon to walk in the midst of the garden. He would commune and fellowship, with His supreme-created masterpiece – mankind.

Adam walked softly over inviting thornless carpets of green. His dominion was respected and the entire creative world responded to his voice as he spoke. With Eve at his side, they expressed a perfect relationship of fellowship to which they had been created. The creator, ushered in by His voice, came: "Walking in the cool of the day." (Genesis 1: 8). His voice penetrated, and reverberated every corner of Eden. It brought a warm assurance to all His creation. It flowed like a symphony of streams and the creative realm lay breathless in the presence of the creator.

Every created creature turned in attentive submission to the passage of Adam, Eve and their Lord. We are not told how long or how many years this tranquility continued before sin laid its evil hand upon the purity of Eden. Daily the first couple would feed on the entire creative supply of food and drink from unpolluted streams, where there was not even a hint of contamination, let alone its presence.

The instructions to Adam were very simple, outlining a clear pathway of creative natural harmony. "And the Lord God commanded the man, saying: 'Of every tree of the garden you may freely eat; but of the tree of the knowledge of good and evil you shall not eat, for in the day that you eat of it you shall surely die'," (Genesis 2: 16, 17).

Daily in the wide expanses of Eden, Adam and most likely Eve 'dressed' or tended to the wondrous exotic garden. Pruned and cared for trees responded under the hand of Adam, and the divine law of growth that was embedded in all species by the creator.

But what was Adam's personal diet of food like? What food provisions did Adam and Eve enjoy on a daily basis? The Word shares about the ability of Adam to eat from the total range of the trees of the garden, with the exception of the tree of the knowledge of good and evil. We can imagine daily, as they tended the great trees of Eden, that they would have gathered exotic fruits, nuts and other food supplies produced by nature as food for their own use.

Daily they would have spread their heaven-provided supply upon a soft carpet of green, so rich in colour and texture, soft to the touch, free of any weed, thorn or intrusion. Nor were the first couple maligned by a hundred annoying insects.

The creative world became the 'Table of Adam.' Beside those colossal rivers, whose purity exceeded crystal-clear, as a contrast to today, a heavenly picnic occurred. It was God's masterpiece feeding and living on God's provisions. This did not nullify the fact that Satan and all the demonic beings breathed in fiery indignation awaiting the hour they would tempt man to fall.

God has always spread a table through His own love and provision. At Calvary was spread the greatest provision that man has ever known. Divinely planned with eternity in mind we may sit at His 'River of Life,' and enjoy the benefits of the Table of the Lord, spread by a loving Heavenly Father.

It is interesting that basically all of the daily provisions of Adam and Eve were from the tree. On every occasion that the Lord's Table is prepared before us, whether in the splendour of a cathedral, or the humbleness of a field, the provisions of the table have been taken from the tree.

On Calvary's tree, Christ died as the greatest provision that man can ever require. Even as Adam sat and ate at his table of natural wonder and beauty, he prefigured what every Christian must do – feed on the work of the tree, the cross of Calvary. The hymn of old says: "Lest I forget Gethsemane. Lest I forget Thine agony. Lest I forget Thy love for me. Lead me to Calvary."

Adam sat bathed in creative wonder and ate of God's provision. The Son of God however died in darkness to become our provision. The first Adam was sustained in his fellowship with his Lord God by the provision of the tree. The second Adam renewed that fellowship with humanity by becoming the fruit of the tree.

God spread Adam's table in splendour. How much less is the Table of the Lord? Can we imagine the first notes of discord, those first aggressive guttural growls of a now ravenous beast, hiding in rebellion in the garden, that rippled through Eden, following the first violation of man with his God? Adam and Eve's eating of the forbidden fruit that eventful day did not satisfy them. It totally changed creation. Potential death now entered into the framework of creation.

Hiding, both Adm and Eve trembled at hearing God's voice on this first post-sin occasion. Adam's mind was in constant agony of the meeting he was dreading. Never before had it happened. The voice of God came walking in the garden, in the cool of the day and Eden was strangely, tragically muted. The shrill cries of ecstatic joy and rejoicing, that had always previously filled the throat of all created species, whenever the creator had walked amongst His creation, were ominously still. Something had changed. A growl for the first time was heard from somewhere.

Adam and Eve could feel the silence of Eden and it seemed the voice of God late that day was more penetrating than ever before. They had partaken of the forbidden tree. Their table was now spread with a recompense of divine judgement.

In honesty, we can approach the Lord's Table fully well knowing our own hearts are not right with the creator. We sense the stillness in the garden of our hearts (Song of Solomon 4: 12), and we know we have offended a pardoning God. The once soft, spike-less growing thistle now seems sharp to the feet of Eden's offender. The animals now held a cautious glance and distance. Mankind was now their enemy. Often we too can find the softness of God, and the creative splendours of God, turning into sharp pricks in our hearts as we draw near to the table with an offending heart.

Adam's table was broken. Unfinished food lay rotting for the first time in Eden as a terror-stricken creation hid. Once docile animals looked for the first time at another species as food, letting out a guttural growl.

But, God's purposes in man can now begin again through the provision of the tree of Calvary. The rotting effects of sin have been dealt with. But, at the table, our hearts must face up to the self-examination spoken about by the Word of God. Communion should leave the individuals reconciled in fellowship with their God again.

Nothing remains of that original table of fellowship, which Adam had with his God. No soft carpet of grasses so green, such as was present in Eden's glory, still exists. Yet, we do have a table of such rare beauty, which can fully meet the total needs of man. I can imagine Adam and Eve in the sweat and labour of their later years, after being expelled from Eden, sitting down remorsefully discussing the splendour of Eden lost.

God created and fully provided for Adam's table. Is ours in this day and age any different? Adam fed on the provision of the tree. Today we also feed on such a provision. The all-atoning death of Christ, on Calvary's tree, prevails magnificently for all humanity. But, we must appropriate it personally and in sincerity.

Study/Meditation 2

CAIN AND ABEL'S TABLE

One of our strongest motivations, when we come to the Lord's Table, is personal self-examination, and the consequent correction of our life before the Lord. Such an attitude reaps a harvest of blessings. Anything less creates an uneasy ground for fellowship. "For if we judge ourselves, we would not be judged," (I Corinthians 11: 31).

In searching for a pattern or shadow of this principle, none seems more relevant to me than that illustrated in the life of Cain and Abel, when as brothers they initially brought their respective sacrifices to the Lord.

Both Cain and Abel would have been fully aware of the lost resplendent glory of Eden, as recounted by their remorseful parents. Both were now living out the severe penalty of sin. Yet, both were moving towards reconciling that relationship with Almighty God. It is interesting to notice that both appear to be genuinely seeking reconciliation with God before any mention of their parents doing the same.

In the initial motives of these two young men, we must be careful not to underplay the heart of Cain in his original devotion to bring a sacrifice. We understand from other passages in the Old Testament that several products of the field were used in acceptable sacrifice or within sacrificial acts in Israel's day. They were accepted. So don't reject the sacrifice purely on the basis of what it was. Although the substance is important, it seems it was the condition of Cain's heart that let him down.

On that eventful day, described briefly in Genesis 4: 3 to 8, we sense something of unity with these two men. They both together toiled to make a living out of the hard ground. The seemingly resistant ground already had become hard, in some places impenetrable. The soft, warm soils of Eden had been replaced with dry weed-infested plains and valleys. Fruit once grew with automatic ease in Eden. A thousand fruits and a multitude of harvests graced Eden's provision. Now that was all gone.

Cain and Abel knew nothing but hard labour. Hard toil eked out a meagre existence in sweat that, through a hard investment of time, they were acquiring skills to cause the soil to yield her bountifulness. The passage tends to imply Cain and Abel lived in close proximity to each other, probably turning their respective hands to their innate skills in the gruelling hours of the day's labour.

Of particular interest is the phrase: "And in the process of time it came to pass." Apparently, there had been something smouldering, burning in the hearts of these young men. Perhaps the conversation between the parents had inspired them. Or, perhaps their mutual discussion and desire to realign themself in a relationship with God had inspired them.

As that day burst forth in golden sunshine, melting away the last traces of the regular morning mist that watered the ground, two young men set out across the ground still moist from the evening's wet blanket. Clearly behind them lay their footprints in the dew-encrusted ground. It is hard often to erase where we have come from unless the Sun of Righteousness rises and dissolves our tracks, till they are but a memory.

There definitely seems to be a common location, a common altar where Cain and Abel brought their individual sacrifices to. That alone illustrates their communal attitudes. But, from that point onwards, individual differences marked these two young men, their motivation and their sacrifices.

A common table or altar stood before them. Yet in every sense, they brought varied offerings, gifts, emotions and reactions. The table we come to is a common table, yet a variety of heart conditions come before it or around it. Make no mistake; your presence at the table does not vindicate your total acceptance. As nice as any one congregation may appear, every heart is distinctively different and personally accountable to Almighty God for the expression of their heart at that time. A common table does not mean a common congregation. Let every heart make a personal examination of its own heart.

On that fateful day one offering was acceptable, yet, one offering was not. We can only allow our imagination to run endless trains of thought trying to conceive how the Lord personally revealed the acceptance of one and the rejection of another.

The emotional scene had changed. The two high-spirited young men that had come with a common purpose to that altar were now not the same men. One was aware of God's acceptance, and perhaps with his face turned heavenward he was lost in the reality that the table or altar had brought him into the right relationship with God.

The other brother, Cain, was sullen, downcast, and facially moved to annoyance and anger that his offering was not acceptable like his brothers. It could have been some minutes before each was aware of the other's state of mind.

Abel was naturally lost in the blessing of acceptance. Cain was left grovelling in the agony and self-pity of the non-acceptance of his offering. Whether words were exchanged or not we do not know. But, there was a growing awareness of the difference between the two.

We must raise something here that I feel is indicative of the heart of God. It considers that whenever one comes around the Lord's Table in a state that is unacceptable, the Lord always in some way tries to share His concern so correction may be made, edemption reached. Note in the 6th verse how the Lord spoke personally to Cain to rectify the situation.

With careful attention to the Word of God, we see that Cain would have been spoken to by God very shortly after the time that he realised his offering was unacceptable. Correction with any child is always needed exactly at the point of disorder or disobedience. So the Lord comes or desires to come, around the table and personally reveal to each of us any disharmony in our hearts that creates friction in the fellowship we have with our creator.

I have often personally found that around the table the service seems to 'soften.' The Lord seems to move into and through our hearts, as we bare ourselves to His holy search.

God certainly wishes to move right into our hearts in holy examination and yet He must have a willing vessel. He must not have a heart like Cain.

God gave Cain an opportunity to repent and he rejected it. Nice Sunday dress, pleasant smiles and rapt attention to the words of whoever is ministering to the Lord's Table do not constitute the necessary conditions of acceptance at the Table of the Lord, as noble as these traits may be. Just as beauty is skin deep, devotion and consecration go much deeper than the exteriors we are so commonly prone to look at.

Note the very gracious admonition of the Lord to Cain. "If you do well, won't you be accepted?" (Vr. 7). But, anger was seated in Cain at the altar that day, not an open, contrite, humble heart. A seething heart turned Cain's spirit sour. Never let us allow our hearts to think that Cain did not have a fair chance. The choice was his. He chose badly.

The totally acceptable sacrifice was already on the altar before him. He could do the same. That which was acceptable had already been slain on the altar of love. As we partake of the Lord's Table the acceptable is clearly before us.

There both men stood, probably dressed in skins as their parents had done. Their very dress spoke of the covering sacrifice, as blood had been shed in Eden to provide skin clothes for the offending parents. The principle of acceptance and covering for sin had been initiated in Eden, through a loving heavenly Father providing skins of animals that He must have slain.

Can you imagine the very emotion of horror rippling like a frightening chill throughout every creature of Eden, as they became consciously aware that blood, blood akin to theirs, was being shed to cover sinful man? Cain knew it yet his heart hardened even as he beheld the acceptable sacrifice of Abel on the altar before him.

Opportunity to correct was extended, yet vengeance bred in the chasms of his dissatisfied heart. He was sovereignly warned that if he did nothing about it: "Sin lies at the door," (Vr. 7). How often do men and women sit in communion services with their spirits cowered by the enemy within, as he maligns their sense of dedication? The right of the altar is immediate correction, rectification and justification. The Lord graciously uses this time to engender deep soft responses with His new creation. How will we respond?

Is there not one of us, at some time, that has not turned a cold heart towards an inviting loving God, who stands at the door of our heart? It is our duty to issue a warning that there is a price to pay for any stubborn rebellion. Didn't Paul himself instruct us along these lines in I Corinthians 11: 28 to 32?

Cain and Abel's Table fell to ruin and Cain to disgrace, as he had rebelled against God, and murdered his brother. Their table had been their altar. Yet one man left the table out of fellowship with both God and his brother.

The Lord's Table was built from human ruin redeeming man back to grace. But, the supreme test is the attitude of the heart that we bring to the table. What lies deep within your heart?

Study/Meditation 3

NOAH'S TABLE

The lumbering colossal frame of wood slowly shuddered from its propped earthly moorings. Beginning to feel the buoyancy of those coursing torrents of subterranean water that were surging upwards, and the heavenly downpours that were swelling around her base, the ark gradually began to lift. The heavens seemed open beyond description or anything known up to that day.

Droplets of water, unheard of before this time, that would later become known as rain was actually falling from the sky with such force that creation was hardly able to stand the onslaught. The water mass that had previously hung over all the earth as a thick blanket, drooping as mist in the morning and blanketing the earth with warmth at night, was now collapsing inward, releasing its moisture. The earth was shuddering as it lurched from being straight on its axis to now a frightening angle.

Literally, thousands upon thousand now crowded the ark superstructure construction platforms. They were banging, clawing, beating with exhausted voices and blooded knuckles to be let into the ark. Hands black with pitch slowly sank into the swirling, violent, surging torrents that broke loose from the bowels of the earth. The desperate left long finger gouges in the pitch on the side of the ark as final marks of their procrastinated desire to get within the ark.

Mr Cynic sank beneath the mud-charged swollen waters. It had been his delight only days previously to lead a heckling session so cutting against Noah, that it had caused the preacher of righteousness to turn on his last trip into the ark with his final collection of animals and commend this sceptic to the mercy of Almighty God.

Madam Worldly Wise, who had danced near naked, in taunting defiance, deliberately provoking Noah as he preached of impending doom, held up her child as the waters sapped away her final strength, and then all was lost. She was gone in the swirling water all around her.

Then the huge craft that defied constructional imagination lifted and moved in graceful eddies, as the flood unleashed its horrors upon unrepentant humanity. The first 'titanic ship' made its way lazily wherever the currents took it.

Within the ark, there was a subdued silence. All eight occupants, although fully believing and depending upon the Word of their God, were strangely mute, divinely conscious that of all of humanity, they alone were alive in the ark.

The animals uttered a shrill cry of alarm as they felt the swell and surges of those mammoth torrents buffet their haven of safety from side to side. Yet, the rain continued its sound just discernible outside those walls of protection so strongly and thickly encasing them.

The animals seemed tamer somehow. That subjugated inner voice that had stirred them to begin their pilgrimage to the ark and file in meekly with serenity was something that hadn't been seen since the days of Eden. They shifted to balance themselves against a rising, buoyant ark. Somehow they seemed to be emotionally involved with that hour as if they realised they were chosen preservation.

Few details are left to us, through the Word of God, as to those unforgettable days that passed in the ark. For forty days the balance of life went on with an order stranger than anything any of the eight humans were accustomed to. Peter, when referring to the people of that day, makes reference when he says: "Who formerly were disobedient, when once the divine longsuffering waited in the days of Noah, while *the* ark was being prepared, in which a few, that is, eight souls, were saved through water," (I Peter 3: 20). Each of us can envisage a wealth of thoughts that would feed our imagination of those awesome days.

Come back into the ark for one day and sit observing a thankful family. Daily the family had various tasks that kept individuals quite busy. The feeding of the animals, the cleaning of the stalls, and the maintenance of the animals and their home, as it was, all took time. But, at that appointed time each day a cry went out throughout the ark: "Dinner, come and get it!" One by one from a variety of passageways emerged the family. Gathering in that area set aside for their own use they sat down at a common table to feed in thankfulness for the preservation of Almighty God.

Before the ark was finished Noah had received instruction not only in connection to its construction to ensure it would float but other intricate design features such as the pitch. A table in their common living quarters was planed and smoothed from rough timber and provided for the family. It was all part of an eternal plan, not part of an afterthought.

Before the horrific hours of Calvary, when salvation began to unfold to meet human needs, the Father destined a table of remembrance that would draw us all to appreciate His gracious mercy.

I cannot imagine a single meal passing, with that original preserved eight, where one would not comment on their privileged preservation. Our God knows the beginnings from the end and fully understood there would be a need for a table within the protecting care of the ark of salvation provided through Jesus Christ to remind us of His gracious deliverance.

Obviously, no individual who was not within the ark could feed at the table. This was the privilege of the redeemed, those within the ark. Of course, there will come those to the Lord's Table who do not understand the depth of their sin and may not be redeemed. There, right there, we have an opportunity to invite them within the ark of salvation to fully enjoy the provision of the work of Calvary and not to eat in condemnation.

God provided by divine order the provisions that the ark was to carry. The table in the ark was daily spread with the provisions of a loving God. Doesn't the Table of the Lord speak in such a way? Could any one of us earn anything of merit that could fully appreciate the efficacy of Calvary, than that which has been left to us in symbolism in the Table of the Lord?

Now it did not matter where they were in the ark, to feed meant they had to come to that table, that commonplace of eating. It was a basic common denominator. The table does not respect, but rather rejects superiority. Every man and woman, no matter where they are throughout the ark, whether in a self-perceived important position or in an obscure place, is brought to a common basis the moment they come to the table.

There is no other place to feed. Provision was only at the table. Can we imagine on one occasion that one of the family of eight was out of sorts with another? It made no difference; they could eat at no other place. Many today feel they can absent themselves with the slightest whim or fancy from the requirement to come around the table. If the eight of the ark didn't come for a meal they weren't fed. There are so many parallels that we can obviously make ourselves here about handling hurts and offences.

Women always love to decorate. Can you imagine Mrs Noah's desire to have the inside of the ark just the way she pleased? Yet the instructions of its completions were divine, not a matter of fashion trends. The order was taken out of the blueprint given to provide for an ark that would preserve them, not necessarily look beautiful.

You cannot decorate the ark of salvation with anything of your own design. It is already perfect.

Can you imagine her exasperated look, with her arms full of beautiful curtains, at seeing the inside of the ark coated with thick black pitch? After all, it was the convention in those early days of shipbuilding just to coat the boats on the outside and between the layers of side planks of a boat. Inside was not normally pitched. Surely the pitch on the inside made its very look rather distasteful. Yet there was divine logic to it all.

We are told that the pitch on the inside was for a very good reason. Nothing God ever orders is without good reason. Pitch absorbs smells and odours and would have absorbed the foul smell of the accumulating animal wastes. So often today, professional filters often use pitch for smell absorbancy.

In the ark, the very presence of animals in such close and crowded quarters created a problem. Yet the Creator of heaven and earth in His infinite wisdom was way ahead of the fashion-conscious whims of mankind. The ark was black and horrid to the sight of man within and without.

It is interesting that the Hebrew word for 'pitch' is a word that means 'atone' or 'redeem.' What a magnificent picture. Christ had died and offered us salvation from the world and sin, paralleling the pitch outside the boat. But also, He has provided an atonement inside the ark, paralleled in the pitch within, saving us from the stench of our humanity, of our own human ways, the wastes of a self-indulgent life.

We can also sense a natural rejection of men and women towards salvation. Paul puts it as follows: "To the Jews a stumbling block and to the Greeks foolishness," (I Corinthians 1: 23). Yet within the ark there was divine order, a model for the church openly enjoying salvation. There is often misunderstanding. We do not suggest that every aroma within the church is a sweet-smelling savour to the Lord.

Yet, just the same as the unsavoury smell of animal waste, so too every unsavoury part of our life can sink into submissive absorption of the ark of our Saviour. Every smell of pride and self must be immersed and absorbed in Christ's life. This is something we must allow willingly to happen to our reactions.

Any unpleasant air within the church, which is within the ark of salvation, can be absorbed in Christ till He reigns supreme. We are all an odd collection of 'animals' of all different shapes, sizes and temperaments. Often it is not easy to relate together in total harmony. Our smell of humanity wafts often through the decks and passageways of the 'good ship salvation.' Yet we are in the ark and the outflow of anything unsavoury behaviour can be, and should be, immersed, sunk deep into Christ by an attitude of true repentance in all of us.

Noah's family sat at their table having a common union because they were in the ark. So too we can come totally secure in the ark of His salvation, being graciously invited to His Table. All our self and humanity that can stink can be absorbed and forgiven, if we let it, into the redemptive work of Christ.

Unity marked that family of eight as they sat to feed on God's foreknowledge and divine provision. Every opportunity should be given to individuals who approach participation at the Lord's Table to do so in unity. If we don't come in unity, then the greatest resources of Christ, in His eternal salvation, can absorb our differences. But, only if the heart is willing to let the 'old man,' and 'the flesh' die and be submitted to the Lordship of Christ.

What was it like for the world outside the ark? It reeked of death, rotting humanity and the flood of divine wrath. The future will have days where we shall see floods of divine wrath. We fully see now how the tide of rotting humanity is eking out an existence in the cesspools of satanic indulgences. Yet, we are in the ark, safe and sound, by the grace of God.

Is there one of us that wants to return to worldly condemnation? Then, allow the priceless privilege of feeding at His Table to stimulate your hearts with a holy love and desire to be closer drawn to Him. Till He Come.

Study/Meditation 4

THE POST-FLOOD TABLE

The colossal ark had rested. Yet it seemed more than settled, more like wedged in a sharp crevice of Ararat's peak. The movement of the hull had stopped days ago. The family of preservation inside were conscious that they were no longer afloat.

The raven was sent out, then the dove, and finally the glorious message returned in the form of a fresh green olive leaf gently held in a bird's beak. Eventually, a released bird did not return. It was safe to go again onto earthly terrain.

As that dove fluttered and swirled in graceful curves in the sky on her final return to the ark she had borne an olive leaf in her beak. This has long been the universal symbol of peace: The dove with the olive leaf. No greater peace can a man have than to be in the ark of safety. The Holy Spirit has shed abroad in our hearts the love of God which in turn brings lasting peace, not because it was merited, but simply because we are in the ark.

Imagine that eventful day when the door was swung open for the very first time from what had seemed like an endless event. God had shut the door as the flood began and it could not be opened again till He desired. But now the heavenly time lock had been released and the door easily swung open. Sunshine splashed onto the wooden floor of the ark entrance. Perhaps the massive instant intrusion of such penetrating light caused the animals and man to squint, blinking at such an invasion of light.

We too have had opened to us an ever-increasing manifestation of The Sun of Righteousness, as He bathes our lives with the golden sunshine of His presence. Often we cannot fully comprehend or receive it immediately. But certainly, we are eternally grateful for being in the ark and being privileged to walk in the light as He is in the light. We know that in that flooding dazzling heavenly illumination, there is no shadow, shade, variableness or shadow of turning.

As that first day wore on a huge ramp was constructed to take the incredible passage and weight of the animals that soon must exit the ark. Yet Noah seemed preoccupied. He was somewhat distant in his thinking and conversation. Burning within him was an unquenchable desire to return thanks to God for such a miraculous deliverance. Slowly he gathered boulders, smothered in the silt of the past flood.

With the ramp finished his sons joined him with a holy purpose to raise an altar in thanksgiving to their God for their deliverance. We too can also identify. The Lord's Table stands between a delivering act, consummated at Calvary, and a thankful heart seeking in some way to return praise and thanksgiving to a gracious God.

Often in the Old Testament altars of Israel are described as using twelve stones, symbolising the twelve tribes. Yet, here with the altar of Noah in Genesis 8, there is no limit set in its size, shape or dimension. It predated Israel's existence. It must have been a huge altar for the extent of sacrifice that was to follow. For us today there are no limits put on the table. No tribal, ethnic, social or whatever restrictions are put on us coming to the table. Israel's altars were for Israel alone. The Table of the Lord is open to all who are in the ark. We can all come and partake.

In my mind's eye, I can see a huge altar for the mighty task that was to be accomplished upon it. The exact number of animals and birds in the ark is unknown. But an offering was made of every 'clean' animal and bird.

So often our minds are clouded and coloured by the worldly pictures and songs about Noah's ark. Children blithely sing: "The animals went in two by two, Hurrah, Hurrah," implying there were only two of every animal. In fact, that was not true. The Word of God clearly declares that of every unclean animal or bird there indeed were two of every species that entered the ark, a male and a female. Yet, it also declares of the clean animals that they went in by sevens, the male and his female in three pairs, plus one spare. This was probably the sacrificial offering.

What a glorious procession of natural wonder came out of the ark. Whether young were born to them in the ark we do not know, and we can only speculate. But, of this, we are certain, as the animals left the ark one of every clean species was doomed to die. Note none of the unclean animals died, just one of the clean species. From the preservation of the safety of the ark to the slaughter of the altar. So too Christ left the eternal security of heaven to take His position and place on the altar of Calvary.

Great themes seem to engulf those first hours when life was resumed again on the earth. Since the flood, the earth has remained relatively untouched by a total worldwide divine judgement, and so it will be Till He Come.

You can almost imagine the excited chatter around the table about the new world before them. This experience made them so grateful to their God. They sat around the table sharing with one another. The family table held them all safe, as indeed does the table of the Lord.

Imagine the stockade of animals waiting for slaughter on the altar. What is more gripping is that they were all 'clean' animals. Only the best were raised as a sacrifice unto the Lord. Of each group of seven one was set aside ready for sacrifice. Of perfection in all its glory, in Christ, He Himself was taken as the perfect sacrifice. In Scripture seven is said to stand for perfection. From the 'seven' of heaven, from the perfections of glory, came the spotless Lamb of God to make atonement for human sin.

The clean died and the unclean were set free. The animals fled the site of the ark and the altar, perhaps with a consciousness of the loss of fellow animal life. The death cry of their animal kin was still ringing in their ears.

Our Christ was pure, clean and undefiled. He alone was the spotless Lamb of God and yet He died for the unclean heart of all humanity. Purity died for impurity. Sinlessness died for sinfulness.

When we consider Scriptures such as Romans 5: 6 to 8 and II Corinthians 5: 21 we are made pertinently aware that the righteous have died for the unrighteous. The clean has died for the unclean, so we may go free.

Blood ran free as countless multitude of animals died that day of being set free. Deliverance was celebrated at an altar of remembrance, at a table of sacrifice. The offering was one of each clean species, symbolic of all their kind, covering clean and unclean alike. Yet, hundreds of years later just one sacrifice hung on a rough Roman gibbet, dying for all kinds, all races, and all peoples of the world.

I cannot help sensing that the multitudes of animals that escaped the slaughter that day, turned as they were in the shelter of the trees, which were just beginning to don a new coat of colour to replace the mudded tones, or they hid in the fresh grass emerging from the silted valleys, as they glanced back at the crest of Ararat. They could see the glow of a holy fire that spoke of sacrifice, thankful sacrifice. They had escaped. They were atoned for.

As we also come from every corner of life, look to the Lamb of God. We can sense the price has been paid. No more altars are necessary. Only the return of thankful praise around a Table of Remembrance is necessary.

In the evening the many valleys were quietened as fauna settled down to the first night back on soil that had been swept so violently away with the wrathful vengeance of God clearing the iniquity of an age past. Up in the mountains, the sun was setting behind lofty peaks. Still visible was the massive silhouette of the ark. It stood like a fortress, impregnable against the wiles of man. The glow of the altar burnt late into the night as sunset came. Twilight eventually penetrated creation with the eerie shadows of the ark standing out against the sky of God's eternal love.

The fire of the altar glowed and the family of eight nestled down in the security of the ark before they moved off into the world again. Much filled their minds. The day's activities still lay fresh upon them. Never had they seen such a display of blood, richly soaking red to the ground. Never had that bow of seven colours arched across the heavens penetrating the blue of the sky with such a brilliant array of colours, that it still thrills an observer today. Tired, yet satisfied eight souls rested.

The next day the first rays of the sun bathed Ararat's peaks in golden sunshine and the altar was bare, but for the ashes of the previous day. It had been a sweet-smelling savour to the Lord (Genesis 8: 21). Noah stood watching his first sunrise. The ark was nestled among the highest peaks. The high alps of Ararat seemed to receive its intruder warmly as if it knew it would encase it in its winter snows and glaciers that were going to show their effects upon the land for the first time in the months to come. For never before had there been a summer and a winter on the face of the earth (Genesis 8: 22).

High in the Alps thanksgiving had been given. High up in Ararat was the evidence of Noah's salvation. Certainly, we do not draw our source of eternal salvation from the gutters of this world. Down from His glory Christ came. But as we view Noah's table of sacrifice it speaks of something higher than the world, higher than what it offers.

As Noah and his family made their way down the valley away from the heights he could look back at deliverance so high above human capacity to understand. The work of Calvary yielded the ark of salvation in Jesus Christ. The altar on the slopes of Ararat's slopes yielded a shadow and an image of the Lord's Table now before us.

I am sure in the months that would follow that the ark would remain a familiar sight to Noah, reminding him of their deliverance. Yet, he had to move further away from Ararat's slopes as the climates of the world began to settle in a changeable mould that rendered parts of Ararat extremely cold, snow-bound and in the years to come glacier bound.

Although we do not live at the location, or even the time of Calvary, the very memory of it is ever kept alive by the devotion of every saint at the Table of Remembrance. Noah would have needed much wood to create the great burning sacrifice, which he offered to the Lord. Whether he gathered the smashed trees of the earth caused by the flood, broken by the raging torrents and drying in the full blazing sun, or whether he used part of the ark we do not know. Neither does it matter.

What is of prime importance is that he needed the product of the tree to yield a pure sacrifice to the Lord. In closing this meditation can we see that it is only by the merits of the tree of Calvary that we can come and be acceptable in the sight of Almighty God. Noah's altar has long since slipped into the glacial majesty of Ararat, yet we can continually bring to remembrance the supreme altar of love, where Christ willingly became the sacrifice for us, through the Table of Remembrance.

Study/Meditation 5

MELCHIZEDEK'S TABLE - Part 1
A Table Provided

For most of us, nothing fires up the imagination like the unknown or the unexplained. The life and references to Melchizedek have such an appeal and quality of mystery. Primarily our section of reading is taken from Genesis 14: 18 to 24. However, one is well advised to study the 5th to 7th chapters of Hebrews as well for further background material and reference to Melchizedek.

We will not attempt to solve any of the unfathomable questions relating to this man, rather emphasising issues relating to the table referred to, which is such a beautiful illustration of the merits of Calvary.

Cast your mind back to those ancient holy battlefields and consider the sight before you. Tired men are walking or riding beside two leaders. Heading one contingent of men is faithful Abraham, perhaps in quiet conversation with Lot, who has just been rescued from a confederacy of four kings. Three hundred and eighteen men from the household of Abraham mill around their leader alive with the conversation about the day's exploits and the battle won.

Nearby another king, Bera, king of Sodom, makes his way back from the battlefield, which had been for him one of defeat and loss, before the arrival of Abraham that turned it into victory.

Yet, in front of them, standing off by several hundred metres stands a king in magnificent array. The retinue that accompanied him and the grandeur of his very presence made a sharp contrast to the war-tired and shabby group of soldiers in front of him.

Melchizedek moved forward and met and greeted Abraham personally as he came from the battle. We are not informed, but there does seem to be some prior association between these two as they greet on the victorious battlefield.

The magnificence and person of Melchizedek embraced the tired, worn, blooded and dirty frame of Abraham. Note Melchizedek has no greeting for or association with Bera.

So often when the battle of life is at its hottest the Saviour comes and again with a reassuring embrace whispers: "All is well!" Can we see the unruffled splendour of the Saviour daily and hourly ready to embrace those who are in the midst of life's battles? No embrace or recognition is even hinted at for king Bera, for he was the king of Sodom. Nor does Lot receive such a welcome. He had at this stage given in to living within Sodom and all its evil ways. Each of us can make our own application on that score.

A tired, battle-worn Abraham, with clothes in disarray from the battle, and with blood still wet on his sword, still in his grasp or dangling at his side, slips down off his horse to find the inviting grass a soft repose. Right there, at the end of the battle, Abraham and Melchizedek would share together. One is the King of Peace, the other the soldier of victory. They shared the day's events in the quietness of their own private conversation before they came to share around the table. Melchizedek was concerned as well as interested in the well-being of this mighty man Abraham.

What a perfect reflection of our relationship to Christ this gives. As the perfect details of a tranquil country scene are mirrored in the still reflection of a lake's waters, here the picture of Melchizedek and Abraham serves to be a perfect reflection throughout the passage of time of our fellowship between the King of Kings and the servants of the Lord, locked in the battles of life, but already victors! They too can share the events and battles of the day.

There was no battle for Melchizedek. He carries no sword of blood. Christ now comes to us, not in the hot pursuit of the battle. For us: "The battle is the Lords." He has already purchased and won that battle and brought perfect salvation to mankind. He now is adorned in robes of victory and leads us into green pastures and by still waters and communes with us as a friend. Then comes the act of a consummating victory as He spreads a table before us in the presence of our enemies.

The grandeur of Christ, like Melchizedek, speaks of His completed redemption and gaining of victory. What a delightful privilege it is to be able to come and discuss with Him daily in the meadows of His leading, His green pastures (Psalm 23), and the priceless provisions He has made for us in the battles of the day.

Yet, lurking at some distance is the king of Sodom. He is always around seeking to contaminate where he can. He has no place in those hallowed moments of communion with your Lord. 'Bera,' the name of the king of Sodom, means 'gift.' Certainly, the world tries its attractions with its gilded toys, gifts and worldly trinkets to draw Christians away from fellowship and intimacy with Christ. But, do not be attracted or affected by any of it.

Bera tried that very same thing in offering gifts and the spoils of war to Abraham. But righteous Abraham would not fall into the trap of owing anything to Sodom. The world may offer, but it is our decision to turn the temporal gains aside so that all we have is what He, the King of Glory has granted us.

Only what Christ has planted in our hearts, and the riches from our relationship with Him, the King of Kings, will last. Take nothing from the hands of the 'kings of Sodom.' And remember, Sodom's gifts can come in many forms. The world cannot make us spiritually rich. The world degrades, debases and subjects, till we like captive Lot, are living in Sodom. Sad be the day when that happens.

The focal point of this meeting of Abraham and Melchizedek centres around the table which Melchizedek spread and prepares himself before Abraham. The food was very simple and certainly similar to that used in an average communion service. Bread and wine simply lay before these two great men of patriarchal importance. How the tired Abraham would have delighted in such provisions after the exhausting rigours of the day. Fresh from the battlefield, if not indeed from the sight of it, they shared together in common fellowship around a simple table spread for victory.

Though the language may be old I like the wording of the King James Version when it says the bread and wine were "brought forth." Didn't Calvary 'bring forth' salvation for us all? Was not the love of the Father 'brought forth' upon all mankind through what Christ has accomplished at Calvary? Simple bread and simple wine graced the table. Yet, it was a soul-quenching provision when you have been in the heat of battle all day.

We are not directly informed but I do not believe that Bera, king of Sodom, shared at this quiet table. Personally, I can't conceive it on the basis of all he stood for. Only the friends of the King are invited. Those of Sodom or the world are not guests at the table till they submit to the Lordship of the King. Neither do we read of Lot being invited to partake at the table. He had already made his choice to live in Sodom's grasp. It is important to note, however, that it is neither the right of any of us to alienate anybody from the Lord's Table. Their own hearts and their walk in life will do that for them.

We note that although we have referred to him as Abraham in fact he is still known as Abram at this point in his life. Soon a great change will come when he will become known as the father of the faithful.

When we come around the table maybe we are not all that we should be, maybe not all that we could be. This is why we must examine ourselves. But thank God we are not what we used to be. There is a divine change in our character and if we are honest with our soul and ourselves, the table if allowed will help us process that change as we continue along life's way.

None of us can imagine Abraham going home and staying in the garments of battle, with the dirt of holy warfare on him. He would have cleansed his body and dressed in the clean garments of the great tribal leader that he was.

When we come around the table we should come with a heart of adoration and worship of all that it really means, and what it can do for us. So after the battles of life let us go home and change. If any place needs change evidenced the most, it is the home. The pious deacon or the spiritual pastor can be far different in the home. Don't leave the table and go home the same way as you came. Be prepared to be different. Go home and change into the cleanness of Christ and watch a little romance, love and respect flow back into the household.

I don't fully understand all the ramifications of the character of Melchizedek, yet it triggers some deep and precious truths about our Lord Jesus Christ. Melchizedek: King of Righteousness, King of Salem, and King of Peace. Hebrews 7: 2 & 3 says he was: "Made like the Son of God." Certainly, we have in Christ the mighty King of Righteousness. He alone is righteous and He alone is worthy to open the books of life.

In Christ alone, we have the King of Peace. Salem means: 'summit,' or 'crowning glory or crest.' Indeed Our Saviour, Jesus Christ, is this to us. He is the very pinnacle of our devotions. 'Down from His glory,' He came to lift mankind up to that same glory. At the table, the realities of that redemption are made even more pertinent as we take time to dwell upon the same.

Can you imagine yourself tired, exhausted and ready to flop down for a good rest and the King of Kings meets you in your weary condition? Yet like Melchizadek that is exactly what the Saviour has done, and is doing, for us and in each of us each every day. Around the table, we meet Him as our righteousness, through all that He has accomplished on Calvary.

At the table, we meet Him as our 'Salem,' our pinnacle and crowning glory. As His broken body was dragged to the summit of Calvary, upon Golgotha's peak and summit, it was further lifted up on a cross. He by that very act of atonement lifted mankind higher than any of us can understand.

At the table, He certainly became our King of Peace. True peace can only be found in the author of peace.

Guard yourself against Lot's position. As stated we are not instructed that Lot had the same fellowship with

Melchizedek as Abraham did. In Scripture, Lot is clearly shown as departing from the pathways of righteousness and sensibility. He knew what evil and filth Sodom possessed, portrayed and represented yet he chose to identify with her.

Genesis 13: 10 shows us Lot lifted up his eyes and beheld the plains of Jordan, in which was the city of Sodom. His interest in the settlement was in areas of easy gain, but doubtful companionship. Be careful if you follow the same course. By Genesis 13: 12 the scene has changed and Lot has now: "Pitched his tent towards Sodom." Don't try to see how close you can live to the world without it affecting you. Keep right away from it. Keep a holy gap, not just a distance, between yourself and the world.

Finally, in Genesis 14: 12, Lot is found dwelling in Sodom. What dire straits this is for any man or woman. Although Peter calls him 'Just Lot' (II Peter 2: 7), that reference also shows Lot was vexed with the corruption of Sodom. Yet he chose to live there. I strongly suggest that living in Sodom had a drastic effect on his daughters and wife as later evidenced by their conduct.

As we draw around the table, if Lot identifies very much with our character, then be on your guard. Perhaps a valiant Abraham may rescue you. Perhaps he may not. The real issue is you should be nowhere near Sodom.

Whether an actual table was used with Melchizedek or not, or it was food laid out on the grass covered with a kingly cloth, we do not know. It is of no significance. It is only important to say this ancient figure stands as a dramatic type of the stature and majesty of Christ, who draws us, tired as we may be, to the table of love and provision.

Study/Meditation 6

MELCHIZEDEK'S TABLE - Part 2
A Table For The Righteous

How long Abraham and Melchizedek stayed at the table of victory we do not know. They both fellowshipped there – the tired and the tireless. The aged and the ageless sat opposite each other and created holy types and beautiful inspiring pictures of faith. One stood in need of cleansing from the battle, the other stood immaculate, the superb figure of kingly stature.

That table not only cemented relationships it created a model that speaks right through to the last table that will be spread – Till He Come. Never has there been a day where we need to draw so close to the Lord in daily fellowship, because of the heat of battle. Yet, He is always there. We may feel unclean and unkempt, but the Table is still spread for us. It becomes a living reality beyond human comprehension if we deal with ourselves in open personal repentance and then go home determined to change.

Something fires in my spirit every time I think of Melchizedek. I cannot imagine him standing in ordinary clothes of the day. His regal and mysterious status exercises my mind. I can only guess what he may have looked like. Royal golds and silvers were laced into exotic patterns on hand-spun cloth as delicate as a hummingbird's wing. Kingly authority upon his face and brow with the humanity of an inviting smile and softness of speech made him a figure of dignity, nobility and grace.

Melchizedek obviously typifies our Lord Jesus Christ, especially as we come around the table. Over time many, especially in the secular art world, have painted a weak and insipid picture of our Lord as if He was a little less than manly. The painters of history have helped perpetuate this far from the true ideal.

Yet, as we gather around a table deep in your heart create a picture that He is the risen Christ, the ascended Christ.

He is the glorified Christ. If you have a limited view of Christ's grandeur take your Bible and read Daniel 10: 5 to 9, and also Revelation 1: 12 to 17. Within both of these passages, we are staggered by the scriptural majesty of the Redeemer. The Christ of glory is far different from the 'Jesus meek and mild' image that many of us have of the Saviour, based so much on our perception of his time here on earth.

Be careful to note that in both scriptural examples cited above the receivers of such a vision of the Lord, Daniel and John respectively had a common response. They were so overcome by the very majesty of their encounter with the Lord that they fell prostrate in His presence.

I do not want to undermine our appreciation of Jesus the babe in the crib, Jesus the kind and good shepherd, Jesus of the cross, or even the risen Lord portrayed at the end of the gospels. They are precious concepts and very valuable to our souls and spirit. Yet, there is definitely something in the meeting of Melchizedek and Abraham that speaks about the glorified state of the Son of God.

When we can see Him, or at least appreciate Him, in this glorified state as we gather around the Table, surely we can understand there is literally nothing that He cannot do, except for the hardness of the hearts of men.

He is all-powerful and all-knowing. He takes us, as we are, weak and battle-weary and embraces us with His very presence. Hungry and tired from life's conquests He feeds us at His Table and on His provisions, with emblems that speak so profoundly of His all-atoning sacrifice in His body and His shed blood.

Tired muscles and limbs seemed somewhat soothed at the touch of His precious hand upon us. He pours in the oil and wine of His great love. Perhaps your own heart can itself be caught up also in the endless pictures and truths that this great Melchizedek can bring to us.

But, as we approach the table it is not a mere mortal we are coming to. It is the glorified Son of the Most High God. Get a vision of His loveliness and it will minister healing to your soul around the Table.

When we do see Him it is more than words can express. Get a vision of the glorified Christ Himself administering the table.

The Hebrews 7: 3 reference to the mighty Melchizedek creates another world of mystery. "Without father, without mother, without genealogy, having neither beginning of days nor end of life, but made like the Son of God, remains a priest continually." How do we get our heads around these concepts?

As we approach the table we are not coming to a human man or woman full of the weaknesses of life. One without beginning and without end tends to our needs and pleads our cause. There are various ways of looking at this Hebrew reference to Melchizedek but that is not our concentration here.

The concern of our heart is to see the priceless comparison and type that Melchizedek was, and is, to the Lord Jesus Christ. We have a beginning and an end. Man has his alpha and his omega and in many cases, both are tragic, as often is the middle of one's life. Yet Christ, the eternal one of glory is now outside the frailty of manhood, which once encased Him whilst He was here on this earth. From His humanity, He understands our frailty. From His glory, He can triumph for us.

But Christ is not 'outside' humanity's understanding. Doesn't Philippians 2: 7 to 10 and many other passages speak so profoundly of the capacity and actuality of Christ to understand and live the very humanity of man? Indeed He walks this road Himself. To understand this setting read Hebrews 2: 18 and 4: 15. It reinforces the wondrous reality that he not only has suffered and overcome but that He fully understands the suffering of humanity from a human perspective.

When all of life and this world will be nothing Christ who is without end will still be. What majesty is ascribed to the Saviour? Note of Melchizedek that He was: "Like the Son of God." Such a rare unique comparison is not commonly used throughout the entire Scriptures. Never has there been one like our Jesus.

We seek not for men to gaze on us. We are mere flesh. As Abraham stood there, on those battlefields of old, there was one standing with him, one like unto the Son of God. Be well assured that when we are in the thick of battle, or resting in the provision that He has made for each and every one of us, He the Son of God is close by our side.

Of the reference: "Abides a priest continually," we sense here that Melchizedek indeed was a perfect type of our Lord Jesus Christ. With time we could look at other references such as Hebrews 5: 6, 10; Psalm 110: 4; Hebrews 6: 20; 7: 11 and 17 and see that the Scripture is replete with references that Christ is considered to be forever a priest after the order of Melchizedek.

We all know that certain sects have taken it upon themselves to set up priesthoods after an order they call the Order of Melchizedek. But I think they are on dangerous ground. That relationship comparison between Christ and Melchizedek is something of holy importance and divine wisdom.

The Melchizedek we meet with Abraham so long ago was not only a king but he was also the priest of the Most High God. None other was called to this honour preceding Melchizedek or after him. Christ certainly arose in such magnificent power to attest to the reality of the type that had been set.

Hebrews 7: 15 and 16 tell us: "And it is yet far more evident if, in the likeness of Melchizedek, there arises another priest who has come, not according to the law of a fleshly commandment, but according to the power of an endless life." Let such impartations in the divine message thrill your soul through and through.

We do not approach the table with a powerless Christ to expedite our cause. We serve one with the power of an endless life, ready, and at the disposal of every believer. We are not told much about Melchizedek to throw light upon the worship of Melchizedek that necessitated him being called the Priest of the Most High God, yet behind every known fact lies a wealth of information and truth that can stir our hearts. Thinking, and meditating on Melchizadek requires depth and insight.

The only actual performance of worship we see in the life of Melchizedek is that which we have now before us in his meeting with Abraham and the consequent table that was raised and shared. What can we know of the depths of Melchizedek's life? Also, we have little except the gospels to bear records of the life of Christ. John attests that of the miracles of Christ alone the world could not contain the books that should be written if all the miracles were to be written about.

John further asserts that his gospel is very selective and that far more could have been recorded. (John 20: 30, 31 plus 21: 25). The greatness of the Godhead, spread out before human view and for human benefit is only revealed in a mere glimpse of what it could be. But of this we are certain it is a display of divine love, culminating on Calvary.

In conclusion in this table study/meditation, we find this priesthood continued in the one of an endless life. An eternal order ratified in one who became the living vicarious sacrifice for the whole of humanity. Presently He is, as a great high priest, interceding for His own (Romans 8: 34).

As you draw around the table there is nothing to spoil your fellowship with the glorified Son of God who is ready and willing to enhance your life with all His blessings, except for one little problem - You! You and I are the ones who stand in our own way in our relationship with the Lord. I can easily blame another. Yet, it is me that needs to be dealt with.

Melchizedek slipped in and out of Biblical records faster than many. Yet his influence and glorious type of our Lord and Saviour Jesus cannot be disputed or denied. The table is spread and the great High Priest of our faith stands beside it to execute glorious provisions.

Study/Meditation 7

ABRAHAM'S ALTAR TABLE

Abraham stood transfixed; tears moistened his aging cheeks as he tried to conceive the human wickedness of the task before him. The low semi-barren mountain was bare except for a crude altar that adorned its crest, and patches of scrub. The patriarch became conscious of the knife within his hand and the searching youthful eyes that lay submissively upon the altar before him.

Mt Moriah had not seen such a spectacle in all of its long history and some may add: "And would never see the same again till Calvary bore a dying Saviour." But, let us seriously consider the gaze of Abraham. His eyes scanned the horizon as his strong yet trembling arm raised in holy obedience bares a crude knife about to perform an act of abhorrent slaughter that defies our comprehension of dedication to God.

There was nothing upon the entire crest of the hill except a heart-rent father and soon-to-be sacrificed son. Not far distant from the peak of Moriah a ram bleated in frantic persistence to free itself from the thicket it had become entangled in.

All was quiet now on Moriah's crest as the hand of Abraham rested upon his son as he listened to the voice of the angel. I cannot conceive the emotional release in Abraham as the aging man burst into rapturous joy as tears flowed freely, as he heard the divine pronouncement to stay his murderous hand and spare his son's life.

Young Isaac, freed from the altar, rubbed his wrists where the cords had held their prey. Unitedly embracing his father, Isaac did not fully know or understand both the immediate significance and the spiritual type that had just been enacted.

Again kindling was set in order and Abraham, directed by the Lord, found the soon-to-be-offered ram. With the sacrifice completed neither, Abraham nor Isaac knew the very import of what would be repeated on this very mountain range not quite two thousand years later.

A little distant from that altar of sacrifice, somewhat in a slight valley to one side lies a small barren knoll. It is rather a crooked outcrop of rock with bare exposed patches of earth and rock. From a distance, it looks like a skull. Little did Abraham know that Moriah's peaks would indeed look down upon a sacrifice that was similar to the one that had nearly been enacted.

That small hill that had held so little attention when he searched the horizon with his eyes would certainly one day hold the attention of the whole world. Some suggest, maybe with romantic impressions wanting a beautiful prophetic type, that the ram Abraham used as his sacrifice, was actually caught in a thicket on a rocky knoll.

Though it is pure speculation could it be that the entangled lamb that Abraham found was actually on what we today call Calvary, for it was but a short distance away from what was to be a blooded altar? Calvary is a name dear to us, but it was nevertheless the place of a skull, in physical description and in its blooded history.

For no idle or indifferent reason did the heavenly Father call a faithful Abraham to those holy slopes of Moriah. We also know of a certainty that for no idle and indifferent reason did the Saviour ascend Calvary's hill. It was the will of the Father.

The sacrifice of Abraham that culminated in the death and shedding of the blood of that innocent sheep, speaks strongly of the wondrous innocent sacrifice of Calvary and the spotless Lamb of God in His personal sacrifice for each and every one of us. Indeed on that day of Abraham, Calvary's slopes were empty. Even today they are the same, except for the religious trimmings of men. But, on that eventful day of Christ's death, full was the cup of divine judgement, justice and redemption for the sins of all humanity. The ultimate sacrifice was made.

Abraham turned to look into those eyes of promise in his son and then turned and pronounced the place where they were standing 'Jehovah Jireh,' meaning 'The Lord will see and/or provide.' That is exactly what Calvary is to us. No one could have known the relevance and importance of what Abraham uttered that day. But the heavenly Father, breathing it in holy desire of prophetic value, through His aging servant Abraham established another unbreakable link in the redemptive story.

The Lord will provide. Imagine the aging Abraham and the young energy-abounding, clean and perfect son ascending the slopes of Moriah together. It may have been that they actually passed Golgotha's rocky outcrop on their way up. At that very moment, the Heavenly Father's heart stirred with holy prophetic vision and He knew one day He would lose His own son to death there, but ultimately to resurrection.

Neither Abraham nor Isaac saw the ram wander into the thicket and begin to push into the bushes for food. They never saw it become entangled unable to free itself.

On that fateful Calvary day that took the spotless Son of God, the Father was not aging, only the sin of man had left an aging effect upon His heart, concerning the tireless rebellion of mankind. A perfect sacrifice was needed so creation may stand clean through a perfect substitution. The clean perfect Son of God followed submissively the plan and will of the Father.

So often the aspect of the near sacrifice of Isaac and the eventual sacrifice of the ram of Abraham has been used to bring meditative thoughts around the Table of the Lord. And it is good that we see just how closely the incident aligns with Christ's actual death on Calvary.

Can we envisage Abraham and Isaac as they walk away from the sight of the servants who had been told to stay at a location well below Moriah's slopes? The old man carries the fire. The young man the wood.

Christ himself carried the wood, on the cross that He would die on. Indeed the Heavenly Father carried the fire and allowed it to fall in holy condescension upon the sacrifice for all humanity evidencing His ultimate acceptance. We are the benefactors of such loving sacrifice.

Holy fire fell on man's sins. Divine vindication of the sacrifice of the eternal Son of God was given.

Abraham and Isaac laboured together to build the altar. Something strong, something firm and able to take a sizeable sacrifice was necessary. Isaac was puzzled at the apparent lack of sacrifice. Divine altars are not carelessly made. They are carefully and strongly built.

To Israel, the building of an altar was something of great significance. To the Father, the altar of love lays bare awaiting the perfect sacrifice of His Son to be an offering for the sins of the world. There was design behind Calvary. It was not an accidental mistake of Roman law and Jewish hatred.

Revelations reveal only part of the great preordained plan of Almighty God to allow His Son to be the sacrifice. I deeply admire the words of Genesis 22: 6 which shares: "They went both of them together." Both were in submission, and both were cooperative in the sacrifice.

The Son of God took upon Himself the plan of salvation submissively and together with the Father they walked literally into the lives of humanity. Man has never been the same since and is not likely to be so again.

Little points continually fire the imagination with the consciousness of the comparison between the altar of Abraham and the supreme altar of love in Calvary. The altar or table of pure obedient sacrifice that Abraham sought to raise to God certainly established him as a friend of God.

When we consider carefully the position of the altar and offering that Abraham raised to the Lord in obedience, we are reminded that the temple one day would grace that very same spot. A temple to house Israel's faith and God.

David was the first to raise a tabernacle in the form of a tent in or near the same place that Abraham had nearly offered his son. Later, the mighty temple of Solomon, which surpassed human comprehension, so magnificent was its structure, would also be built here.

After the exile, Ezra and Zerubbabel would again raise a temple that eventually Herod the Great would embellish and restore. But eventually, such a building would stand with cold indifferent eyes of heartless religion, while the actual Son of God hung on a Roman gibbet on a hill not too far away. It was not an act of the whim of Jewish hatred. It was the Father's love and plan.

Today, no such holy temple stands. Yet Christ fully knew that although the temples of the earth may fall He would be established in love in temples that do not fall – temples not made with human hands. Temples of the heart. These temples will stand forever. Perhaps you have never had the privilege of looking at the site of Moriah and standing where Abraham once offered his son or turned your eyes towards the actual hill of Calvary.

But, make no mistake about it: "Blessed are those who have not seen and yet believe." There is in every one of our hearts an immovable fortress temple of the Most High God.

Isaac spoke to his father just before the sacrifice. So too did Christ within the Garden of Gethsemane. However, the prophetic words of Abraham spoken hundreds of years ago pinpoint, if not nail, the very eternal purposes and provisions of God through Jesus Christ.

"Son," says the aging patriarch as he contemplates the very brutality of his impending act: "Son, God Himself will provide a sacrifice." God did indeed provide a lamb for a burnt offering both on that day and in the future a sacrifice that was beyond cost.

The table centres our attention on the glorious redemption of that sacrifice. It seeks to create within our hearts a holy understanding of the divine victory that the Father has indeed purchased through His Son. The table remembers. So do not allow the heart to be so neglectful in being slow to remember.

As we gather around the table and remember the altar of love and dedication that Abraham raised so long ago, we need to realise that a bride for Isaac was not sought till after he had become the sacrifice. Although we on this side of Calvary realise God did provide a lamb in the place of Isaac, and a pure lamb upon Calvary. The Lord needed to pay the supreme price and then through that act realise a bride.

The Bride of Christ meets throughout the world on various occasions to remember with love the sacrifice of the one that has made them His bride. No bride was possible till the sacrifice is complete. This is the lesson of Genesis and this is the pattern of Scripture concerning Christ and His church.

The ram was caught in the thicket. No thicket was ever so holding as that of sin. Christ was not caught up in the thicket of sinfulness through His own unrighteousness, but rather ours. The illumination of Scripture is: "He became sin for us." I know we like to consider He took our sins upon Him, and that is valid, but the Scripture says: "He became sin."

Seething wickedness crept over Him as the thicket of man's iniquity caught hold of Him till the Father had seen the blood flow for the redemption of all mankind. As Abraham's tiring aging eyes looked there were three focal points each expressive in the spotless Son of God. They were the altar, the son and the ram. In that 22nd Chapter of Genesis, nothing is said of the immense struggle that must have gone on in the mind and heart of Abraham between verses 2 and 3.

Thank God for holy courage, which I again say, is beyond most of our comprehension of dedication. Oh, that we may sense the call for holy sacrifice around the Lord's Table and that we may serve the Lord from that perspective. The table is one of remembrance. As we gather to remember our redemption let us add our lives as a continuing sacrificial dedication as a sweet-smelling sacrifice to the Lord Himself.

In conclusion consider what God's Word says in Genesis 22: 16 and 17: "By Myself, I have sworn, says the Lord, because you have done this thing, and have not withheld your son, your only son— a blessing I will bless you, and multiplying I will multiply your descendants as the stars of the heaven and as the sand which is on the seashore, and your descendants shall possess the gate of their enemies."

It states: "Your son, your only son." Certainly doesn't this also speak prophetically so loudly of our Saviour? Who amongst us would be brave enough for such a sacrifice? When Jesus became the sacrifice of the whole human race then added the bride and a family beyond counting. As the sands of the sea, both in extent and number, the Saviour has redeemed Himself a great family.

The table draws the family together to fully appreciate His supreme display of love. And we 'will' be victorious right at the very gates of the enemy.

Study/Meditation 8

THE WILDERNESS TABLE

Moses stood watching patiently, gazing upon what appeared to be a mass of moving life in the distance. Heads were hardly visible as the backs of the children of Israel bent heavenward. Children ran around in tight, excited circles chasing small quails that ducked and cornered in equally tight circles. Adults were doing the same, heads and hands bent down.

Little squeals of delight from children pierced the hum of voices and activity as they caught hold of their feathered prey. Yet as Moses beheld this almost childlike hilarity, that had swept adults as well as children, his eyes moistened and he turned to walk meditatively back into the camp of Israel.

Could such happiness be so genuine as to drown the cost of their murmuring? He mused upon their rebellious spirit. He paused and glanced back at the masses of Israel moving on the desert floor, watching their coloured coats blend as one, as a flag unfurled and flew in the desert wind.

"The flag is one of a rebellious army," he muttered. Moses then strode determined back towards the camp. He had things to do.

What were now the wild excited cries of happiness, at the newly provided 'table,' had hours earlier been a deep curdled cry: "Can God furnish a table in the wilderness?" Such challenges and outbursts had cost them dearly.

Numbers chapter 11 shows a people driven to the end of their hunger lusts, crying out against the provisions of God. God had answered them back with fire. Judgement fell throughout the camp. Yet with the memory of the dead fresh in their minds, they lost themselves in a wild selfish frenzy to gather on that day quail as well as the daily manna.

We suggest 'that day' for it is unclear if the quail were a daily provision like the manna. The reference is in the setting of the 11th chapter of Numbers, in which the episode of Israel's provision of quail has its mention. Reference to the quails is also found in Exodus 16: 13, then Psalm 105: 40 and Exodus 16: 35 for reference to the manna. The references tend to imply Israel ate the manna for forty years. It does not say the same for quail.

The disturbing cry of the children of Israel is recorded in Psalm 78 and it would be good to carefully read the whole Psalm to see the overall development of the journey of the Israelites.

Verse 19 declares: "Yes, they spoke against God: They said, 'Can God prepare a table in the wilderness'?" Such disbelief is emphasised throughout the Psalm as it basically deals with the incredulous rebellion of the children of Israel and their consequent disobedience. God provided a bountiful daily ministration of food in the manna, yet they were still rebellious and dissatisfied. The Psalm so beautifully depicts the priceless privilege of Israel to be led by God (Vr. 14). No other people had been literally led by the omnipresence of God.

Flaming fire by night warmed those under it from the harsh-cold desert nights, and a sun-blanketing cloud by day protected God's children. Yet Israel matched it with rank disbelief and dissatisfaction. Living water was provided (Vrs 15, 16 and 20), yet their response lay like stagnant pools of mistrust. Manna daily and quails often graced their desert table.

Food finer than was present on many a mighty king's tables in the manna was theirs. Yet, they are tired of divine provision. They cried out in arrogance: "Can God furnish a table in the wilderness?" Twice such a challenge to the Almighty provisions of God is heard and twice the children of Israel paid for their disbelief.

Numbers 11 finds the faithless cry and hankering after Egypt's cucumbers, melons, leaks, onions and garlic answered by fire and death. Note their lame petition in verse 6 of Numbers 11. "But now our whole being *is* dried up; *there is* nothing at all except this manna *before* our eyes!"

How arrogant an attitude for what the Bible describes as "Angel's food" (Psalm 78). Yet, Israel loathed the almighty provisions of God. Quails in this instant were given in wrath and verses 31 to 35 have graphic detail of those that so rebelled.

Fiery serpents slithered along the ground. Men, women and children equally were subject to their fiery bite. Thousands lay dying and why? The cry of their course godless throats was: "Can God furnish a table in the wilderness?" This Numbers 21 episode shows the people as saying: "And our soul loathes this light bread" (Vr. 5). When will they learn that such rebellion brings a consequent costly price. Death was the ending of such an attitude?

But, is the church any less rebellious today? Doesn't the church in many quarters hanker after the false food of Egypt? Consider the listing of Egyptian foods. They certainly would leave a stinging taste in your mouth, but their presence would easily be discernible by those around. Feed on the world and all around you will be affected by its foul aroma. A stench of death breeding in what should be life. What a contradiction.

God certainly did provide a table in the desert for the children of Israel. Thousands had perished throughout the desert, yet they could have passed through the very heart and severity of the desert being totally fed. But, they had to rebel.

There are many alive today living parallel experiences of rebellion. They speak to our hearts as they uniquely parallel this sad episode. So often many consider the great redeeming work and power of the Table of the Lord, and yet still hanker after the world, Egypt's pleasures, demanding: "Can God meet my need in the midst of this arid desert of life?" The answer is always: "Yes!"

The Table of the Lord provides and satisfies all who will unfold their wills to its provision. Consider three simple little analogies from the context of Israel's challenge for God to furnish a table. These are taken from the Psalm referring to this sad episode.

Firstly: The table came after their deliverance from Egypt. Consider verse 12 of Psalm 78. God indeed did marvellous things for Israel. Yet, the wonder of those things was evident in their deliverance. God not only set them free but took them out of Egypt. The provision of manna was part of their deliverance.

Christ has indeed provided magnificent salvation with more than a mere remembrance associated with it. The table is living proof of the efficacious nature and work of Calvary. But, one has to come out of Egypt to enjoy the furnished provisions of God's provisions and this table in the desert. Indeed Egypt's leeks may be tasty at the time, but they leave a reeking odour of the judgement to come. The table has been spread. Though the way ahead of us may be desert we need to remind ourselves that the provision is called 'Angel's Food!'

Secondly: The table of provisions exists whilst they are journeying. Long were the years and hard was the way to the Promised Land, mainly because of their rebellion, not the plan of God. But, all the time the provisions of the table were theirs. Their indolent challenge as to whether God could provide a table in the wilderness was mirrored by the reality that indeed God did and would continue to provide a table of His provision in the midst of their journey. He would never abandon His own. They had known Egypt's snare and deprivation, now they were experiencing God's provisions.

Sometimes Israel camped, at other times she was on the move. But, at all times God provided her with food and met her needs. Notice how the children of Israel were to collect provisions for six days but, not on the seventh, the Sabbath.

Wouldn't it be great if every Christian were thorough in spiritually gathering for their personal needs six days of the week? Then on the seventh day, they would come into the church, resting on the provisions of the table. However, the last fifty years have turned working patterns upside down. What blessed times the Lord has in store for every believer, as we collectively meet with Him on His day. But in the nitty-gritty of life, meeting six-day needs in work; we have a faith where individuals should learn to deepen themselves in their growing relationship with the Lord.

Thirdly: The table was also provided after the Red Sea was crossed. Now Israel was separated from Egypt. God's children need to realise the sea of God's forgetfulness and mercy separates them from their old life, habits and bondage.

The table was furnished for those separated by the waters. Allow daily the water of the Word to wash over our hearts cleansing and keeping the holy separation from Egypt. Psalm 78: 13 points out a glorious separation. Praise the Lord that at Calvary, His love was heaped up and an effective way was made through life's difficulties for each and everyone who will come the way of the cross.

The table of provisions waited for Israel on the other side of the Red Sea. Let us realise that His provision is just the same. Abundance awaits those wanting to put a clear distance between themselves and Egypt and its ways and wiles.

In conclusion, let us remind ourselves of certain basic truths of the wilderness table. It was in the midst of the camp of Israel. God's provisions are always in the midst of His people. Today many splinter groups want to break off from church fellowship and do their own thing. Remember God provided His table of provision amongst a collective people not an isolated group in a corner.

Do you want to enjoy real life? Then belong to a fundamental, Bible-believing church and feed with them on God's provision for you. Loners and the arrogant die in the desert. The provisions of God for Israel were met within camp. Be part of it.

The actual table God prepared for His people was in the midst of the tabernacle. Here it consistently held a living remembrance of the manna that was being provided daily, except on the Sabbath. Whether out in the desert of life or right in the holy place, manna is found. Search diligently for the provisions of the table.

The wilderness tabernacle was attended by a priestly order. Even though they were out in the desert they still acted, dressed and presented themselves as priests, before both the Most High God and the people.

Can we do any less with the provision of the Lord's Table? His atoning work, fresh before us daily, and remembered collectively at communion, should be lived both before God and before the people. And that demonstration should be daily.

No matter whether you feel you are in a desert, beside still waters or in the glorious tabernacle of His presence, you still have to feed on the manna. The work of the cross is just the same as yesterday, today and forever. We all need to realise whilst we journey to the Promised Land that He provides a table in the wilderness for His people.

Study/Meditation 9

TABERNACLE TABLE - Part 1
The Table of Shewbread

The air was still outside the tabernacle. One of the priests stood transfixed amid his nightly duties. He stood quietly gazing up into the heavens hardly able to comprehend the colossal column or pillar of fire that rose up from just above the tabernacle and spread out like an embracing warm blanket till it covered the very last tent on the outskirts of the camp of Israel.

It was warm beneath the covering of God's provision. Normally the nights could become excessively cold in that desert area, with snow possible in seasons. There was stillness throughout the entire camp as the priest began to move again about his duties. Moving slowly, as if every step would be his last, he moved into the temple's holy place. He quietly mused on the wonders that lay inside.

From the far end, a pulsating glow emanated from beneath the veil. It was not fear, that affected the priest, but holy awe and heaven-bred respect for the actual omnipotent presence of Almighty God that lay just on the other side of the veil.

The holy place where he stood was in subdued light. The candlesticks or menorah of Israel to his left sent seven flickering flames into the air. The flame and glow were constant, except for the flicker caused by the passage of air created by the movement of the priest and his garments throughout the holy place.

All was in order. All was set in the divine pattern that God had committed to Moses upon mount Sinai. The priest moved from item to item in a systematic check that seemed routine, yet something accomplished with a fearful reverence of the one whom he served, who existed in shimmering Shekinah glory behind the veil.

The oil feeding each of the flames had to be checked, wicks trimmed and the lamp stand positioned correctly. Moving through the holy place the priest stood before the altar of incense and then realised he was only a short distance from the veil and God's glory.

The mysterious presence of the Shekinah glory and glow seemed to ooze out from under the veil and bathed the corner of his garments with a fresh warm light. He hastily jumped back. Leaving the altar of incense he moved to his right and unknowingly touched the Table of Shewbread and ran his fingers along its golden border with a sense of holy fondness.

The priest seemed lost in thoughts of all that surrounded the table now before him. He carefully checked the supply of shewbread that it held. Little did he realise the great Table of the Lord this tent tabernacle table was to speak of in later years.

The Bible includes many passages that deal with the Table of Shewbread. To further our knowledge the passages of Exodus 25: 23 to 30; Leviticus 24: 5 to 9 and Exodus 40: 22 and 23 will help your understanding. Ponder deeply over the richness and splendour of the Table of Shewbread. It was constructed with the precise design set down by the Almighty Himself. In terms of size, there was nothing pretentious about the Table of Shewbread, yet its intricacy of design and its wealth of meaning leaves paper cold in a vain attempt at explanation.

The Apostle Paul in I Corinthians 10: 11 adds to our understanding that all within the Old Testament were an example or type to us. He refers that those things of old were patterns to us of new things to come.

The Table of Shewbread carries some profound teaching about the vicarious death of the Lord and parallels the communion table. Human words are inadequate to convey the splendour of comparison from the holy place of Moses' Tabernacle to our day and age. Yet, if we take time to open the Word of God, then open our hearts and bend the knee in prayer He will reveal His truths through it all.

Too often we read the Word of God superficially. Great is the reward of praying over your readings and taking time to meditate.

Let us consider the Table of Shewbread itself before we move on to the actual shewbread and the customs surrounding its use and administration. As stated, the table itself was not large. But believe me in today's values it was priceless. The table was just two cubits long by one and a half cubits high. The width was just one cubit.

We fully understand there is disagreement about the size of a cubit as it was commonly taken as the distance from the elbow to the tip of the finger of the king. King's arm lengths obviously differ. But generally, it is accepted as close to and rounded off at around 45cm in length. This would make the table dimensions just under a metre long by just around 70cm high and a width of just 45cm.

The Table of Shewbread obviously wasn't impressive in size. In fact, it paled in comparison with later tables, such as in Solomon's temple. Congregations around the world meet around a variety of tables. In some places they are large. In other places small.

Persecuted Christians meeting in secret have often used the fields and meadows of hillsides as their table. In some places, the home has turned its own kitchen or dining room table to the purpose. For others, the bed of a failing sick person has carried emblems, a table nonetheless.

It is obviously not the actual table that is of prime importance. It is what it stands for and brings to our attention, and what it holds is the value under study.

We are told in the Scriptures that the table was constructed of 'shittim wood.' This was common acacia wood used frequently in that area for the construction of many things. Yet it was overlaid not just with gold, but pure gold. The very common and basic wood of life was taken and literally turned to gold, pure gold that glistened and reflected the lights and flames of the menorah. Whenever the high priest passed through the veil to the holy of holies that pure gold and the table shone with the illuminative splendour of the Shekinah glory of the Lord that had just momentarily shone out with the unintended innocent parting of the curtains.

The old hymn catches a pertinent point: "Heaven came down and glory filled my soul." That presence of God that once was hidden away now should emanate from every single Christian. The veil has been rent and the table should be a place where we literally reflect the glory of the Lord and shine with His magnificent presence.

Christ became the very common acacia of humanity. But don't be deceived. He was, and is, pure gold through and through. Calvary's great act is complete and He has completed the immense transaction of redemption for our souls as He stands in divinity, pure gold divinity, over the garment of humble humanity.

We all sense the frailties and weaknesses of humanity and tend to shudder at the thought that it could contain or be contained in divinity. But, indeed our Saviour triumphed in humanity and so wears divinity as a garment of assurance to all mankind that we can also succeed through Him whilst still mere mortals. One day like the Table of Shewbread we will wear pure gold in the grandest of ways.

Can we fully comprehend the absolute wealth of the gold that adorned the table of the tabernacle? The very hope of glory, our Lord Jesus Christ, the greatest investment that we can conceive came from the wealth and majesty of eternity and divested Himself of the wealth of heaven to join the poverty of mankind, for the benefit of humanity.

A crown of pure gold formed a border surrounding the edge of the table. A handbreadth in on the table surface there was another crown of gold forming an inner border. Inside that border lay two gold dishes upon which lay the two piles of shewbread, six on each dish.

On each corner of the table was placed a golden ring through which golden staves could be placed to bear the Table of Shewbread on its way when the glory of God moved and Israel also moved in obedience. The table could be moved.

There was no absolute common location. Its only common location was God Himself.

We need to understand that if we celebrate the Table of the Lord, where God is not literally present in our hearts, then it is all ritual, it doesn't bring life. It is because He rules in glory in our hearts that makes the table so relevant. Exodus 25: 30 tells us: "And you shall set the showbread on the table before Me always." It was a living and symbolic celebration and remembrance. God had to be there.

Has He moved on in your life? Have the purposes of God been picked up and shifted yet you refused to move? Then it's time we picked up our life and tabernacle and moved to where God is and let His glory attend our hearts.

Let's move our hearts to God. If we are not as close to God as we once were, then don't ask God who moved. Are there 'rings' on our table in the sense that we should be urgently concerned about moving ourselves to where the presence of God is?

The Sabbath came around with its usual regularity and duties as the priests rendered their service to the Lord. But one duty that befell the priest each Sabbath was the replacement of the shewbread on the table within the holy place (Leviticus 24: 5 to 9). Weekly the sacred bread would be taken by the high priest and his sons and eaten right there, within the holy place.

Only those within the sacred confines of the priesthood could eat the shewbread. Upon thinking on this I am sure we can sense something of what the Lord is sharing here. The consumption and feeding from the table should be in His holy presence. Sadly, we can be outside of Christ and be in a meeting where the presence of God is literally throbbing. Yet, if we approach that table, and we are not personally in His presence, and are not enjoying a living relationship in His priesthood of believers, then watch out for the consequences of coming onto the holy ground with unholy motives.

For the priesthood alone was reserved the right to eat the shewbread. Only in King David do we find another eating of it, and then it was in extreme circumstances of survival. When the seven-day-old shewbread was consumed fresh shewbread was brought out to be laid out and lie before the Lord for the next seven days till it was again consumed and replaced.

The provisions of God lie within our grasp at all times. Yet, there is a time when we need to consume or realise them. Weekly the word of God is preached and it is our prayer that fresh bread may be presented. Something that God has laid in the hearts of ministry before the Lord can become life, as it is broken consumed and fed to receptive congregations. Then the ministry must replace it with fresh bread that will again become the people's food next week.

As I Samuel 21: 6 implies the shewbread was only to be replaced by a fresh supply and often it was hot from its preparation. It is spoken of as being prepared overnight by the Levite priesthood to be brought fresh on the Sabbath to the Lord.

Certainly, within the darkness of men's night, the Saviour gave the supreme sacrifice of His life to become that fresh supply that new life may flow in the greatest of Sabbaths. Rest for human hearts comes in renewing afresh the memory and reality of the atoning work of Calvary.

There were twelve cakes made each of two deals per cake. Made from fine flour and frankincense. The 'meal,' or flour, speaks of the sacrifice of the humanity of Christ. The frankincense expresses the sacrifice of the Kingly Christ.

The prepared shewbread was reserved to be consumed only by a holy order of priests. Even after the division of the tribes, to take up their inheritance in the Promised Land, the twelve cakes were still being prepared. Although God's people may be many and diverse tribes (denominations and fellowships), some self-made, some God-made, His table stands as a complete identity to draw men back into unity itself.

Of special note was the sweet aroma of frankincense that wafted throughout the holy place from the fresh shewbread. Used in its preparation, and anointed with the same whilst it stood upon the table, the spice of frankincense speaks of wondrous kingship mixed with humanity to redeem mankind.

Yet it showed His kingship living through the garment of mankind because of His prevailing death.

There are many lessons from the Table of Shewbread of the tabernacle that are pertinent comparisons as we gather around the Lord's Table. Our communion table may not be lavish in terms of wealth. Yet, it is priceless in terms of the value of what it does to the souls of mankind.

Study/Meditation 10:

TABERNACLE TABLE – Part 2
The Position Of The Table

God doesn't appoint anything without purposeful meaning. Even within Moses' tabernacle of old the placement of the furniture speaks throughout the centuries. Messages to believers can be seen and understood who are alert to the Word of God. Where exactly was the Table of Shewbread? What were its surroundings and do they have anything to teach us today?

For a moment let us slip back into the past, don the dress of the priests and quietly come into the Holy Place to see what is about us. Interestingly the Word of God is full of fine colourful descriptions, which we often completely miss. Through the Word, and a fertile mind, allow the full majesty of the table's location to come alive and teach truth, accompanied by the challenge.

The curtains that separated the Holy Place and the outer court of the congregation of Israel were of exquisite craftsmanship. The priest as he entered held the curtain aside as he pushed past, but then stopped to behold the splendour that was in his very hand.

Curtaining made of the finest of linen, fine twined linen as the Lord commanded. He traced his finger over the cunningly devised patterns of the cherubim that seemed to cascade throughout the entire length and breadth of the curtain itself.

He let its softness slip from his grasp as he moved further into the Holy Place. The break of natural daylight that had slipped in when he entered through the front curtain was now shut off. The brilliant desert sun is now muted and his eyes blinked to adjust to the subdued soft light of the Holy Place.

After touching the curtain of the door his eyes followed its graceful lines right through to the ceiling. Often he had seen it, yet afresh today he was enthralled by the splendour of the tapestry over his very head. That fine twined linen, with cunningly worked embroidery of cherubim, stretched from one side of the tabernacle to the other forming a ceiling of such exquisite design that it was breath-taking.

Alone in this Holy Place, the priest began to sense the very import of its name. Before him was the veil that stood between the Holy Place and the Most Holy Place or Holy of Holies. The veil also hung from the ceiling to the ground and like the ceiling tapestry above him was of fine twined linen of blue, purple and scarlet with the dominating embroidery of cherubim.

From the ceiling to the ground, the priests knew that they were surrounded by living images of God's protection. Stepping cautiously he reached out and touched the great inner veil. He again cast his eyes from ceiling to ground admiring again the gorgeous fabric. From the lofty heights of the ceiling, the cherubim looked in mid-flight heading towards the barrenness of the desert floor.

Still touching the veil he whispered, breathed, almost prayed: "From heaven to the earth." He affectionately patted the veil and moved to attend to his duties.

The embroidery and the cherubim denoted the expressive heart of God prepared to leave heaven's glory to walk the dusty trail of humanity. Through Christ, the great aspiration of the Father was that heaven had come down and was dwelling with man. He is our Emmanuel: "God with us."

Our Emmanuel has come to dwell with man, as man, to redeem man. This is the beauty and setting of the Table of Shewbread. Underneath the glorious canopy of a rare tapestry, speaking of God's omnipotence, standing alone one can fully appreciate these beauties.

Understanding the beauties of the table requires we are in the Holy Place with Him. So as you are drawn there, through a desire to serve Him, we begin to realise how grand a place He has called us into. Heaven has come down and touched the barren desert souls of man. God is perceived as love.

Behind the internal fabric lining, Table of Shewbread and behind the Golden Candlestick was the solid boarded walls of the tabernacle. Gold to the eye and gold to the touch. The Holy Place stood ten cubits high and twenty cubits long and every bit of the surface was gold.

The priests had grown accustomed to the wealth around them, yet there was an atmosphere of great honour to be serving the Lord in the midst of such wealth. Each of the boards that side by side made up the length of the walls were covered in gold with each plank set in two silver sockets.

Stooping to the floor the priest touched the silver sockets. He examined them. Silver, pure silver. Then it gave way to golden walls, which were crowned, by a ceiling of finely embroidered linen. What wealth. What a display.

"To think this is ours, given to us by a divine plan." The priest was muttering gratefulness as he mused and tried to take it all in. He understood that the children of Israel had given all the wealth of their homes to provide the material for the tabernacle. Moses had been specifically instructed by God in Exodus 25: 1 to 3 to encourage, even command and exhort the people to contribute to the beauty of the tabernacle.

In a sense, as we approach the Table of the Lord we can create our own atmosphere. For the tabernacle, the children of Israel gave all and God inhabited their gift. Doesn't this challenge us to give all we are and let God inhabit it?

Read both the 25th and 26th chapters of the Book of Exodus to fully understand the surroundings of the Table of Shewbread. It will give you an understanding that space does not permit us here.

Just three items stood within the Holy Place and except for the occasional daily presence of a priest the sanctuary was otherwise bare if one could dare to say that after looking at the splendour around them.

Before the veil to the Holy of Holies stood the Altar of Incense. As the priest came through the front opening from the congregation of the people into the Holy Place the Table of Shewbread was on his right-hand side and the Golden

Candlestick or Menorah was on his left-hand side. But, the Altar of Incense was immediately in front of him.

Consider the continual use of 'three' throughout the tabernacle construction. Three items in the Holy Place and three metals were used (gold, silver, and brass). There were three colours used in the embroidery (blue, purple and scarlet), and three points of access (into the courts of the tent tabernacle, into the Holy Place and finally into the Holy of Holies). Three as a number is often regarded as a symbol of the perfection of God's character and His planning.

The two accompanying items that stood quietly with the Table of Shewbread speak volumes even today. What do we make as our 'companions' around the Lord's Table?

The Candlestick reflects more than light. Beaten from one solid piece of gold it was a craftsmen's marvel (Exodus 25: 36). What I like is that it burned continually before the Lord (Exodus 27: 20). Daily it was trimmed, but it continued to burn.

Our service centring on the Lord's Table mostly also centres on the Word of God. In an atmosphere of worship, the Word is honoured with the table. We can see that pattern existing in Acts 2: 42. The three items in the Holy Place speak of the integration of facets of our relationship with Christ.

Clearly, the Table of Shewbread illustrates the Lord's Table in remembering the sacrificial death of Christ. The Word being central is accommodated in the image of the Golden Candlestick. Worship flows from our lives as prefigured by the Altar of Incense. There is no idle accidental occurrence to this pattern. All was in order before the universe was flung to its extremities.

The Candlestick was of wondrous creation and design. Careful Scripture research will show it had sixty-six parts within its whole structure. The Word of God stands also to attest in sixty-six parts – the exact number of books in the Bible. It is many books but one truth. Christ is the living Word. As the candlestick illuminated the Holy Place for the priests to perform their duty so the Word of God illuminates our life so we may serve the Lord. Christ is the light of the world (John 1:

4, 8: 12). The Candlestick was the light. Beaten from a single piece of gold it was literally battered into shape. Was not our Saviour as the Living Word beaten and bruised for the iniquities of us all?

The Table of Shewbread stood directly across from the Candlestick and in a real sense attests to the reality of the light that is shed. Aaron and the priests could not eat the shewbread if there was no light to see what they were doing.

So today we feed on His provision by the virtue of the fact that the Holy Ghost sheds His light and love abroad in our hearts. The Candlestick not only illuminated the beauty of the inside of the Holy Place, but it also exposed the desert floor for all it was.

I am exposed when I come to the table. Let only the rich beauties of heaven be seen in me as I am made more like Him each day. Fed by oil, so symbolic of the Holy Spirit, the lamp burned eternally before the Lord. We too should daily trim our life by allowing the Great High Priest access to our inner thoughts.

The Table of Shewbread was nothing without the Candlestick to illuminate its worship and its meaning. So today we cannot fully appreciate the Table of the Lord without the full majesty of the living and written Word of God.

The Altar of Incense was at the end of the Holy Place before you passed into the Holy of Holies. The Scriptures again give us insight as to the significance and operation of that altar. Exodus 30: 1 to 10 is useful as a wider reading, but pay attention, particularly to verses 7 and 8. Always remember that the Word of God is its best commentary.

Every morning when the lamp was dressed and trimmed a fresh burning of incense was made. Every evening when the lamps were rechecked, trimmed and relit the incense was again offered.

Throughout the day what had been offered on the altar slowly smouldered before the Lord as a sweet-smelling sacrifice. The Scriptures show that the burning of the incense was: "A perpetual incense before the Lord throughout your generation." Note that the association of the main pouring forth of the incense on the altar was when the lamps were being attended to.

Prayer, praise and ardent love and attention to the Word of God go hand in hand and also increase our devotion, purpose and meaning at the table. Whenever Aaron and his sons came to attend at the Table of Shewbread there was the sweet smell of the Altar of Incense.

Whenever we come around the Table of the Lord it should be accompanied by great worship and praise of our hearts individually and collectively as a congregation. They should rise as a sweet-smelling fragrance. The altar not only speaks of our worship but that our Saviour is the great intercessor (I John 2: 1 & 2; Hebrews 7; 25, 9: 24 and Romans 8: 26).

The altar was four square. Christ too has reached down into the four corners of the earth. It was the horns of the external altar that were grasped in desperation by one who sought God in prevailing prayer and fasting. Certainly accompanying the Table of the Lord in the Holy Place should be a life prepared to wait on God, to lay hold on God.

Much more could be said about the setting of the table. But sufficient is conveyed to understand that the table is not something of flippant mindless remembrance. Ordered and administered in holiness the tabernacle of old encourages us to only present our finest to the Lord.

As you come to the table remember this; the tabernacle was right in the midst of Israel. It was covered above by the glory of God. The majestic handiwork of unbelievably glorious design adorned it. Attendance at the table had the illumination of the Word and the praise or incense of the altar. Anything less from us is unacceptable.

Study/Meditation 11

TABERNACLE TABLE – Part 3
Service And Servants Of The Table

The air was crisp with activity. People stirred from every direction as they anticipated the voice of Moses. Families everywhere had already seen the cloud of God's glory begin to slowly shift, to gracefully lift off the tent tabernacle. In the distance, deep with the camp, a clear forceful cry penetrated the air. All ears attentively turned to listen: "Let God arise..." Its message trailed off as the camp burst into an instant seizure of activity. It was the unmistakeable voice of Moses.

God was on the move again and the camp of Israel was to follow submissively and yet joyfully. Every family gave attention to their pre-planned departure procedures for their own tent and belongings. Systematically they found their place in the customary assembling of Israel as it moved forward with God leading on.

But, deep within the very heart of the camp of Israel, there was a very much different movement. Camped immediately around the tabernacle lived the children and descendants of Levi. They were organised in family groupings according to the Word of the Lord to Moses.

Here instead of personal preoccupation with their own removal and preparation of their tents for travel, the men who were priests suddenly disappeared within their tents the moment they sensed that God was on the move. By the time Moses, from some high vantage point, had cried out the call to move most of the priests had appeared dressed not in work clothes for house moving, but dressed in the fine clean array of the priests.

The Word of God declares that all the Kohathites from thirty to fifty years of age were dressed and ready for service to the Lord. Kohath was the second son of Levi and from him had sprung a line of descendants that were to be the attendants of the tabernacle as it was being moved.

Aaron himself was of the Kohath sub-clan of Levi and as such you could understand that he would have been a natural choice to be instrumental to direct certain of the activities of the removal of the tabernacle. However, God had appointed a direct descendent of Levi to oversight the plan.

Levi's son was Kohath. Kohath's son was Uzziel and Uzziel's son was Elizaphan. To Elizaphan was committed the sacred responsibility of the oversight of the removal of the tabernacle furniture, which of course included the Table of Shewbread.

God is concerned about every aspect of the service of His own house. Background reading about this situation before us can be gained from Numbers 4: 4 to 33; 7: 3 to 9; 10: 17 to 21.

God understood the need for organised living and worship and had therefore designated the whole camp of Israel with respective responsibilities and duties. The Kohathites were to attend the tabernacle. Elizaphan's own name means 'God is protector,' whilst that of his father Uzziel means 'God is strong.' From a holy line and people, God selected His workmen and servants.

Numbers 4: 4 is of importance as it speaks of 'the service,' which the Kohathites rendered to the Lord as a definite calling and administration to the Lord. In actual fact the term in its origin is synonymous with, and associated with, military service. Here it is used in a special sense that the service of the Levites, and particularly the Kohathites under study, was regarded as being a particular militia of God, an army of priestly servants to God Himself.

They were directly used by God to move His holy presence-filled tabernacle to its new resting place. There would have been those men under thirty years of age, and over fifty years of age to attend to the removal of their private dwelling places. But these particular Kohathites were needed and used to move the dwelling place of God Himself.

There was a particular manner in which each item was to be handled as the tabernacle was being prepared for removal. Within our reflective thoughts here we are only concerned with that section that relates to the Table of Shewbread.

Quietly the priests worked, with little chatter but with holy awe pulsating deep within their hearts. They were keenly aware of the reality that God was moving and they singularly were required to assist in the movement of the house of God.

A priestly hand stretched over the table and took the dishes off the table that carried the shewbread. With a gentleness that accompanies a nursing mother, other priests laid a clothe of blue over the entire framework of the table. Covered gold lay beneath that simple yet exquisite colouring.

The softness of the blue lines draped gracefully to the sides. Then the dishes of shewbread were returned to the table. It does seem from a reading of Scripture (Numbers 4: 7 and 8), that the table was moved with the existing shewbread in place upon it.

Fresh priests were waiting calmly to one side with a cloth of a rich scarlet hue. Glistening in the sun of the desert now breaking through after the protective cloud of God, which had acted like an air-conditioning cover had moved. The scarlet robing of the table placed over the table, already covered in the blue cloth, held every eye in its rich colouring.

Finally, a covering of badger's skin was gracefully draped across the scarlet cloth already showing the pattern of the dishes below it. Blue, scarlet and rough badgers hide. Not just any old cloth or covering. God had ordered cloth of blue, scarlet and badger skin.

Blue as a colour has often been associated with the expansive omnipotence of Almighty God Himself. It lay across the Table of Shewbread. We sense here God in His divine foreknowledge, planned before the time a living example of salvation. He understood there would be a table that would stimulate holy fellowship and relationship. Notice it was spread or covered before the items on the table were returned to sit in their position.

Christ was slain before the foundation of the earth (Revelations 13: 8). The Almighty omnipotence of God undergirds the sovereign act of Calvary. Their love and provision were spread before all the world. Calvary made God's embracing love complete.

Then the scarlet cover came next. It has often been taken as symbolic of the covering of the precious blood of Christ. Also at that time, it was a timely reminder to Israel their sins were purged with the shedding of blood. Remember if it doesn't cover all it doesn't cover at all. Allow His redemptive covering to be consciously draped across all of our life and be covered by its cleansing power.

The Table of the Lord, which we celebrate as often as practical, speaks of the all-atoning sacrifice of Christ and His shed blood. It has penetrated every period of history, age, creed and race to bring the love of the Saviour.

Then finally came the badger's skin. Hardened by weather and the glare of the elements beating down upon it, often unmercifully from a scorching desert sun, the covering of rough badgers skin may have looked unkept and lacked the finesse, or look of wealth and beauty from the outside as it was finally placed over the table.

Certainly to the outside world, the power of the gospel may look to be lacking dignity, wealth, beauty and aspects that may make it important enough to be bothered with. But, like the Ark of Noah, the horrid outside covering of pitch only helped to protect the beauty of that which lay inside. The Lord's Table may not seem pretentious, and indeed we should never aim to make it so, yet it is what is carefully preserved inside that is of wondrous import.

No infant or novice was allowed to attend to the removal of the tabernacle. Only those between the ages of thirty and fifty were given the sacred right to transport the habitation of God. Should anything go amiss it was the responsibility of these Kohathites to render an account to Moses and directly through him to God Himself. They were select people for a select job.

God always seeks dedication and consecration even in the simplest tasks and ministries that come our way.

Everything about the transportation of the sacred table speaks of the overriding rule of Almighty God.

Finally, two staves were slipped into place through golden loops or rings and they kept the overlaying clothes from shifting or blowing off. These poles or staves were not just common timber but the fine timber poles were each overlaid with gold. Golden staves were made to move a golden table upon the shoulders of human priests.

The ministry of the Kohathites was by divine appointment. Throughout the life of any church, there are several jobs that are handed to various people with an express purpose. It is trusted that they may realise their divine place and connection with the framework of the entire church of Jesus Christ. We shouldn't see any task as insignificant.

The New Testament lists various types of ministries within the operation of the church. Paul in I Corinthians 12: 28 mentions the ministry of 'helps.' The Kohathites could be satisfied with the knowledge that everything else in the camp of Israel was being attended to, as long as they attended to the matters of the tabernacle.

Every one of us can fit into a useful and divine place in the church. We all have a function to help the church move forward hopefully under the cloud of His presence. Within the church of today, there is a more open attitude to involving as many as possible in meaningful service in practical as well as ministerial areas. The care, preparation of and administration of the Lord's Table should be seen as an incredible opportunity to serve the Lord.

Nothing is worse than a last-minute rush with nobody really knowing who is in charge of the table and its preparation. Nothing looks as bad as not enough communion glasses/cups being provided for normal situations, or the eventuation of an overflow crowd.

Then some indelicate attendant makes a noisy fuss. It is generally more about their self-perceived importance in solving a crisis, about being noticed than actually getting a correct count and bringing the needed extra cups or bread to the table quietly. Some people interestingly use disorganisation to assert their own position and prominence.

Great grace should accompany the ministration at the table at all times. I'm not talking about a religious, legalistic piousness that is not rooted in grace. I'm talking about the fact we are here to celebrate, remember and assimilate afresh Christ's atoning work. Then let's do so realising we are coming into the presence of the king.

Have you ever been to a service where nobody is quite sure who is waiting on the table distributing the elements? Or have you seen the table hasn't actually been prepared? I have. What respect does that show for the ultimate sacrifice for mankind?

If in the Old Testament context, extreme care was to be taken in personal preparation of the Shewbread Table and its movement, then how much more does that apply to those of us privileged to walk in the light? After the service is over who is attending to the clearing up of the table and the washing, if necessary, of any items, and their storage away? These matters may seem trivial but to a God who desires everything to be done decently and in the order, I do not feel they can be overlooked. And, at the same time, we want those assisting to genuinely know how important their sacrifice of time and talent has been.

I am not of the opinion that all of the tasks surrounding the Lord's Table are somehow meaningless services to be given to those of little ability. Every man and woman is divinely instrumental in serving in any church service.

No task is too menial that all in the administration of His Table be conscious that they are serving the very God of glory. And, we are to act, as if He is attending every action of our service in and for the Body of Christ. Grace and dedication should always accompany serving the Lord, no matter the task we're asked to do.

Paul is talking about how we can all grow up together in Christ when sharing: "From whom the whole body, joined and knit together by what every joint supplies, according to the effective working by which every part does its share, causes growth of the body for the edifying of itself in love" (Ephesians 4: 16).

Every man and woman in the church is supremely important. The Table of the Lord emphasises that time and time again. If your ministry is to 'serve,' often called a 'ministry of helps,' to prepare, tidy up and administer the table then you are in good company. You are spiritual Kohathites of the Lord. Stand straight in your task to wait at the table. Seek a divine anointing for your humble duty and seek to be of service as the presence of God continues to move on.

Study/Meditation 12

TABLE OF RECOMPENSE

'Lord of Lightening!' The very name seemed to strike terror into the hearts of people. The king who bore the name, Adonibezek, ruled the city and country region of Bezek. He rose and stood still watching from his window in deep contemplation. The fortifications were now manned around his city walls.

Always before this day, he had been the undisputed king and conqueror. The one who bore the name of the power of the gods had ruled with an iron fist. Adonibezek had defeated and humiliated seventy other kings and towns. In those days single cities, really towns, had their own king. So seventy towns had been overcome by the conquering king of Bezek.

Now, this mighty king of the Canaanites and Perizzites was under siege himself. He turned his back, hands clasped in a wrenching fashion behind his back. He moved to the table where his generals sat waiting for fresh orders of war.

He seemed embarrassed. Never before had his authority been challenged. Outside the city walls lay but a small division of the host of Israel. They stood ready for battle. It was enough to cause the city gates to close and be barred. Judah was armed and waiting to attack. The warriors of Judah were the smaller rank, but nonetheless deadly as soldiers than those of the tribe of Simeon.

It was thought that Caleb, who was possibly still alive, after the death of Joshua, could have led this conquest against the city of Bezek. This king Adonibezek was doomed to be defeated this day. He was well known for his cruelty and his unconquered record.

The assault began. The walls shuddered under the valiant attacks of the Israelite soldiers. Judges 1: 1 to 7 give us insight into the battle of that day. The armies of Judah and Simeon had already swept through the surrounding rural area in victory, which was connected to the city of Bezek. Terrified villagers and farming families had retreated to the safety of the city walls. Or, so they thought. "The Lord delivered the Canaanites and the Perizzites into their hand," attests to the successive victories of Judah/Simeon.

Already Adonibezek had suffered uncountable losses with the tide of God's children, as holy liberators fought to gain Palestine for the Most High God. Before that day was finished ten thousand men of Bezek would lie dead and the price of stubborn rebellion would be fulfilled. When you look at the passages defining the military strength of the respective tribes of Israel you are amazed to think such a small contingent as Judah and Simeon could take the walled city of Bezek.

The thought of this insignificant army about to destroy his city throbbed in the mind of Adonibezek as he paced impatiently around his palace throne room. "Defensive. Purely defensive," he roared at his commanders. "Is that the best that Bezek can offer to these marauding nomads?"

The chiefs of war hung their heads in shame. They too understood the humility of the moment and their impending defeat. As the king continued to ceaselessly harangue his military leaders, communications from the battlefront continued to arrive. The generals looked even more concerned.

A military commander entered the room. "Your majesty. Forgive me that I should ever interrupt you. But, the north tower has fallen. The wall is breached and the enemy like a flood is overrunning the city. We must get you away to safety."

The other commanders and generals sat quietly putting their heads in their hands and did not quite see the colour drain from the face of their ruler. It must have been only a second, yet the silence seemed like an eternity. Then Adonibezek spoke.

"Let us flee the city for she is lost." With a small elite group of guards and key soldiers, the king and his family fled the palace and headed towards a part of the wall relatively unmolested from outside attack. The enemy was now content to swoop into the city via the lesion in the wall to the north.

Death reigned within the city. The valiant defence was no match for the all-conquering spirit of the children of Israel. Victory after victory had been impregnated within the spirit of Judah and Simeon. It was an unyielding spirit. They fought as if defeat was unheard of.

"The king has fled," reported one of the soldiers that had stormed the palace with three other brave warriors with the determination of taking the king himself. Soon it was revealed the manner of the king's escape and a party was sent to hunt him down and recover him.

The streets were already gorged with blood. The king's palace and houses of city leaders were already alight with fire. The city was dying and a king with such a fierce reputation and past military glory was fleeing before the army of the Lord.

The chase must not have lasted long as the Scriptures declared they caught him as they pursued after him. Somewhere on the plains, the conquerors committed what may seem to some the greatest of horrors. They cut off the king's two thumbs and his two great toes.

I can imagine the tempers and hostilities of the Israelite soldiers would have run high. Around the king lay his contingent of protection dying and slain. Yet, he was allowed to live. Most likely the decree to cut off his thumbs and toes would have come from Caleb. The king was then returned to the burning conflagration of Bezek a defeated, humiliated and now mutilated leader.

In some small way, we can trace the origins of the Canaanites from Scripture. The Perizzite's origin is however a little more obscure. Whether Adonibezek was an actual Canaanite or Perizzite ruler is not quite clear. Yet, we do know God caused victory to flow to the children of Israel. The origin of much in this world is very doubtful. Yet of this, we are sure, we are the children of the King and we are more than conquerors!

Adonibezek's own origins are uncertain. But, our origin is certain. Nothing hidden or unknown surrounds us. We are children of the King of Kings. So let us move on in faith and obedience and take the 'Adonibezeks' who seek to destroy the work and progression of righteousness.

Brought back in disgrace Adonibezek was returned to the city. Either at the point of capture when they cut off his thumbs and toes, or later on his return to his destroyed city he utters these illuminating words.

"Seventy kings with their thumbs and big toes cut off use to gather scraps under my table; as I have done, so God has repaid me." (Judges 1: 7)

If we are disgusted, with our perception of sensibilities, at the thought of Adonibezek having his thumbs and great toes cut off, imagine the inconceivable horror of King Adonibezek's own inhuman actions. He had personally defeated seventy kingdoms, or cities/towns, and subjugated their leaders and their kings, in exactly the same fashion as he is now being punished.

The context of the Judges passages seems to imply that this was an act of holy retribution for the inhumanities that he was personally responsible for. When you read wider of this horrendous practice you will find that in the times of feasting by conquering kings, the defeated kings or great leaders that had been so mutilated, as now Adonibezek was, would often be brought out to be made sport of.

Samson is a clear case in point as seen in Judges 16: 25, though we are not implying he had his thumbs and big toes cut off, but certainly, his eyes were gouged out. They paraded Samson to make fun of him.

Can you imagine the impossibility of kings trying to walk into the presence of Adonibezek's feast with their great toes cut off? Your great toe gives you balance. It was gone. They stumbled, wobbled, and even fell into the feasting chamber to the raucous hilarious laughter of Adonibezek's guests.

Food was thrown to them from the table to the floor and beneath it and they were commanded to eat. You cannot grasp without your thumbs. They are vital in holding power. Some researchers feel the captives were actually starved for these special occasions to heighten the humiliated individual's craving for food. As they tried to grasp food they would fall, not being able to stand properly, and become objects of ridicule unable to grasp the food.

Such sport was exceedingly cruel and Adonibezek was himself now to taste of his own indecencies. No thumbs and no great toes around a table that would one-day demand recompense. No grasping and no balance around the Table of Recompense.

As we come around the table of communion there is a need for grasping and balance of truth and divine guidance that comes from the time around the table. But, we have not been brought here to be mocked or to be made sport of, but rather to be whole. We have been given back a true grasp of life and truth. We now have proper stability. Truly we have found balance in life and Christianity. The world and its Adonibezek rulers seek to make sport and cut off man's grasp for truth and life inclusive of his balance and stability.

But, around the table, we celebrate the reality that sin has no more dominion over us, through Christ's death on the cross. We celebrate knowing the Adonibezek of man's soul, Satan himself has been rendered grasp-less and without standing because of Calvary.

The table of Adonibezek was one of violence, evil and an inhuman display that was destined to be recompensed. Adonibezek could not be allowed to continue his evil domination. The Word of God stands to answer such indifference. Galatians 6: 7 states: "Whatsoever a man sows, that also shall he reap. Do not be deceived, God is not mocked; for whatever a man sows, that he will also reap." It is a principle as old as man himself.

When we come around the table we cannot be indifferent. What we sow we will reap. A heart of conceit can sit and smile whilst at the table, feeling smugly accepted by all, but he/she will reap recompense. Adonibezek's cry should temper our hearts: "As I have done so God had done to me!"

The heart that is cold and unbending around the table will one day have the recompense of the Almighty to answer for. There are none of us that can be anything but cautious and soberly aware of the paramount importance of the attitude of our hearts. This is the critical balance as we come to the Table of the Lord.

Listen to the teaching of Paul in I Corinthians 11: 27 to 32. "Therefore whoever eats this bread or drinks *this* cup of the Lord in an unworthy manner will be guilty of the body and blood of the Lord. But let a man examine himself, and so let him eat of the bread and drink of the cup. For he who eats and drinks in an unworthy manner eats and drinks judgment to himself, not discerning the Lord's body. For this reason, many *are* weak and sick among you, and many sleep. For if we would judge ourselves, we would not be judged. But when we are judged, we are chastened by the Lord, that we may not be condemned with the world."

These are ever-powerful words speaking their own vindicating judgement deep into the recesses of our hearts. We do not have to be apologetic. If the Word declares that an incorrect attitude at the Table of the Lord may be responsible for certain sicknesses, both in the body and in the spirit, then we had better believe it. How careful we ought to be.

Self-examination is the order of the communion service. If not it may become a Table of Recompense. What are we bringing to the Table of the Lord and attempting to hide? All is exposed and seen for what it is. Are our own actions making us have an inadequate grasp or balance in life, truth and the fullness of the Christian life? Are the blessings of God too hard to grasp, or do we seem never able to stand upon the blessed ground of perfect liberty?

There is a Table of Recompense. What we sow we will reap. Therefore let us sow liberally to the Spirit.

Hosea cried in 9: 7 in his day and age: "The days of punishment (or visitation) have come; The days of recompense have come." We desperately desire a visitation of God. We can have this at His Table. Yet, if our attitudes are not right it may result in recompense. It all depends upon our hearts around the table.

In conclusion, it is important to remember that we should be satisfied to know that if we judge ourselves we will not then be chastened. Be hard on yourself for the sake of your soul and the health of your body. You don't want to deal with the Table of Recompense.

It is our desire that none may come to know the stinging, soul-destroying, none-grasping, none-balanced reality of the table of Adonibezek. But, our desire is that we should indeed be blessed as pureness of heart takes over our entire attitude at the Table of the Lord.

Study/Meditation 13

RUTH'S TABLE

Eyes that quivered with nervousness peered hesitantly across the table that had been spread in view of the fields of Bethlehem's country slopes. A man stately and strong stretched across the table and personally handed provision from the table to a little maid still feeling her own intrusive insecure presence. Then the words of Boaz again reached the recesses of her mind.

"At mealtime I want you to come here and eat of the bread and dip your morsel in the provisions," (Ruth 2: 14). In other words eat at my table.

That little maid was Ruth. Jewish teaching says Ruth was of the royal house of the Moabite king. Now impoverished and needy she was being exposed to the kindness and generous, gracious hospitality of Boaz. This same, seemingly insignificant young woman would become part of the lineage of the Lord Jesus Christ Himself, the King of Kings.

When we pause to muse on the import of Ruth 4: 21 and 22, in conjunction with Matthew 1: 5 we sense something of the great love of God in gathering each and every one of us into the fold of His family.

Ruth by birth was a Moabitess and Boaz's mother was Rahab the previous Canaanitish harlot who was brought into Israel's ranks following her brave support of hiding the spies at Jericho. The combination of these two lines of ancestry would make any true, self-righteous Jew's blood run cold and shudder with indignation.

As we trace the lineage of Jesus back to David's great-grandparents we find a mother who was of Moabite extraction and the father was of half-Canaanite extraction. Not the most impeccable 'Jewish' credentials for the Messiah.

So too, as we gather around the Lord's Table out of every tribe and nation have we been called. No ethnic group is superior to another. We are 'all' what we are by the grace of

God and the all-atoning work of the cross, not our racial identity. There is nothing of a 'pure' lineage that alone qualifies for the continual love and blessing of God.

Some who come to the Lord's Table come from backgrounds as sordid and deep-dyed in sin as Rahab's. Yet, He saves and He cleanses us. Others were quiet and demure as little Ruth. Yet, we still needed the saving grace of God.

We were aliens from the Commonwealth of Israel, as the New Testament puts it, and strangers from the covenants of promise, having no hope and without God in this current world. But now, those of us who were once a long way off are now in Christ Jesus. We have been brought close by the blood of Christ (Ephesians 2: 12, 13 free translation).

Certainly, Jesus is our peace. He has welded both the righteous and the unrighteous into Himself through His atoning death and resurrection. So as we gather around the table perhaps we feel like Ruth, a stranger in a foreign land. Yet He, our Saviour, reaches out His hand and feeds us from the provisions of the table.

From the marriage of Ruth and Boaz, Obed was produced, who was himself the father of Jesse, who in turn was David's father. Clearly, we can see Christ as the royal descendent of King David coming directly from the lineage and marriage of Ruth and Boaz.

Shouldn't it be the aspiration of every Christian heart that from our relationship with a loving heavenly Father, Christ will come in all of His glory, through our lives? Also more pertinently shouldn't it also be that out of every Christian marriage Christ should be seen as an evident product of the glory of God?

We only want that which is of Him to shine forth. During her first marriage, Ruth was barren. But when her husband died she moved from a land noted for its immorality into God's territory. She joined herself to God's principles and was blessed with children.

Whilst we are in the world we may have a measure of success and happiness. But, many times we remain barren and unfulfilled till we move into God's territory and are joined to the lover of our soul. Then through Christ, the full meaning and purpose of life begin to flow.

Around the Lord's Table, there should be an expression of completeness that He has drawn us unto Himself. We celebrate that redemptive wholeness together as a family. We are all drawn from less-than-perfect ancestral, domestic, social or sin-soaked lives. What a wonder to be brought into a relationship with the Lord of Lords and King of Kings.

Our concentration in this meditation is drawn from those incidents around Ruth and the table prepared by Boaz in the field. There are many principles that we can readily identify with. Ruth had to come to the table of Boaz. There was no other spread for her or us than what has been spread.

From the conversation with Boaz, we understand that Ruth had two types of companions in those days in the field working alongside her as she gathered the grain that was purposefully allowed to fall. There were the 'handmaidens' and there were the 'reapers' of Boaz. Both are expressive of the church in various phases of its life.

Ruth was invited to come to the table with the workers, those already of the household of Boaz. We are invited to a table that should be attended by those who are already of the household of faith. Ruth 2: 8 and 14 show us the good company that Boaz was pleased to leave Ruth with.

The sharing of life, and the casual conversations she had with those in the fields as she gathered food led her to more and more appreciate the might and benevolence of the one in whose fields she was gleaning. Naomi left her in no doubt as to Boaz's standing.

Note they were workers and dwellers in the Master's fields. They shared her great love of the master of the harvest. There are some people we would do well to stay clear of in the Christian life. Their conversation and behaviour don't reflect the ethics of our Master and Saviour, Jesus Christ. They are not a good example to the household of faith. I do not mean to be unkind but there are some Christians who cannot leave others alone in their negative conversation.

The handmaidens and reapers of Boaz communed incessantly about the graciousness and majesty of their master. Both the handmaidens and reapers were called to Boaz' table. His provision was for all that were called his workers and for all that were in his service.

In the heat of the day, he shared with all his provisions who were in his service. Within the very heat of the battle of life, where we are both harvesting and gleaning in the fields for the master, He provides. He in the midst of life's challenges calls us to His table to feast on His provision.

That which was spread before Boaz's workers certainly speaks so much of the elements commonly used on the Lord's Table. The King James Version identifies it as bread and vinegar. The vinegar would have been a mead drink made out of grapes half solid half primitive wine base. Some say the vinegar was a freshly pressed grape of the field that had not quite ripened. Other suggests it was sour or unripened grapes.

Indeed our Saviour Himself partook of the bitter cup that the host of the redeemed may feast on the provision He has graciously provided. What we are called to feed on around the Table of the Lord are but emblems of the sacrificial work Christ bore alone on Calvary for each and every one of us.

Ruth sat down to this kind of provision. I cannot say I would be delighted to eat the bitter taste of what she dipped her bread into. But, we understand that it also satisfied thirst far more than a sweeter drink. Sharp and possibly bitter to the taste it left a clear consciousness of its presence in the mouth of those that consumed it. Never let us take for granted our salvation. Let communion become almost a sharp taste, a timely reminder of what He has done for us.

One of the warmest images is when Boaz personally picks out some provisions, dips them in the centre dip and stretches over the table to hand them to Ruth. Along with the dipped bread, he handed her parched corn (Ruth 2: 14). With such personal attention, she blushed, ever so slightly beneath her veil. Kindness was extended and received personally from the hand of Boaz.

Around the Lord's Table, there can be both the generalised appreciation of what has been provided for us and also those special moments when Christ reaches over and personally imparts to our life.

Others around the table were busy with the chatter of the day, yet Boaz was moved with compassion to meet Ruth's needs. Others carried on as if nothing had happened, yet the eyes of that couple met and the benefactor expressed his desire to meet her needs with holy and pure love.

Amid the clatter of the church, the Saviour stretches across, at the time around the table, and touches us personally at our point of need. Often in church, there can be much noise (mental, social, relational, attitudinal), and plenty of talk. A hum of human conversation yet often really little Saviour-to-saint contact. When He reaches into our life we flush, sensing our inadequacies. Yet, He comes right into our hearts and touches us.

Amidst the songs around the table, amidst the words being spoken by the one administering such a table devotion, the Saviour can speak personally to each and every one of us – If we will let Him.

No doubt we all react as Ruth did to the lavish display of love that was extended to her. She fell down at his feet on one occasion and from her lips was uttered something that is a testimony and challenge to all who come to communion.

Ruth implored: "Why have I found grace in your eyes that you should take knowledge of me seeing I am a stranger." What a true response for every Christian. We too were strangers from the Lord. But, He has loved us and extended Himself unto us. Is it any wonder we should be found at His feet?

Again in Ruth 2: 13 she expresses the humility of her heart when she says: "Let me find favour in your sight, my lord; for you have comforted me, and have spoken kindly to your maidservant, though I am not like one of your maidservants."

As the Table of the Lord is spread before us shouldn't the cry of Ruth be our conviction? For, without Him, where would any of us be? Boaz invited Ruth at mealtimes to come to his table. Certainly, every one of us as Christians is invited to come and dine. But sadly many are at the table, but few are dining.

For Ruth, it was simply responding to Boaz's invitation that meant she came to the table and received what he offered. So too with us. Take time to come. Take time to sit and wait on Him. Take time to eat His provisions. Don't be in a rush to hurry back out of His presence.

There was a mutual exchange between Ruth and Boaz as they sat at the table. Into her empty hand, he placed his full provision. That which was given to Ruth speaks of the all-atoning sacrifice of Calvary. Boaz further reached over and gave her parched corn. This would have been any of the grains roasted with fire and eaten. Often, though called parched corn, it was a full ear of barley lightly roasted.

Christ, Himself took the full fire of indignation of the wrath of God for our sins. He became the sin offering for the world, the roasted lamb of the flock. The iniquity of man had come to a full ear and He received it graciously Himself and died in our stead. As Ruth ate at the table she ate something that nourished her. So we ought to do. Also, we note on the basis of the relationship developing between Ruth and Boaz that he gave his reapers instructions concerning her. How lovely that the Saviour has mutual concern over us and shares it with his reapers, his workers that they too may tend to our welfare along the way.

Ruth 2: 14 takes pain to point out that Ruth was satisfied and full from her meal. Full satisfying provisions lay in the table spread for her and the other handmaidens and the reapers of Boaz. What Ruth received fully satisfied her and she was able to go on in the strength of that meal for the endurance of that day till she retired at night.

Also in verse 18, it implies in the last phrase that she took home to Naomi provisions from the table. After she was satisfied she reserved something for her loved one and spread it before her at home. We cannot stress enough the vital truth of the home being the place where the full provision of God should be enjoyed.

Let your loved ones see your bountiful portion. Be a giver. Let your children see what Mum and Dad have received from the Lord as they share God's goodness. What you receive from the table should work itself out at home. Ruth is shown as being satisfied and then leaving. In John 10: 9 we are shown as able to go in and out and find pasture. Let us whether in the church around the table or out of church at home, work or in the community communicate the life principles of the Lord's Table.

Ruth initially thought it to be an accidental occurrence that brought her to the field of Boaz. Ruth 2: 3 shares: "And she happened to come to the part of the field *belonging* to Boaz." God had directed her every footstep till she stood in the field of the only one who could meet her every need.

Throughout the Book of Ruth, in fact, nine times, Boaz is referred to as the 'kinsman.' The Hebrew word 'gaal' is used which literally means 'one who can free or redeem.' The fact that the word is used and is restricted in this specific meaning to the Book of Ruth, except for one other reference in Numbers is highly significant. We can all make our own spiritual application.

None but Christ is our true kinsman, and how we are loved by Him. He alone has the power to free and redeem. And how incredibly he has done this.

As we leave Ruth, ready to become the wife of Boaz, it is lovely to sense so much of the fire of their romance was triggered off around the table. Let it be so in our life.

Study/Meditation 14

THE TABLE OF SAUL
The Table Of Ulterior Motives

The face of Jonathan was livid with anger, he began to speak again but rather than continue he snatched his robe to his shoulder and with deliberate heavy movements and tread stormed out from the presence of his father, King Saul. Saul sat fists clenched, heart pounding from the encounter he had just been through with his son. His orders to his servants measured his anger as he himself stormed from the table.

The king's table now was empty, except for the spread and provision that still lay upon it. Others in the king's household had moved from it talking together in groups and discussing the violent family quarrel that had just erupted.

The table had been spread as at other times for Saul, his sons and those of his royal household. Yet on this occasion, the heart of Saul had hatched a scheme more deadly than being caught in a viper's nest. Saul planned on killing David at the meal. Both David and his bosom friend Jonathan had discerned something of the evil intent in the heart of the king and so David absented himself from the table of Saul.

The table of Saul was not one of family love and kingly provision. It was demonstrated here as a table of ulterior motives. Although the provision of the table was resplendent, the condition of the king's heart was decadent. Although the dress of the king and his attendants were majestic, the garb of the intentions was sinister beyond imagination.

'Death to the shepherd youth.' 'Death to the supposed anointed David.' These thoughts and others bred in the heart and mind of the king whilst he tried to engineer the presence of David to his table, to take his life. Reading I Samuel Chapter 20 and verses 24 to 34 will give you adequate background to this table study.

Days earlier the shepherd boy and future king, along with his close companion Jonathan had sat and discussed the impending danger of David's presence at the table of the king. Their mutual decision had been that in the interest of David's safety and life it would be better if David weren't present at the feast that was intended to be his appointment with death.

David chose rather to be at the table of his natural family than at the table of the king, which was none other than the 'Table of Ulterior Motives.' What a glorious delight it is for every believer to be coming to the table of the King of Kings. Yet, we must be on our guard that we are not drawn there and exposed to the ulterior motives of our own 'soulish' life.

Think about this issue. Often our life before the Lord is in drastic conflict with the Holy Spirit over many things. These differences may not be visible to the rest of the household of faith, just as the intentions of Saul were not fully understood by his entire household except Jonathan. Such an individual may then approach the table and partake from it with suppressed ulterior motives, thinking that their very presence qualifies them to share with the Lord in remembrance.

Beware! God is not as fickle as the slighted souls of mankind. I have had people in my congregation who have on occasions not partaken from the Lord's Table because they feel God is dealing with them over some little issue. You notice different ones just holding back and letting the emblems pass because God is speaking to the very depths of their heart, and they do not want to offend a Holy God. I would rather have it this way than see all just glibly partaking, without the conscious challenge to their motives.

Children watch. Families know. Mum and Dad can sit in church and partake of the emblems and families know of the intense, deeply disturbing quarrel, between Mum and Dad that they overheard just prior to coming to church, or in the car on the way to church. Many people partake of the table and yet there is the ulterior motive of acceptance before the eyes of all those around. They are more interested in what others think of them than what God thinks. Mark my words idle attention or attitude to the Table of the Lord does not go unseen by the 'One' who is closest to us.

Jonathan knew the very diabolical evil that was brooding in his father's heart, and that it was hidden behind the presence of the provision of his kingly table. You cannot hide behind the cup and the bread and sing softly and sweetly the melody of worship and not be pertinently aware that He sees, and that He judges us according to the words of our heart, not just our lips.

Different people in the church may feel others in the congregation are just wonderful people. They partake at the table of the Lord all the time. Unfortunately, after the service in the quiet of their homes, they begin to make accusations against the minister or others in the congregation. They run fellow Christians down and their children sit and listen and hear this and measure up that Mum or Dad was at the same Lord's Table also with these same people. Children quickly associate this with hypocrisy.

Is it any wonder that so many children leave church life and even their Christian faith and walk, sensing the falseness, that too much of the table has become a mere sham, a table of ulterior motives? People would rather partake of the table publicly being seen or perceived as 'holy,' than have the table undertake and do probing work in their own life. A table is a place that calls for real heart-searching. The attitudes displayed at Saul's table set the entire family at variance with each other. It left its mark, and so do attitudes at God's divine table.

The princely Jonathan, with robes trailing after his indignant body stormed through the corridors of Saul's palace, through into the courtyard and to the city beyond. Anger was seething in his heart and the thought pounding in his temples because his father had treated him shamefully in attempting to trap his dear friend David (I Samuel 20: 34). The very next day, even after the heart of the table incident had settled down, the offended prince mounted his steed early in the morning, even as the golden rays of the morning sun began to splash through the Judean hills.

Accompanied by his servant, Jonathan left the city. The city walls were just turning from steel grey to sun-drenched granite white with the morning sun. He rode to the predetermined place to meet with David. The behaviour at his father's table the day before had irrevocably sealed the fate of David and the behaviour and promised love of Jonathan.

Standing on the grassy slopes of the hills, Jonathan shot the telling arrow that communicated to David the very plight of his soul. After the servant had collected the arrow and then been dismissed to the city, a fond response and warmth of fellowship was shared between David and Jonathan, such as would not be repeated, as it was most unlikely that David ever met Jonathan in such a meeting again.

David left that hallowed meeting to endure the life of the hunted. Jonathan left to return to the palace of the hunter, his father. The table was still daily spread, yet David never again was catered for at the table of the king. Are there any of us who personally do not feel we have a place at the table? If the ministry were led to ask different people to sit in various areas of the church I'm sure some would rather sit next to certain other people, whilst others would not want to sit next to them.

How very careful ought we to be in our personal estimation of who has the right or not of attendance at His table? Do we wrap a cloak of pretence around our supposed saintly shoulders, yet find a heart inside intending hurt and harm in thought if not in deed? Would we all be happy to serve everyone in the church with the emblems? To be the servant of all is an honour. Or, would there be slight arsenic traces of discrimination coursing through our being?

It is always very easy to blame another. That was King Saul's approach. 'Thou son of the perverse rebellious woman' (I Samuel 20: 30) he thundered across the table to Jonathan as he sat internally fuming over his father's scheme of death. Saul blamed another for what was his own violation of human dignity.

Do we approach the table with anger, hostility, pride, revenge, and family trouble brooding in the heart filling our very presence at the table? Can we alleviate all of those worries? No! Rather, it surfaces in all of us to be dealt with. The table is the place where we can put bad attitudes to death.

It is a table of remembrance of the glory and majesty of Calvary. Don't turn it into a Table of Ulterior Motive.

Study/Meditation 15

PSALM 23 Table – Part 1
What A Preparation

There would hardly be a person within the confines of the church that has not read and come to love the immortal Twenty-Third Psalm. Its ministry surpasses that which pen can write or imagination can conceive. Men and women in their time of trouble and upon their deathbeds have found ministry and solace from this one single Psalm.

People blessed with victory have sensed the divine blessing that meditation upon this Psalm can bring. As preparation for this study, it would do every reader well to settle back for a quiet time with Bible in hand and take time to read slowly and pray earnestly verse by verse over this incredible Psalm 23.

The two meditations we shall share with you over the next few pages are shared with you with the desire that truly the Lord, the Good Shepherd, will minister afresh in your life.

In this first part we will unfold something of the background colour that the Psalm has, and the basic spiritual applications with special emphasis on the table. Within Pt. 2 there will be a more in-depth treatment of the richness of the meaning of verse 5 reference to the table.

Come with us now into the land of Israel and share the Twenty-Third Psalm.

****

David lay fully stretched on his side upon the grass. He picked a remnant of dry grass hanging lonely within the fresh green carpet that mantled the hills as far as the eye could see since the winter rains had begun enriching life. He chewed the end of the grass with the wispy end making quiet circles in the air. Occasionally he reached out to pat the sheep that browsed beside him. He played with the odd lamb that nudged and nestled into his back. Though resting his eyes scanned ceaselessly the circuit of his sheep, ever alert to guard the flock.

On occasion he arose and followed after one or more of the sheep that were crossing the brow of the hill, quite unaware that they were foraging themselves out of the watchful eye of their shepherd. David gently turned them back into the dell that enclosed his flock as a natural fence. At the base of the dell ran a crystal clear stream, which broke from its babbling course to form quiet pools whose surface was only disturbed by the occasional circling dragonfly, or the ripples set up by a sheep that had moved to its banks to drink.

David rested again this time upon his back and it seemed the golden rays of the sun melted away every trace of disharmony that racked his land. The whole of the valley was bathed in sunlight that seemed to accentuate every colour. A ripple spread across the valley. David sat up and watched the heads of grass move in rhythm swaying from one side of the valley to the other as the fresh winter breeze brushed passed his face and sent a shudder through his being and a gentle flurry through his golden locks of hair. It made him pay attention to his sheep and again become conscious of his task.

David rose to his feet and in the circle of sunshine that was exposed through now white billowing clouded skies, he skirted around the flock checking the sheep as he walked. Finally, he stopped at the stream and stooped. Cupping his hand he drank of the country-tasting water purity. The sheep not more than five paces away seemed to be refreshed in a similar manner.

"Beautiful isn't it?" David said, speaking to the sheep by name next to him. God's provision filled his mind as he looked around finding spiritual expression and application to everything his eyes set their sights on.

With one hand gently upon the shoulder of the sheep and kneeling beside it, he ruffled its wool and snuggled his head into the sun-warmed coat.

"The Lord is my shepherd." The words came softly and yet like a liquid flow from heaven. The impulse of those words fired his very soul. He looked up and around repeating them and felt at the same time a Holy charge and impetus coursing through his mind and heart.

David had felt this before and had often been caused to lapse into prose that had been a blessing to his own soul. Strolling among the sheep his heart gave vent to a heaven-sent melody. "The Lord is my shepherd I shall not want." He paused to stroke one of the flocks that blissfully lay half deep in the grass, feet tucked under her body. "Yes, He makes me lie down in green pastures."

Turning towards the waters he watched the sheep and contemplated. "He leads me beside the still waters." Noting the refreshment that both he and his flock received from such water provision he continued. "He restores my soul: He leads me in the paths of righteousness for His name's sake."

The voice of the Holy Spirit was now beating strong in that young poetic mind. Holy meditations were being laid in a human heart and hundreds to thousands of years later the world would still be remembering those sacred moments of revelation.

Dark winter clouds began to now cast their cold dreary shadows across the valley. David sensed it was time to move the flock back to the safety of the fold, closer to home. As he gently led them he did so under a mantle of increasing grey ominous clouds. Again his mind quickened by the impulses of the Spirit earlier began to crystallise the events around him.

With his rod in his hand, he climbed the undulating hills unafraid of the impending storm. David began to think of a real valley called the 'Valley of the Shadow of Death,' which led towards Jericho via an ancient and important path known as Wadi Qelt. It was understood to be dangerous and difficult to get his sheep through to pastures on the other side.

David continued: "Yes even though I walk through the valley of the shadow of death, I will fear no evil: for you are with me: your rod and your staff they comfort me." Often he had encountered both wild beasts and the occasional robber in the dangerous crossing of this valley. Within his mind, pregnant with Holy visitation and revelation, the comparison of this land began to quicken within him. What he breathed out as a Psalm were real places to him.

He had spent the best part of the day basking in the presence of God. The darkening of the clouds heralded the approach of the storm. It brought reality to his mind that indeed his land was itself in the midst of a storm. As David made his way toward home the visible country skyline slowly filled with threatening rain clouds. Winter rains were upon them. David mused that although he could walk through the darkest of trials and situations, his own people still had not learned the secret of trusting in their God and riding out the storm with Jehovah in control.

David was in the fields with the sheep because his brothers were away at war. The Philistines oppressed the land. From the natural darkness that was creeping into the late hours of the afternoon, the mind of the young shepherd wandered to the battlefront.

He had heard of the exploits of old. Men of courage standing against incredible odds. He had listened to men of renown speaking of fighting battles conscious of the fact that the battle was not theirs, it was the Lords.

On one occasion David had heard the soldiers talk of their preparation for battle. The children of Israel had been so confident of victory that they had prepared their victory feast before they even went into battle. The thought came to David: "You prepare a table before me in the presence of my enemies: You anoint my head with oil; my cup runs over." David was confident in his God.

The same God that had previously enabled him to slay a bear and the lion that was marauding the flock, whilst he was protecting the sheep, was the same God that could stand by His people if they would simply trust in Him. They simply needed to acknowledge His sovereignty over the battle and their lives. The young shepherd boy was supremely confident in his God. Such trust was to be put to the test often in the future, but it never let him down.

David strolled home with the day's meditations filling his heart and mind. He tended to every last sheep till they were all bedded down in the fold, away from the driving wind and rain.

"So my God cares for me," he thought. "He protects me, and cares for me just like my sheep." He patted the last little newborn lamb into the fold next to its mother. "Surely, goodness and mercy will follow me all the days of my life; and I will dwell in the house of the Lord forever."

In those last few minutes as he walked home there came a presence of what God had shared with him. It collected in his mind. Either that night or shortly afterwards, he would pen those immortal words into poetic prose that would outlive him by thousands of years.

Indeed the Twenty-Third Psalm seems to have two vital parts or aspects. It begins with hallowed meditation on the wondrous provision that God provides to the sheep of His fold. Then it turns to consider the conflict and victory that all of the fold of God have in their God, as they trust Him to be their shepherd and the captain of their salvation. We can spend hours in meditations about the resplendent glories of our salvation. But then still buckle under when the storm clouds lower.

Fundamentally there are two challenging aspects of our Christian Life.

1. The majesty of salvation as we can appreciate it day to day. Sadly though for many this is only often when things are going well.
2. The days of conflict and trial, when the storms of life and the shadow of the enemy fall across our pathway.

David beautifully expresses in Psalm Twenty-Three that irrespective of whether they are good or bad experiences that we pass through, our Almighty God has made ample provision for us on the way. The verse dealing with the 'table' falls in the middle of the Psalm and expresses the victory of the Lord in both the good and bad experiences of life. Understanding the victory around the concept of the table was not only important to David, but to each of us.

The Table of the Lord stands as an icon pointing backwards to all the embracing victories that Calvary has won. This is the easy bit to praise God about. When all goes right we can sing. But, when the chips are down and the enemy comes in like a flood, then remember the 'table' is spread as a victory feast over the enemy of our soul.

This is where our view of life is forward towards battles already by faith won.

This Lord's Table is an expression of the victory that Christ has bought for us, once and for all. When things are going well this 'table' thunders out the praise to the one who brings us victory. Then when things are not going well this 'table' stands defiant against the wiles of the enemy.

The table is spread in the face of opposition and the enemy of our soul and clearly, it prophetically says: "These, my children, are victors and over-comers already through what I have provided for them. Before you bring their souls into a life and death struggle, know this Satan, the enemy of all mankind – The battle is the Lords, and the victory belongs to the King of Kings, and through Him to His redeemed."

May we take note that this Twenty-Third Psalm is a personal Psalm? There are seventeen personal appellations within this Psalm alone, which, as you know only has six verses. 'My' occurs five times (Vrs. 1, 3, 5, 5 & 6). 'I' occurs four times (Vrs. 1, 4, 4 & 6). 'Me' occurs seven times (Vrs. 2, 2, 3, 4, 4, 5 & 6). 'Mine' occurs in verse 4.

Don't relegate this Psalm to everybody except you. This is a sensitive portion of God's Word, majoring upon the personal position. It applies to 'you' personally. Don't negate its importance, assigning it to the one alongside you, or to the church generally, or some other identity, without fully accepting its impact in your own life.

As this Psalm speaks of trouble-free moments as well as trouble-filled moments, the Table of the Lord stands to isolate both victory and struggle, as having their absolute victorious strain in the work, which Christ has accomplished for you. Some consider there is a break in the harmony of the Psalm once you begin to read verse five.

I trust you have not considered there to have been a lack of reverence in the way I scripted the possible background to this Psalm. Certainly, David's victory was something that belonged to God's children through thick and thin.

The Table of the Lord stands to assert your victory rights. So in the face of the enemy, or in the face of bliss, let there be rejoicing that: "The battle is the Lord's." What preparation has been made for us? What a remembrance and ongoing victory the 'table' stands for. What a preparation. What salvation!

Study/Meditation 16

PSALM 23 Table – Pt. 2
What A Victory

In Part 1 I tried to share something of the background of Psalm Twenty-Three that occupied that Study/Meditation. Now we want to unfold something of the magnitude of the meaning of the beauty of the table in verse 5. Here is what it says: "You prepare a table before me in the presence of my enemies; You anoint my head with oil; My cup runs over."

We see a table spread. In it, we sense supreme victory in that the prepared table before us is a 'table of victory.' It celebrates overcoming but interestingly is spread 'before' the battle is engaged. Right through the battle to come it still sat as a memorial as the 'Table Of Victory.'

From the lips of David (I Sam. 17: 47) to Jahaziel (II Chronicles 20: 15), in the days of Jehosophat's mighty victory, comes the standard of the Christian, both in conflict and in peace: "The battle is the Lords."

God preserves His people and His purposes in victories that are ordered of Him. It would be good to continually refresh ourselves in the truth and confidence that the Lord fights on behalf of His own (Deut. 1: 30 and 3: 22).

The Table of the Lord, which we celebrate weekly, fortnightly or monthly, or as often as you celebrate it (in church or at home), stands as a table of victory. It is spread for the entire world to see. My captain, Jesus, never lost a battle and is not about to do so now. The individuals that do lose battles are the rank and file who fail to recognise their captain has already won the victory for them.

Napoleon once was overwhelmed in a particular battle on the Russian front. He turned to the drummer boy standing by his side. "Beat a retreat," he ordered with coldness in his voice. Silence reigned for a moment. The lad looked puzzled. His sticks were held up, but there was no action. Napoleon turned again to the boy and repeated his order. With fury in his voice he ordered: "Beat a retreat I said!"

"Sir," said the lad in trembling fear. "I don't know how to beat a retreat. My drum major only ever taught me to beat a charge, an advance, an attack." "Then beat a charge, an advance and attack," Napoleon said in desperation. The little lad played his hardest. The French troops with fresh hope after hearing the drummer's message stormed an attack and their seeming defeat turned into a magnificent victory. This occurred all because a little drummer boy didn't know how to play or beat a retreat.

Christian, there is no retreat with the Captain of our Salvation. In situations of uncontrollable odds, it is His destiny to win the victory every time.

Perhaps the most important concept that we want to leave with you in this study surrounds the word 'enemies,' in the fifth verse. Throughout the Old Testament, you may safely say that the word 'enemy,' or its derivatives, occurs hundreds of times. In fact, it is used in excess of three hundred and fifty times. Yet, the meaning behind the word 'enemies' in Psalm Twenty-Three is reserved for only fourteen or fifteen of those three hundred and fifty-plus references.

The selective, special references only occur in the book of Esther and the Psalms, inclusive of Psalm Twenty-Three. The word has a much deeper meaning than just a physical enemy in front of a soldier. It means: "To straighten, or distress." It is 'Tsarar' in the Hebrew. It rather refers to the negative position the enemy will bring your soul and thinking into, than an actual physical enemy.

It is the negative state of mind and soul that the enemy's psychologically destructive actions have caused. The word is better understood as the circumstances of an enemy attack and the state of mind engendered by the enemy attack, rather than the visible tangible enemy. To straighten is: "To make straight, or narrow, restrictive distress, to afflict or press with poverty."

The enemy within this Twenty-Third Psalm is the lowest form of attack. It is the bondage of mind that the enemy can bring us into when we give up.

Psychological warfare goes on throughout the world today. But, Satan is the master of it. If he can in any way attack the people of God through their minds, to think that they are in bondage, that the battle is lost, and that the enemy will triumph in situations, then he has an advantage. Nothing is irretrievable to the Saviour. But negative individuals are putting themselves outside of Christ's triumphant presence and victory.

Consider how this almost took over David's thinking and ruled his life, especially contacting his brothers as soldiers of king Saul. Israel's troops had lost the battle already in their minds. It almost coerced David into thinking that way when I Samuel 17: 24 shows "All the men of Israel running," David included. Note it was 'All,' which must have included David.

The sides of the hills were lined with tents, on both sides of the valley. Banners of two nations flapped in the breeze. Israel and the Philistines were at war. And, in the narrow confines of the Valley of Elah, Saul the king, was face to face with the very same enemy of Psalm Twenty-Three.

No, the Twenty-Third Psalm is not talking about the Philistines, but rather the level of bondage mentally that they had already inflicted upon Israel. At the stage when David arrived to visit his brothers (I Samuel 17: 1), Israel had sunk so low in their morale and fighting spirit that there wasn't a man who would step out to take on Goliath. Now let's not be too hard on them, for I hazard a guess that you and I would not be quite prepared to take a stroll out to face the giant. The enemy had in fact won the day. Fear, the 'Tsarar' enemy ruled.

Come let us look at another situation. Twelve men stand before all of Israel and Moses. They are all princes, the finest representative from each tribe. Two, standing slightly to one side, are disgusted at the fearsome report that the other ten spies have given of the ability of Israel to move in and conquer the promised land (Numbers chapters 13 and 14).

It was fear that had gripped the heart of the ten evil spies, not a physical enemy. The giants in the room were not the physical giants in the Promised Land, but the real giant was fear. And it was this same terror that caused them to lose the battle concerning entrance into the Promised Land before a single blow was landed by either side. The narrow constricting fears that the enemy of our soul will bring us into if we let him, is illustrated here.

In the face of the enemy would I rise up as a warrior? We need to remember that in the face of whatever Satan wants to inflict upon the mind, we are already conquerors. In over 90% of all encounters, the victory or loss thereof has been accomplished in the mind, a long time before a single blow has landed.

So shouldn't our hearts rejoice to know God has already prepared a table of victory before our enemies and us? Before everything that would bring us into bondage, the Saviour has spread a victory feast. The Table of the Lord is spread as a signification of the past victory of the cross. Nothing that Satan can bring to the area of our minds should be able to stop us from demanding: "Get behind me, Satan. I've got the victory now, through Christ my Redeemer."

Certainly, we should exercise our minds more to know or realise that we are victorious and will continually be in victory through what Christ has accomplished for us. Boldly the Word declares: "Let this mind be in you which was also in Christ Jesus," (Philippians 2: 5).

Again it is the Apostle Paul that encourages us: "For though we walk in the flesh, we do not war according to the flesh. For the weapons of our warfare *are* not carnal but mighty in God for pulling down strongholds, casting down arguments and every high thing that exalts itself against the knowledge of God, bringing every thought into captivity to the obedience of Christ," (II Corinthian 10: 3 to 5).

Beloved we can't reinforce enough the captivity that the enemy of your soul will bring you into through a careless, undisciplined mind. Set the mind as a flint against Satan, by living the principle that we are more than conquerors in all that comes our way.

David knew that this issue of fear was Israel's trouble. That is why he, through the direction of the Holy Spirit, chooses the specific word for 'enemy' that we are looking at. God has meant to set forth a table of remembrance not merely celebrating a past event, but also of constant victory in our life, and in the future to come. Note the table was 'prepared.' This word means: "To arrange, to set in array." Calvary has certainly openly displayed and manifested the greatest array of love and victory that the world could know. Before the world was created the work of the cross on Calvary was set in array. And the table of victory, past, present and future has been spread. None can argue with the efficacious work.

When we gather around the Table of the Lord, it is to accept and live out the victory that it so expressively speaks of. Jesus knew the value of the table. That is why He commanded mankind to do so often, in remembrance of Him and the victory of the cross. Let the table speak to our hearts of the banishment of the enemies of the mind. Satan has one purpose – to choke our spiritual life. We must not allow it.

Consider that the table was spread so lavishly so that I might feast, whilst He has fought on my behalf. That may seem to you to imply a non-participant attitude, but it bears some meditation. By our lives of victory, we will be a testimony to the world of the power of the Christian life. Our witness is important. The world will know Christianity is viable when they see the anointing and Christ-like nature that is upon us. It will see an overflowing cup of blessing that we drink from. When we clearly identify it as the outworking of the cross it will draw people to Him.

May we never just indolently approach the Table of the Lord with a mere performance attitude? Participation should bring liberty to every believer every time they celebrate it. We should realise its power, positive confession and positive position that every partaker is potentially placed in. Lord thank you that: "Thou prepare a table before me in the presence of my enemies." God doesn't prepare it behind us but before us. This is an ongoing experience, pressing forward the fight into the camp of the enemy, knowing that he is defeated before we even begin.

Study/Meditation 17

THE TABLE OF DAVID FOR MEPHIBOSHETH

The court of the palace was silent with chilling anticipation. The throne of David was filled with a king of compassion. On either side stood the courtiers standing silently awaiting word from their master.

Before the throne was a pitiful sight. A young man, lame in both feet, lay prostrate before the throne in obeisance, fearing for his very life. His clothes were not the royal silks that had once graced his father and grandfather. Poverty was his clothing and pity for his companion.

Mephibosheth looked up to the throne and although it was mere seconds since he has prostrated himself before King David, it seemed to him and the hushed court that an eternity of judgement had transpired. The king smiled and looked intently at Mephibosheth who lay before him. Something about his mouth and face reminded David of Mephibosheth's father, his dear friend Jonathan.

There was such a comparison and likeness that David's heart and mind turned to reminisce of the 'soul-knit' fellowship that he and Jonathan, had enjoyed before he was slain in the battle of Gilboa. Moving from his throne David moved to the still fearful, quivering form before him. Gently he raised Mephibosheth and embraced him in a warm welcome. It brought back memories of his friend's embrace with Jonathan.

As they sat in intense conversation with each other Mephibosheth uncovered the story of his lame feet. He recounted that at the death of his father Jonathan and grandfather Saul, and fearing for the safety of the baby Mephibosheth, his nurse had fled with the baby in her arms. On her journey to safety, she fell heavily and the fall was so serious that the little young prince Mephibosheth, then only five years old, was made lame by the injuries of the fall.

Moistened kingly eyes lovingly beheld the nervous Mephibosheth, as he slowly told his story and with certain gestures and mannerisms the young man made David see again, his dear departed friend Jonathan. Jonathan seemed again to live as he relived a thousand mannerisms now through his son.

The account of the meeting of David and Mephibosheth is beautifully dealt with in II Samuel 9: 1 to 13 and II Samuel 19: 24 to 30. David had initiated the search to find any surviving relatives of the household of Saul to exhibit kindness. How this mirrors Christ's initiative to bring hope and salvation to the lost seed of Adam.

Love initiates, it does not passively wait to be motivated. David in kindness reached out to the decimated and stricken family of Saul, expressing the love of a benevolent king. This raises in our thinking the comparison of the King of King's love for us. How graciously Christ has reached out when we were unworthy. He stepped out of glory into humanity all for our benefit.

In David's search, he discovered there seemed to be only one left in the household of Jonathan, son of Saul. This descendant lived in the household of Machir the son of Ammiel. Machir means "salesman," whilst Ammiel, his father means: "My people are strong." Certainly, before Christ rescued us we were being held, or as it was sold to the salesman of this world. Then Jesus touched and liberated our hearts. We were amongst people who were strong in their own ways. We could find no way out till the Master called us out.

David called Mephibosheth to come to the palace and so he was brought, probably carried. How a lame man could make the journey I do not know. We too are often typified as seriously lame in our feet (Hebrews 12: 13). Yet divine love undergirded our life and brought us to Christ.

It could have been a combination of his efforts and the assistance of the king's servants that eventually brought Mephibosheth into the presence of the king. So often when we come to Christ we do so by a combination of our own search and desire and the capable assistance of servants of the King.

When Mephibosheth was first born what delight he was to his parents, but what a horrid name was afflicted upon him. We say this not so much in our ability to pronounce it but in the real value of its meaning. Mephibosheth means: "From the mouth of shame," or "destroying shame." What a negative meaning for one's name. Why would you give that name to your darling child? How do you live with that? In Mephibosheth's manner before David, it actually seems like he was living, or acting out the meaning of his name.

Another obscure meaning to his name is: "Utterance Of Baal," The curse of Baal tagged this young man from the cradle. Yet, he was called into the presence of the king.

It also is true that each of us was part of this evil world, some with less than honourable reputations and a name of disrepute, yet Christ's great love took hold of us and drew us into the palace of the king. We became seated with Him to share the glorious inheritance He has provided.

David extended kindness beyond what was considered normal. Not only did David receive Mephibosheth into the palace and acceptance of his realm, but also he restored to him all the property that once belonged to his grandfather, king Saul. From a pauper to a prince and rich man in one gracious decree.

Mephibosheth came in fear for his life and left with the inheritance of the king. Ziba, an old servant of king Saul was made responsible for the management of the property bequested to Mephibosheth, for two reasons. Firstly, because of the incapacity of Mephibosheth to care for his own property due to his injuries and secondly, because David desired that Mephibosheth should remain within the palace and be his guest at his table as long as he lived.

Carefully examining the passage in II Samuel Chapter 9, with particular emphasis on verses 7, 10 and 13 you can see the repeated love of David to draw Mephibosheth to his own personal table, to feast on the king's provisions. Imagine the great contrast that has just taken place from being dependent on others for his food and well-being to now being brought into the domain of the limitless provisions of the king of all the land.

From the meagre provisions of his own table, that catered for the single needs of a family to the limitless provisions of a king at his glorious rich and more than an adequate table. Food beyond description. Provisions beyond measure. Although the table of David does not rank with that of Solomon, which we shall look at later, it was nevertheless one of extensive magnitude, because of the size of his family and the range of his servants.

The king's delight for Mephibosheth was: "Come and feast at my table." The great delight of the Father's heart is for us to come and feast at His table, which is provided for our benefit and fellowship. It is not a single table where we eat alone. This table of provision embraces us all as spiritual Mephibosheth's lame in our spiritual feet. But we are called to sit in heavenly places with Christ Jesus.

We are called to come to the table of the King, in the presence of the King, in the kingdom of the King. What a contrast and what a present-day application to each and every one of our lives. Notice that Mephibosheth did have an inheritance, yet he lived with his daily needs provided in the house or palace of the king.

We certainly do have an inheritance in Christ, but we must remember to live daily with the King. Crave His very presence as the token of His acceptance, rather than being preoccupied with an inheritance, as grand as that might be. Some may talk till their blue in the face of eternal rewards, as good and precious as they may be, but understand that to be in His presence right here and now is so precious and real.

Before becoming Christians we were lame on our feet, we had lost our standing before the Lord, and our ability to look after our own interests. We were lame and a victim of an enemy stronger than us. Then the precious love of Jesus reached out to us and issued an invitation to come into His presence. Oh, the awesome apprehension that accompanied that call.

With fear and trepidation, we approached the Lord full well knowing that our just reward was death. Yet, He reached down and loved us so deeply and drew us out of the house of the enemy of our soul and brought us to His banqueting table, where His banner over us is love. Our delight is now to feast continually at that table.

For many Christians, the weekly, fortnightly or monthly gathering around the Lord's Table comes as a religious part of their background. Yet, it should be something of a rare delight to every believer. Imagine in your own heart a beggarly individual being drawn into the palace of the king and then invited to feast at his table.

As we approach the sacred bread of His body and the wine of His blood, we ought to have a holy ripple energise every area of our soul. May we be fully aware of the import of what a great privilege it is to be drawn by love, not a ceremony, to His dear table.

Some people view troublesome times as direct onslaughts of the devil. Others see them through the eye of experience, to know that in every situation God can be glorified if we trust fully in Him in times of opposition.

Later in life, Mephibosheth would be taken advantage of by Ziba. Through guile Ziba, the servant of Mephibosheth, caused his master to be seen to act in a way that later brought discredit to him, even assumed rebellion against the king. But, at all times Mephibosheth's intentions were honest before King David and his kingdom. Ziba had deceived David and set Mephibosheth up to look guilty for not supporting David in the terrible rebellion of Absalom.

II Samuel 16: 1 to 4 describes a little of this incident. David was on the run from Absalom and Mephibosheth was accused of attempting to regain the throne for the line of Saul. When the civil dispute and rebellion of Absalom ended with his death, David then eventually returned to Jerusalem. Then the entire diabolical plot of Ziba's deception was uncovered.

However, it is worthy of note that although Ziba had wronged Mephibosheth, the lame prince had in fact only ever exhibited the greatest of devotion to the king in his absence.

Later in II Samuel 19: 24, shortly after David's return to Jerusalem, we see the unkept, haggard, wasted form of what appeared to be a lame beggar before the presence of King David. This is how Mephibosheth came to the king. In all the time that David was forced on the run from his rebellious son Absalom, Mephibosheth had wasted away. He adopted a position of self-neglect till the king was rightfully restored to the throne again. From the day David was forced to leave Jerusalem till he came back to the throne in peace, Mephibosheth grieved, not caring for himself. He literally wasted away. His life was incomplete whilst ever the king was not on his throne.

This raises a challenging point. Is the king in residence in our life? If we feel wasted and lacking it may be that we are not recognising the king in His rightful place on the throne of our hearts. II Samuel 19: 11 clearly shows the devotion of Mephibosheth. The cry of his heart was, let all my inheritance pass away if needs be, but grant always that your servant may abide at your table. Mephibosheth's attitude was to let Ziba take all, even though he had been dishonest, but give me the right of access to the king so that I might feast at his table.

Do we always so tenaciously hang onto the temporal inheritances of this world so that we lose sight of the eternal value of fellowship around the table? Like Mephibosheth let the world take all, but give us Jesus. The world cannot remove the king from residence deep within our hearts. He is on the throne.

Later the Gibeonites sued for justice and required the death of the last living descendant of Saul's house, because of the great injustice that Saul had inflicted upon them whilst he was king. Yet, David spared Mephibosheth and preserved him from any harm. David wouldn't allow anyone to touch Jonathan's son. The king preserved his life and so will he yours as you totally abandon yourself to Him.

A greater king than David stands now on our behalf to preserve us in the battle of His Table. II Samuel 19: 28 carefully crystallises the devotion of Mephibosheth. Can we copy it? Do we yearn for fellowship around the table of the King? Seeking only His smile and the favour of His presence is our satisfying joy.

Study/Meditation 18

SOLOMON'S TEMPLE TABLE

On the porch of the temple and throughout the Holy Place priests lay prostrate, unable to stand in their service to the Lord and the dedication of Solomon's Temple. They were alive, but it was discernible only by the praises that were rising from their lips in somewhat of an accord with the music and singers outside the temple. Thousands upon thousands of Israel had flocked to the dedication of the grandest building that Israel had ever, and would ever raise.

Instead of an audible excitement that would accompany such occasions the fear of the Lord was rippling through the congregation. Little children buried their heads in their parent's shoulders unable to look for the childlike fear that gripped them. Normally vocal adults stood speechless almost in mute unbelief, at the site that confronted them.

Only minutes before they had seen a company of priests slowly wind their way through the rest of the people to ascend the steps to the great temple of Solomon. Upon the shoulders of the priests was carried the Ark of the Covenant. Simultaneously when the ark was deposited within the Holy of Holies and the golden staves were withdrawn, as the clothes of covering were removed, the air had been pierced with the triumphant note of one hundred and twenty heralding priests upon trumpets signalling the note for the great throng of singers and other instruments to join in the praise of Jehovah.

Whilst the priests were just returning from the Holy of Holies the visible, almighty presence of God flooded down in the form of a unique cloud covering the Holy Place and the magnificent sanctuary that had taken seven years to build. When the priests were coming from the Holy Place towards the Most Holy Place, ministering to the Lord they had been struck prostrate by the divine Shekinah glory of God. Priests lay in every direction, visible to Solomon on the porch as he stared inside the temple precincts, and to the amazed and awe-struck congregation behind him.

Like an invisible wind, a ripple went through the people as they sensed the hand and the presence of God. They bowed before the Lord. Children asked parents what was happening only to be met with tear-filled faces saying: "God has come among us." The crescendo of praise upon instruments and priestly voice penetrated an otherwise silent sky. Across the valley that surrounded Jerusalem could be heard the praise to a people-inhabiting God.

One by one the priests emerged from within the temple where they had laid before the Lord. Their faces were soft with weeping, their garments ruffled and lacking their fresh crisp press. Yet, they had met with God in such a way, as had never been their personal experience before. Solomon had at this stage been blessing the people before him and reiterating the sovereign responsibility of the people to walk in a holy state before the Lord.

As the night fires of Israel burned, and thankful souls returned to their own homes, many a priest was still quivering from the overflow of the presence of God that they had literally seen, partaken of and been consumed by. Excited little children sat at their father's feet as he tried to recount what had happened in the temple when God came down upon his people.

The temple was an incredible structure. Even now as people moved about the streets of Jerusalem in the closing hours of the day, they looked up to the crest of Moriah to see that colossus of an edifice, raised to the glory of God, black against the crimson, orange sky behind it. Solomon rested within his palace satisfied and thankful with his mind wandering back to the time when many years previously he had been summoned to the presence of his father King David. His father looked both happy and yet regretful on that day.

Slowly David unfolded the burden of his heart to erect a temple to the glory of God. Yet with sadness in his tone, he told his son that God would not allow him to complete the task because he had shed much blood. This still lingered in the mind of Solomon. Often they carefully they went over the plan together and David recounted to his eager son how the Spirit of God had implanted the very concepts and design of such a temple within his heart (See 1 Chronicles 28:11 and 12).

From a plan born of the Spirit, the Temple of Solomon was raised to the glory of God. Before his death David made full provision for the temple to be built by his son (1 Chronicles 28:16). Gold and precious items were amassed and set aside for the construction of the temple. David left an ample supply of wealth and building materials at his death for the temple to be a glorious structure.

We can appreciate that in Christ, He has left in his death an abundant, wondrous supply of resources to ensure the temple, that is created, is a glorious one. And that temple is us!

The temple of the Holy Spirit in every born-again believer could not be consummated till Christ's death and resurrection. Even before his death, Christ knew that His provision for humanity was mankind's redeeming feature. Revelation 13:8 says: "The Lamb slain from the foundation of the world." All was made ready because he died. And, such a provision has been made for each and every one of us. The pattern or design externally and the worship internally in Solomon's Temple were all ordered by the Spirit of God. Is it any less in the Temple of The Holy Spirit?

The Temple of Solomon, for so it is called, was much grander than Moses' tent tabernacle of the wilderness. Solomon's temple was noted for its lavish beauty of detail rather than for its great size. It was totally built-in parts away from the crest of Moriah. All the building components were brought to the holy site of the temple. The finished stones were placed one upon the other. The wood was all cut and shaped outside the domain of the temple precinct.

It was said that the sound of iron was not heard upon the crest of Moriah as the temple was being built. Its magnificence can really only be discerned from Scripture as no archaeological evidence remains of its glory. The temple stands as a perfect example of the Church of Jesus Christ that is being raised to His glory throughout the world. From every quarter they brought material for the temple, even from lands afar.

So the church of Jesus Christ has gathered material in humanity from every tribe and nation. How God fashions us in the sea of life, even as the timbers of Solomon's temple were floated through the sea to the shores of the Promised Land. How in the valleys of life and the hard rock quarries of endurance Christ is cutting Himself out a Church that is true and straight, one that can weather the storm and fit edge to edge with his fellow saint.

Each Christian is an essential part of the glorious Church of God. I am so thankful that the Lord said: " I will build the Church." Building the church is God's business and the pattern of example in Solomon's temple creates many trains of thought for our spirit.

Within the tent tabernacle of Moses, there was one Table of Shewbread. But, within the Temple of Solomon, there were ten tables. Ten pure gold candlesticks or lampstands flanked one side, and ten pure gold tables flanked the other side of the Holy Place. When you think of Solomon's Temple one is sometimes inclined to think that it was his personal grandiose idea to have a such lavish display. Yet remember the Word. Solomon only followed the plan that was committed to him by his father David the king, who in turn was only following the plan directly from the Spirit of God Himself.

God ordered ten tables, not of shittim wood overlaid with gold as in the Tent Tabernacle but pure gold through and through. Cost cannot be conceived of the value of the tables within the Temple of Solomon (II Chronicles 4: 8 and 19). Why ten tables some may ask? God is a God of order and so often He revealed His perfect government or governance and way amongst men by the use of the numeric ten.

In Biblical numerics 'ten' represents original perfection, or perfection in order. God's perfect plan was outworked through human agencies here on earth. Consider there were

Ten Commandments; Noah was the tenth through Seth. The tithe is a tenth. The Holy of Holies was ten by ten by ten cubits. There were ten plagues of God's wrath and ten kingdoms (Daniel 7:24). Ten virgins, ten lepers and so on through God's Word continually affirm this pattern.

God is a God of order and He was establishing His perfect government amongst mankind when the ten tables were introduced to the House of The Lord in Solomon's day. God was saying to the children of Israel to abide and reside in Him in the divine order He provided. We understand that if the children of Israel had listened to the Lord at all times throughout their life, after the erection of the magnificent temple of Solomon, then they would have walked in perfect order knowing the actual presence of God with them always.

Yet they departed from God's ways and the magnificent glory of God departed from the Temple of Solomon (Ezekiel 9, 10 and 11). God was expressing His perfect order in the tables. Because the children of Israel did not walk in that order did not negate the sovereignty or order of God in itself.

The Table of the Lord God has created a perfect order that He desires all of His people should share. Yet, it is not His fault that sin-ridden humanity often does not love His table or its instruction of it.

Under Solomon, Israel reached the zenith and heights of cultural and political importance. Into this cradle, God nestled the perfection of His plan in the temple. Because Israel grew up thinking it was too big for God, did not mean that God's ways were outdated and obsolete. Adherence to His ways would have saved them much agony, captivity and depravity. God's order was complete and the Ten Golden Tables speak of the total perfection of a perfect God among His less-than-perfect people.

The Table of the Lord before us is perfect. Are we, its participants mirroring that same perfection? It shows us up for our imperfections. Do we feel prostrated and levelled out when we approach his Holy Presence as the priests of old were? Or, is there a reserve that holds a barrier between our

God and us? In many places today you would be regarded as fanatical to be prostrate before the Lord. But in God's way of doing things, it is nothing more than worship.

There was of necessity an increase in priesthood participation within the Temple of Solomon than what had been experienced in David's Tent Tabernacle, where the Ark of God had been kept. In the Tent Tabernacle, only a few priests could eat the shewbread each Sabbath because there was only one table.

Now within the Temple of Solomon, there were ten tables. A multitude of reverent, thankful priests could eat of the provision of the table. Prior to Calvary, there was only one table of acceptance and that was Jewish. But through Calvary, the table is available to every race and creed. A multitude of priests is invited to come and feast at His Table with Him. Nationalities of a hundred ethnic backgrounds are called to be part of the royal priesthood that is drawn to the Table of the Lord.

Tragically Solomon's heart, later in life, was turned from closely following the Lord by his attachment to many strange wives. His example, as cancer, affected the entire spiritual structure of the children of Israel. Don't let us be involved with any relationships with the world that pollutes the Church with spiritual adultery, so debauching the meaning of His perfection at the table.

Pure Gold. The ten tables stood as an example. Ten in a dead straight row, each solid gold. Indescribable value. Certainly, the perfection of our Saviour is of a value inaccessible by our feeble minds. He always desires us to be vessels unto honour (II Timothy 2:20).

Every time you approach the Table of the Lord, remember its perfection its absolute God-breathed order and thank God as a priest upon your face that He has called you to share at such a table.

Study/Meditation 19

THE TABLE OF SOLOMON – Part 1
The Magnitude Of The Table

We begin now a series of five studies on the Lord's Table, taking the magnificent Table of Solomon as the central pivot upon which we will hang these meditations. It needs to be mentioned here that we feel it wiser, for continuity and understanding that the reader sequentially takes the studies from Part 1 through to Part 5 rather than reading at random, out of sequence.

Each successive study to some degree relies upon the background of all preceding studies centring on this same theme. We trust that your meditations will be as rewarding as ours have been over the many years when we have sought to bring enrichment to all our devotions around the Lord's Table. May we all be encouraged as we progress further.

I Kings 4: 22 to 23 shares: "Now Solomon's provision for one day was thirty kors of fine flour (around 150-195 bushels), sixty kors of meal (around 300-390 bushels), ten fatted oxen, twenty oxen from the pastures, and one hundred sheep, besides deer, gazelles, roebucks, and fatted fowl."

I Kings 4: 26, 27 continues: "Solomon had forty thousand stalls of horses for his chariots and twelve thousand horsemen. And these governors (officers), each man in his month, provided food for King Solomon and for all who came to King Solomon's Table. There was no lack in their supply."

I don't think there's a mind that can properly conceive the magnitude of the Table of Solomon. Servants milled about by the score, arranging and setting out the entire length and grandeur of the tables, for indeed multiple tables would have been needed. Their dress marked them as almost royalty themselves. They worked quietly in preparation for the usual daily dinner of the king. Solomon's household, and those especially invited, feasted in a manner that defies the imagination.

The finest of silk curtains hung in graceful folds around the banqueting chamber. Gold taches clung to their satin textured festooned drapes. Here and there maidens of fair beauty stood gently adjusting the drapes and flowered arrangements that certainly spoke of the presence of a mighty king.

The chief steward spoke sternly to certain of the servants and they moved instantly to obey the dictates of this domestic overload. Goblets more exquisite than could be found singularly anywhere in Israel lined the length of Solomon's Table/s. The seating was plush, oriental but regal. In pre-eminence was the seat of the king. Cascading from it were the various honoured seats of dignitaries, till the lowliest seat, of richer taste than of any court today, was found.

Below in the underground chambers of the kitchen, the sight was unbelievable. It defies our understanding of how such a large volume of food as the Scripture outlines could be prepared for consumption in one day and every day. Dissected bodies of animals lay on preparation tables, as they were skilfully prepared by the best butchers, chefs and food artisans that Israel had.

The finest of meat was prepared in the finest of ways. Thirty oxen alone were taken daily and slaughtered for the table/s of the king. One hundred sheep and an unspecified number of deer, gazelles and roebuck also graced the table/s. The I King's passage only refers to 'fatted fowls,' but these could have numbered hundreds of pheasants, quail, ducks and chickens that had been specially fattened.

Twelve thousand hunters divided into a thousand hunters per month scoured the hills and valleys far from Jerusalem to bring in the game meat. Such an organization was in place just for the daily provisions of the table/s.

Even the kitchen servants, as they busied themselves with their tasks, wondered at the magnificence of a table that could hold the majority of this feast. Yet, a feast it was not, for this was only the daily provision of Israel's most luxuriant king. The servants and those engaged in preparation must have numbered hundreds.

Throughout the entire palace of the king, the glorious odours of sweet delicacies rose to tantalise both guard and guest alike. By the time the entire table was finished and the vast amount of food was prepared, hundreds, possibly thousands of man hours had gone into the preparation of meals for one day for the mighty king Solomon.

Not only were meat dishes prepared singularly but entire beasts were prepared as exotic dishes. Arrangements of the meal and flour-based delicacies graced the table/s of the king. From the soft flesh of venison and fowl to the rich red-blooded meat of oxen, garnished in ways that make our Sunday dinners look more like a mere snack. Pastries, bread, cakes and meal dishes with the wafting spiced aroma of the east were in abundance.

When one looked at the table/s it was very difficult to see what was embellishment and garnishing and what was actual food. The spread of the table/s was unbelievable. 'Fit for a king,' in more ways than the proverb could imply. There was hardly a section of the table/s that was not laid out in such an exquisite design with food, that the guests when approaching it for the first time may have felt almost guilty for disturbing the display.

The implication of Scripture is that the setting of the table was also something that was beyond the normal realm of the king's court. If you have a problem now, selecting the right knife or fork to pick up at some prestigious banquet or restaurant, then Solomon's Table would have left you dazzled. There was greater wealth on the table in silver and gold than we would see in a lifetime. The grace of the presentation was enhanced only by the presence of the king, which we shall discuss in later studies.

The Scriptures that deal with the provision of the Table of Solomon clearly state that it was the provision for just one day. Every day such provisions were brought and prepared at the palace to feed the great household and servants of the king.

Although the provision was spread over the entire day's meals, indeed the majority would have been presented at one single time and meal for that main meal as is taken and customary in the east.

Meat and flour with meal, are the two basic divisions of the provision of the Table of Solomon. If you carefully read the types of foods presented they fall into one or the other of these two categories. Nothing, we repeat nothing, is included in the Word of God as an accidental occurrence or reference. God's sovereign design is upon each word and meaning.

If there are two things that speak so deeply of the dual aspects of the redemptive work it is these two types of provision. Meal, flour and grains speak so much of the manhood and humanity of the Lord Jesus Christ. Rember he was the 'Bread of Life,' (John 6: 48). It displays His humanity in a profound way, which we will develop later. The meat substances, the slaying of the meat, and the shedding of blood speak so intensely of the Lord's work and sacrificial death on Calvary as the: "Lamb slain from the foundation of the world."

As we unite these two aspects of the wonder of the work of Calvary and see them spread upon the Table of Solomon with inconceivable magnitude and seating an equally inconceivable large number of guests. We sense something of the shadow of meaning in the Table of the Lord.

The greatness of Jesus is in this sacred comparison. His divinity took on humanity, till the great redemptive purposes were accomplished. Certainly, Jesus was the Son of God, certainly, he was the incarnation of divinity, and yet let us always remember it was mantled in the frailty of human flesh. Not that we suggest he was frail in the human sense. Christ redeemed mankind from frailty. Humanity's other name ought to be 'frailty and weakness.' And into this mould the Saviour allowed Himself to take shape.

"But Jesus made Himself of no reputation, taking the form of a bondservant, *and* coming in the likeness of men. And being found in appearance as a man, He humbled Himself and became obedient to *the point of* death, even the death of the cross" (Philippians 2: 7 & 8). This is more than our human minds can contain and fully understand. Yet the Saviour walked, veiled in human flesh, living out His humanity to become the meal and flour personification of The Bread of Life in the all-atoning sacrifice, through the shedding of His blood, that bought humanity back into acquiescent fellowship with an omnipotent God again.

Jesus, Himself often referred to His association with this shadow/type from Solomon's Table. As previously stated: "I am the bread of life," are the words of the Saviour in John 6: 48. Perusal of the whole context of John chapter six is interesting to illustrate this humanity in Christ. Early in the sacred script the type seen in Genesis 3: 15 refers to Christ as the 'seed' and again in Mark 4: 28 Christ alludes to Himself as the 'corn of wheat' that must die. He is the 'measure of meal' that has been sacrificed to bring the provision of the Table of the Lord. The perfection of humanity was realised. Only Jesus Christ with that perfection has wrought salvation available to all of humanity in return.

Let us consider the meat and blood provision of the Table of Solomon. We can see in our mind's-eye such colossal numbers of beasts. Instantly there lies a comparative model. Was there ever a sacrifice that can compare with that which Christ has wrought for every one of us at Calvary? He was, and is, the spotless Lamb of God. His sacrificial offering was in real blood, yielding the unsearchable fruits of eternal life for all who will simply trust and live in the power of that finished work.

As the Saviour sat at the meal with His own disciples at the Last Supper he referred to His own impending sacrifice when he said: "This cup is the new testament in my blood, which is shed for you" (Luke 22: 20). I Corinthians 11: 24 puts it this way: "Take eat, this is my body which is broken for you." There is enormous merit in what Christ has done on Calvary.

Christ's shed blood was a human and eternal sacrifice. It has spoken now and will ever speak of the favour man has been granted in God's love. John expresses it even more penetratingly: "Then Jesus said to them, 'Most assuredly, I say to you unless you eat the flesh of the Son of Man and drink His blood, you have no life in you. Whoever eats My flesh and drinks My blood has eternal life, and I will raise him up on the last day. For My flesh is food indeed, and My blood is drink indeed. He who eats My flesh and drinks My blood abides in Me, and I in him.'" (John 6: 53 to 56). Christ has become all in all to the human race in every way. Life is now lived through Him and the work of the cross.

As we gather around the Table of the Lord we are called to remember the body and blood of the Lord Jesus Christ. Solomon's Table was full of symbolic meal and meat images, speaking of the humanity and sacrificial atonement nature of our Saviour.

Can any one of us ignore the fact that the Saviour overcame sin whilst garmented in mortal humanity? Can any one of us ignore the fact that through the work of Calvary, the shedding of His own blood and the yielding of His own life, there has been created the cure of man's sick, sin-soaked, soul, spirit and body?

Solomon's Table was immense, yet it dwarfed in comparison with the virtue that the Table of the Lord speaks about. It is beyond our ability to know the grandeur of the guests when it came to Solomon's Table. Can any one of our minds fully grasp how many blood-washed saints meet in a hundred different ways every week, in millions of communion services, to remember and glorify the finished work of Calvary?

Indeed the magnitude of Solomon's Table can only be surmised. Yet summaries are very poor meditations of the wonder of the Table of the Lord. Live it, enjoy it, and sense the fullness of what God is doing throughout the world. He is calling more and more to the greatest memorial feast of the ages. The manhood of the Lord Jesus Christ in His humanity and the sacrificial death on Calvary are spoken of in shadow in Solomon's Table. But don't live in the shadows, enjoy the real substance of all that has been prepared.

Study/Meditation 20

THE TABLE OF SOLOMON – Part 2
The Incomparable Table

Throughout the life of Solomon many people of low and high rank, prophets, priests and kings as well as commoners were to find themselves at his table. When special dignitaries were expected and arrived we can imagine that special arrangements were made with respect to the meals. It seems inconceivable that they were not specially catered for, in the light of what one day's provision was for the Table of Solomon, as was shared in Part 1 of these Solomon's Table meditations. Yet, whether palace or home, both have this common quality... guests require special attention.

Perhaps the greatest single visit that Solomon had from regal lines outside his own country was that of The Queen Sheba. The Sabean Empire to the south, of what is today Egypt, had become extremely wealthy through astute and sometimes rogue-like trading. Others would suggest they almost held a trade embargo and acted unmercifully in matters of trade.

Yet the majesty and reputation of Solomon attracted the Queen of Sheba. His reputation had filled the earth. His name had become associated with greatness, power, supremacy, wisdom and wealth. This single visit raises certain spiritual comparisons that would be good to review in light of our table studies.

The court was still, quiet and yet static with an air of expectancy. To one end of the royal throne room sat the supreme ruler of Israel. Mounted on his throne that seemed in magnificence itself to enhance its seated monarch. Through the doors, carved deeply from cedar, in relief so skilful that the approaching queen had stood for some seconds just to behold their magnificence. The mighty queen of the south stepped into the light and splendour of the throne room.

Two superpowers stood facing one another before the exchange of greetings in formal eastern fashion had cleared the air of the expected anticipations. She stood for a moment, slim and every inch the stance of a monarch. Where her subjects were rough-skinned people of deep brown hue, having spent their lives in the fierce sun in the heart of their trading links, she personified the very aspects of her royalty. Her skin was clear yet touched deeply with the brown of her people.

Being of non-Jewish extract her hair and body were bedecked with jewellery that spoke of her country's wealth. Maidens attended her, ensuring every fold of her silken garments, fell in just the right way. Embroided tapestry of a design that was not common in Israel clung and yet stood out on the delicate silks and exotic materials that adorned her gracious body. Her train of dignitaries stood silently behind her. It seemed her very presence was graciousness itself.

Rarely, even in the splendid court of Solomon had such a ruler been present. The discussions between The Queen of Sheba and Solomon were both political and cultural as well as her probing him with questions. She had heard, as had all the then-known world, of the fame and wisdom of this monarch in whose presence she was now seated. We are not exactly sure whether Solomon himself was married at this stage.

Solomon's lust for women does not appear till the eleventh chapter of 1 Kings. Readings that surround this incident before us come from two passages of the sacred canon, being 1 Kings 10 verses 1 to 13 and II Chronicles 9 verses 1 and 12. Also for those areas of spiritual application, we shall make reference to the comparisons from the Old Testament with the reference in Matthew 12: 42. It is very interesting.

Possibly days were spent by The Queen of Sheba, in the courts and house of Solomon. She was shown all the majesties of his empire. How far she was permitted to enter into the House of the Lord we do not know, yet she was stunned by its magnificence. Solomon's own house, whether the one in Jerusalem or his summerhouse to the north, in modern-day Lebanon or both was fully appreciated by the queen.

She was staggered at the greatness of the king of Israel. She had come with an enquiring, one might even say critical mind, yet she went away incapable of knowing or even beginning to understand the glory that was Solomon's.

Daily she would have feasted at the great Table of Solomon and the Scripture takes time to specially mention how she was overwhelmed by the status and magnificence of that table. It was the magnitude of his table plus the glory of his empire that caused her to be without spirit. There was nothing left that she could be critical of.

Many had spoken of the great Solomon in her own country, and yet it had hardly been believed. Now she found that his greatness had been tragically and grossly understated. Whenever she sat at his table she was stunned by its size, its provision and its luxury. All pertaining to it left her with this consciousness – there is nothing like it on all the earth.

There is nothing like the provision of Calvary on all the earth. Let us get our perspectives clear and straight. The table only reminds us of what has been already accomplished. The magnitude of the table was not the only thing that stayed in the mind of the Queen of Sheba. The crux of the matter was that it all belonged to the king in whose presence she had earned grace. She sat with that king in fellowship and relationship.

We come to the Table of the Lord, knowing there is nothing to compare with it in the entire world. However, it is the living relationship of feasting and being seated with Jesus that thrills our souls ever deeper.

Throughout both of the detailed passages in the Old Testament, you will find certain similarities and spiritual lessons. The Queen of Sheba came because she heard of the fame of Solomon. Truly a greater than Solomon, as Matthew 12: 42 stated, is our Lord Jesus Christ. He is here amongst us right now. If the fame of Solomon was great, then that of our Jesus exceeds Solomon's by degrees in comprehensive.

We are coming to the table of the King of Kings. Imagine being invited to share at the table of a king, let alone realising it is the King of Kings that draws us to full and perfect fellowship with him. The fame of our Jesus is immense. Imagine yourselves getting an invitation from a natural king or queen to dine with them. Before long the whole street and neighbourhood would know. Yet we have an invitation from the King of Kings to share at His Table and how often do we share it in testimony, that we have a living relationship with the King?

Besides assessing his fame The Queen of Sheba sort to prove Solomon with hard questions. Whether in matters of state or mind we do not know. To prove something is to establish its worth. Of the things of God, the Word declares: "Taste and see that the Lord is good." God establishes this principle to come, prove and establish questions of life in living expression in your life. So we know daily the things of God are real and lasting.

Whether the matters that concern you are spiritual, emotional or material the Lord, our greater than Solomon, will prove them in our lives. The table is spoken of in 1 Corinthians Chapter 11 as being a place where we can "prove" the Lord. In 1 Corinthians 11: 26 the literal meaning of "show" is to prove openly.

At Solomon's Table, the Queen of Sheba leant over and communed all that was in her heart. Can we not see also how we can similarly come into such a place of confidence with the Lord? His table provisions are incomparable, as we share them with Him. She was awe-struck by Solomon's provision. The more she saw and partook of as his guests the greater was her amazement.

Are we similarly so much in love with Jesus? Do the things of God mean so much to us that we are without the actual ability to express all that we desire to express? All of Calvary's blessings are ours. The table speaks of these provisions, no wonder there is no spirit left in us to fully explain and capture the wonder of His redemptive purposes.

Deep in the heart of the land of the Sabeans, the Queen had heard of the fame and majesty of Solomon. Yet she had to come out of her own land and come to where the king was, to feed from his table. This is the same with us. It is no use thinking you can live in the world and then feed on the finest of God's provisions. No, indeed you have to quit the world so you may come and be speechless and awestruck at the glorious provision of the cross, through Christ.

It may be noised abroad, the fame of the King, as it was of Solomon, but hearing it is not enjoying it. Come to the King, sit with Him. Feed with Him. Fellowship with Him and you will return to your walks of life having no spirit left, for the King of Kings will have captured your whole heart and being.

If anything is known about The Queen of Sheba it is that she recognised and stated that the half had not been told of the magnificence of Solomon and his household, his wisdom and incomparable table.

Can any mortal pen dare to assume that in the volumes that should fill ten thousand libraries we would even begin to catch a glimmer of the majesty of the redemption Christ has wrought for us? John the apostle himself captures this and expresses the same in John 21: 25. The apostle Paul further adds: "But as it is written: *'Eye has not seen, nor ear heard, nor have entered into the heart of man the things which God has prepared for those who love Him."* (The 1Corinthians 2: 9 passage is quoted from Isaiah 64: 4).

I cannot fully conceive what my Jesus has done for me. There are never enough keys to hit or letters on my typewriter/computer to fully express what He has done for me. There are too few words available. The table stands as an expression of that work. All glory to the bleeding Lamb.

Gifts were brought from the queen and laid at the feet of Solomon. The gold was valued in excess of three and a half million dollars alone (some say five million). Wealth beyond our comprehension. So too is the spiritual wealth that Chrst brings to us.

Yet one single heart before God given in simple service and love to the Lord in appreciation of what he did for us, is a richer token by far. We can pay out of our pocket often what we are not prepared to pay for with our hearts. Give to Jesus your whole life and love for indeed He has given everything to you. Notice what King Solomon gave to The Queen of Sheba.

I have summarised the two passages with respect to what she seems to ask for. They are:
- Given all that she desired
- Whatever she asked
- Of his royal bounty.

We are abundantly endowed in Christ. Don't live like a spiritual pauper when you are a child of the King. As you draw nigh to His table realise He will supply all of your needs according to His riches in glory. Just think you can enjoy the royal bounty you can enjoy the delights of your heart in Christ because of the great love of the great King.

The Matthew 12: 42 reference to the Queen of Sheba is interesting. How fascinating that as a figure of speech Jesus says that the Queen of Sheba will rise in judgement of those who don't attest to the greatness of the Saviour. So be warned by the Queen of Sheba's breathless enraptured appreciation of Solomon's greatness, that there is even a greater one than Solomon, and His name is Jesus.

To me, the saddest part of this episode, with The Queen of Sheba, is where it shares that she: "Turned and went away to her own land." Now I know that she had to return home, but let the spiritual implication override in this dimension as an illustration. Let us stay and linger in the presence of the King. Let us feast at His Table all the time. Let us receive from His hand the good things in our hearts. Don't turn back to your old land and old ways. Stay close to the King. Extract from the table its fullness and truly you will be left with no natural spirit within you, for you dined with the King.

Study/Meditation 21

THE TABLE OF SOLOMON – Part 3
The Standing Of His Servants

Eliab stood motionless. There was not a single flicker of an eyelid. He was as rigid as the marble sculptures that lined the Hall of Pillars within the House of Solomon. The Queen of Sheba eyed him with wonder and perused, for what must have been seconds, yet seemed minutes, the fineness of his stance, dress and total appearance. She turned toward certain of her own emissary, compared their dress and refinement, and felt somewhat embarrassed at the contrast.

By this time Solomon was crossing the glazed floor of the hall, with the form of his person and robes reflected in a hazy fashion off the highly polished surface. He stood before the young soldier and began to speak to him of the provisions that the officer had just delivered to the palace. For that entire month, Eliab was commander in chief of an elite group of soldiers. He led one thousand horsemen soldiers, whose sole responsibility whilst on duty, was to deliver the daily provisions of wild game to the palace for Solomon's Table.

Everything about the young man was the finest that Israel offered, from his personal youth and stature to his apparel. So immaculate was the standard of Solomon's soldiers and servants, that the mighty queen from the south was heard to remark that never in her life had she seen soldiers and servants attired like those of Solomon. The conversation completed, the orders received, the officer snapped to attention, sending a crisp ring of obedience and discipline across the chamber.

His turn, the sway and flow of his robes and his exit left the visitors from Sheba somewhat stunned at the par-excellence of the servants of Solomon. Such discipline and superiority of dress, manner and stature, with Solomon being able to communicate in such a loving friendly way. There was no familiarity, but there was a deep bond between the king and his servant household.

Throughout that month Eliab masterfully ordered the household needs and requirements of Solomon's Table. The next month a fresh one thousand horsemen took on the task with an equally efficient attitude. Twelve thousand horsemen alone were set aside and throughout the cycle of the year were engaged, at a thousand per month, in bringing the provisions, especially the wild game, to Solomon's Table.

Soldiers expert in the art of horse warfare took to the hills daily to bring down the treasured game of fallow deer, gazelles, roebuck, game birds and other delicacies for the table. Then men dressed in the refinement of Solomon's household would take the catch to the palace precincts where they were prepared for the mighty Solomon and his table.

Within the palace servants, both male and female moved about engaged in their particular chores, aware of the privilege and honour of being a servant of Solomon. Their dress alone was something that has to be imagined, as records do not include details, yet sufficient to say the Queen of Sheba had never seen the like. When the main meal was served the whole of the staff that was in attendance looked more like royalty themselves.

Standing quietly behind the guests' scores of maidens and young men waited at the table. These servants experts in attention and service satisfied every desire and expression and want of the guests. The neatness and cost of their apparel can only be speculated, yet indeed few if any courts of kings before or after Solomon's could duplicate this array of exquisite refinement.

Even the stance and stature of these servants must have been something worthy of note to find a place in the holy script. If the apparel of the entire servants of the king was worthy of note, the cupbearer was singled out in Scripture and the Queen of Sheba's comment and thoughts, to be beyond description. That honoured servant stood quietly behind his king and waited upon his every desire and thirst requirement.

Scripture does not imply that these were chores that were something of the drudgery of work to the servants. Happy were the servants of Solomon because of their lot, who they were with, and what their lives were exposed to. Indeed happy are the servants of the Lord.

Before we lead you in some of the spiritual applications of those servants of the king remember this: The provision of the table was also the provision of the servants by virtue of the fact that Solomon included them in his household, and as such the provision of his table was for them also. On occasions, certain feasted with the king. On most occasions, they partook of their meal in the chambers of the servants. But always it was the same provision that the king was sharing with his guests.

That colossal quantity of food that was brought daily to the palace was for the household. Privileged men and women waited at the table. This was one of the things that staggered The Queen of Sheba in that the king made provision for his servants in such a gracious and loving way. This is why they were counted as 'happy' and their standing was beyond anything that she had seen or known. Praise God that the servants of the Lord feast with Him at His Table whilst still in the midst of service for Him.

The Queen of Sheba noted that the: "Sitting of his servants," was beyond anything that she had seen or known before. This referred to them seated with Solomon's table provision. We too are: "Seated in heavenly places." It is through Christ, that we are in such a privileged position. Of the household of faith, it can be applied: "Never have we seen the servants of the King seated in such majesty."

Let us glory in what will be ours in eternity, but above that learn that we can enjoy it in the here and now. The setting of the Lord's children is indeed great. With this in mind what a shame it is to see many Christians going around as if they are in continual defeat, showing long faces of despondency.

You're a child of the King. You're an heir and joint heir with Christ Jesus. You have a sitting that even exceeds that of Solomon's household and servants. Because it is referred to, as their 'sitting' the implication is they could take partake of the provision of Solomon's Table. Indeed the Lord has spread for His servants a table of magnificence that we do have the right to partake of.

"The attendance of his ministers," was something that has a spiritual parallel in the Church today. We are called to serve the King of Kings. So, look like you're an ambassador of the King. Act like you are part of the royal household. You're in attendance upon the King of all ages. Hold your head up high, with pride in what He has done for you.

The King of Eternity, time and man has servants of the highest order wearing outstanding garments. Your apparel too is unparalleled. Although you cannot see the garments that you wear in the spirit they are really exquisite. "Robes of Righteousness," "Garments of Salvation," fold in graceful lines from your life. Stand up straight, look the part of the King's privileged servants.

Gone are the old garments of the filth of sin. The "Garment of Praise" has replaced the spirit and shroud of heaviness. In fine array as a bride prepared for her wedding is how Isaiah paints his impressive picture of our garments before the Lord. I believe every Christian should make an effort on every occasion to look neat, but we here refer to the spiritual garments that are seen by the Lord. As we wear them humbly, yet proudly the world starts to notice the difference.

How sad the Lord must be to see the saints, children of the King laying aside the "Garment of Praise" with its shimmering embroidery and costly display, only to pick up the sin-soaked, filthy garment of the spirit of heaviness, despondency and downcast nature. Reject such. Stand like a regal son and daughter of God, you're a child of the King.

Dress accordingly in the Spirit and attend to the table with that garment message in your conscious mind. What a reproach and travesty it must be for saints to approach the Table of the Lord, in the presence of the King of Kings, and they are still dressed in the filthy garments of despondency, sin and of this age. Come to the table; wait upon it and your Lord, looking every part a proud servant of the Most High God.

As stated, the apparel of the cupbearer warranted special note within Scripture. As we draw into active service around the table, to bear the cup to others or to seek to make others aware of its meaning and worth, watch your dress before the Lord. Be garmented in meekness, humility and grace that the beauty of the King may be seen deep in your lives.

I am sure you have sat on rare occasions at the Table of the Lord, and the life of the one administering it has been far from straight and honest. If you are called to bear the cup, remember to keep your life clean and straight. It could affect the entire significance and power of the table remembrance.

If there was one quality woven into the fibre of the servants of Solomon it was happiness. The Queen of Sheba specifically noted it and it is recorded in both of the accounts of Scripture. Be happy, and smile, it doesn't cost you anything, and it is the state of inward expression. Happiness is to know the Saviour. Solomon's men and servants are listed as being happy. Let every Christian be full of the joy of the Lord. We can be joyful of the significance of the table, at the same time as being soberly reverent. Reverence is not a long face, and happiness is more than a 'state of lips.' God loves happiness. Rejoice for you're a child of the king called to celebrate the table with Him.

The servants of Solomon were said to be standing continually before him. In such a position they would become exposed continually to his wisdom. As we stand daily before the Lord, certainly he lovingly and wisely guides our every way. God sees us at all times, we are consistently before His presence. Let us remember that being around the table is being under the scrutiny of the eye of the Lord.

Whilst reading about The Queen of Sheba you would have picked up the scriptural base for this meditation. To refresh your mind II Chronicles 9: 4 & 7 with I Kings 4: 27 gives the basis of consideration. However, to conclude, let's review an interesting point. The servants of Solomon did not finish their lineage when that great king died.

If you turn to Ezra 2: 55 & 58 with Nehemiah 7: 57, 60 and 11:3 you will see the continuation of this special line of servants, named: "Children of Solomon's servants." Those named in these passages are certain Jews that returned to Jerusalem under the return of Zerubbabel hundreds of years after Solomon had died. Solomon's servants are specifically named amongst them. Indeed they were still identified in that context.

King Solomon was dead, yet his servants carried on in the glory of that position of the name the king had given them. Our Jesus was thought dead, crucified by mortal man, yet we know He ever lives. He is risen from the dead but abides in a physical sense on the earth no more. But the lineage of His servants goes on forever and will continue to bring glory to His name.

We will forever be coming out of Babylon to build and be built into the Temple of God. Even those exiles that returned met around the Table of Nehemiah (see later study so named). We are coming out and yet we are coming into. Let the table speak of the unsearchable riches of the servants of the Lord as they remember Him.

In conclusion, I Kings 4: 27 says of those Servants of Solomon: "They lacked nothing." Indeed as we are in Christ Jesus we lack nothing. Let us so rejoice as we gather continually with Him around the table that the provision is complete. There is nothing in all this world to compare with the standing of the servants of the Lord. Let us live like heirs as we have been born again to that calling.

Study/Meditation 22

THE TABLE OF SOLOMON – Part 4
Descending From The Throne To The Table

The forests were a soft green as the typical approaching winter rain licked up the slopes of the Lebanese mountains well to the north of Jerusalem. The cedars stood stately and snow-capped as the fresh snow heralded the approach of winter's hand. Within a sector of the foothills stood a colossal house that should more correctly be called a palace.

The Scripture simply calls it: "The House of the Forest of Lebanon." Into this dwelling went the most luxuriant furniture. We are not exactly sure if the great throne of Solomon was housed here, or back in Jerusalem, but from the contextual flow of I Kings 10:14 to 21 it may appear to be in the 'House of the Forest.'

Cedar was carved deeply and with craftsmanship that was not repeated again throughout the ages. The cedar supports seemed to be suspended, yet it was supporting, the fine structure of the roof.

From the spade of the archaeologist we have learnt that besides the royal quarters that abounded in size and luxury, there were two major halls. The Hall of the Pillars and The Hall of the Throne which is referred to as the Hall of Judgment. In this haven or retreat, Solomon spent a great deal of time and settled a great many of the matters of state.

The gardens and the natural setting beggared description. The servants in their usual majestic fashion were almost an adornment themselves. As one walked through the entrance to the house of the forest you were aware of the fact that you were in the presence of no ordinary ruler. Solomon's majesty and political might had risen to such a height that much of the then-known world was subject to his fame if not his rule.

It took thirteen years to complete the palace of Solomon in Jerusalem and we can only guess how long the palace in

Lebanon took to construct. Reading I Kings 7:1 to 12 will help you understand its magnificence. Precious cedar, priceless stonework and the finest of tapestries and materials all went into the construction of this house. Only the best was used.

God only uses the best when He is preparing His Bride. He is gathering from the four corners of the world so that He may prepare the Bride of Christ as the most exquisite creature that graced heaven.

As you swung around the main entrance and headed for the Hall of the Throne you were aware that the king must be of mighty rank to effect such glory and architectural splendour in just his 'House of the Forest.' Golden shields hung in rows along the hallway. The doors swung open into the Hall of the Throne, and if it was the first time that you had entered through those doors then you were hardly able to move or speak from what you saw within.

There was only one central thing in that room. The throne of Solomon was central. The throne was paramount. It captivated the room, interest, conversation and especially the imagination of all once it was seen. The Bible is specific in saying there was nothing like it in all the kingdoms of the earth.

The Scripture simply lists and mentions the throne in passing. But no individual could pass it off as anything usual. It rose from the floor of the Hall of the Throne, which itself was highly polished, probably marble, in what seemed a cascade of six steps. On the sixth step, the throne was mounted. They were not ordinary steps. They rose in such a manner that they accentuated the throne at their apex. It could have been that they swept around from side to side.

Six steps or terraces each holding two intricately carved and specially designed ivory lions. All before your gaze was carved from pure ivory. From either side of the throne on the sixth step running down to the last step stood twelve massive carved ivory lions. There were six lions on each side of the throne, running down the six steps.

The throne itself had a canopy or round covering at the top or back and was endowed with two armrests on either side of the seat. A footstool was immediate to the front and this was attached to the throne itself. The entire throne was carved and constructed from pieces of solid ivory. Then as if this was not enough to speak of its ceaseless wealth, the throne was overlaid with the purest gold that came to the land of Solomon.

Yearly the Word of God declares Solomon's acquisition of gold was worth over $700-1,000 million in today's value as of 2022/23. The best gold was acquired and used on the throne. It was smelted purer than any in the land. It was used to overlay the throne and the footstool. We do not know whether or not the lions were overlaid with gold, yet their very degree of carved craftsmanship left no doubt as to their worth.

Singularly any lion would be worth a fortune in today's markets. Consider that the researchers' Brent Hardaway and Lambert Dolphin state that David left his son Solomon around $25 billion in gold to complete the temple. He also valued the 666 talents of gold that came to Solomon at over $700-1,000 million (upgraded to today's value, from Hardaway, Dolphin estimate) as per above. 666 talents are equal to 540,000 to 600,000 troy ounces. The Tuesday [04/10/22] gold price was $1,700 an oz (which may be a slightly high amount). This gives the gold price of Solomon's 666 talents between $918 million and $1.02 billion.

We do not know if the lions and the steps were similarly constructed of ivory or just the lions. It would appear that at least the lions were. Imagine the worth today of one of those lions, let alone the entire twelve. Such refinement of features carved into their form. Ivory, the finest that Africa could yield used in such lavish priceless ways. The replicas of lions that was closer to the original than some real lions themselves.

Then within this breathtaking display of wealth and majesty, the mighty Solomon was seated. Is it any wonder that there was no more spirit left in The Queen of Sheba after she beheld these sorts of wonders? How sad that such a treasure has disappeared from the face of the earth.

From this seat of magnificence, the mighty Solomon brought judgment and justice. Thrones speak of authority, exalted position and majesty. Certainly, all of these things were present in Solomon. Yet the King could not remain upon that throne indefinitely.

Judgement and justice were certainly meted out from the throne, but the king was also present and officiated at his table. Solomon had to leave his throne to come to his table. We have seen that in fact, the table was of such magnificence that it really defies description. The king, however, had to purposefully attend to his table. He had to physically leave the throne to officiate at his own table.

In a real sense here is the crux of our meditation. The Saviour had to leave the realms of glory to effect such glorious salvation that can be remembered, celebrated and lived out in the power of the table. The glory of the King upon his throne was laid aside when he came to attend to the needs of his guests invited to his table.

Psalm 45: 8 speaks of Christ leaving the: "Ivory palaces." Hebrews chapter 1: 6 to 9 confirms that the 45th Psalm was a Messianic prophecy of Christ. Christ left the ivory palaces and realms of His throne to inhabit human form. He came down the six (Biblical numerics usually indicates 6 as the number of mankind or humanity), steps into humanity's form for us all.

We could not be partakers of the Table of the Lord, had not the Saviour laid aside His eternal glory and come and stood in human flesh and died for each and every one of us. Divinity became humanity. This is something greater than we can imagine or contain.

When thinking about the Saviour we are nearly always forced by our humanity to see Jesus in some guise of humanity. To us, he looks and is a man. We would do well to read Daniel 10: 5 and 6 in association with Revelation 1: 13 to 17 to really appreciate something of the literal eternal glory which the Son of God had before he took on the form of a servant, a man of this earth.

Such was the glory that the apostle John fell, prostrating himself as dead when he saw Christ's presence and glory. Such is the majesty and splendour, even mortal ink and paper cannot correctly describe that glory. Yet the Saviour laid all aside to come down to earth, to come and stand by me, and is identified with mortal humanity.

What love, what redemptive purposes, is outside our minds to conceive? Christ freely laid it all aside that He may come and be identified with mankind and in the commonness of our flesh, overcome and bring salvation to mankind.

Notice Solomon had to come down those six steps to get to the table of provision. Six is the number of mankind, the number of humanity. Jesus had to come down to the universal identity of a man. Divinity though He was. Humanity from divinity yet he lived for each of us. He came into a framework that understood our weaknesses and strengths. Christ came into the human mould and would suffer, be tempted and yet without sin. Into my shoes, He trod that I might ever tread in his pathway.

The table speaks of such a wondrous provision in Christ. But never let us lose sight of the eternal cost in that the 'darling of heaven,' and eternity, had to leave the glory to effect that necessary redemption. With folded wings and breathless anticipation, the angelic hosts beheld His entry into human form and flesh. No wonder they heralded His birth in such a way.

Do you realise that when Luke details: "The glory of the Lord shone round about," this was the first time that the 'glory of the Lord,' being the glory of God, had been seen or heard of since the Shekinah glory of God had departed Israel in Ezekiel's day (see Ezekiel Chapters 9 to 11). "And the Word was made flesh, and dwelt among us, (and we beheld his glory, the glory as of the only begotten Father,) full of grace and truth," (John 1: 14).

Heaven came down and glory filled my soul. Though heaven was stilled at His departure, to affect the wonder of Salvation, to crystalise the provision of the table, yet it was rejoicing with a heartbeat that had originally begun in eternity's dawn.

Solomon left the glory of the throne to attend to the glory of the table. This table was within the majesty of his house. Now today the situation finds a similar parallel. His table is celebrated within His house. Not that exterior house of God of bricks, timber and natural materials. But the living house of God's making is gathering together everywhere throughout the world to meet with him around His Table.

Christ stepped out of the position of pre-eternal glory, out from the praise and worship of angelic beings, into a human form despised and spat upon. Love beyond our comprehension. When we read and reread these passages dealing with the throne of Solomon (1 Kings 10:18 to 20: & 1 Chronicles 17: 11 to 15) our minds can themselves make many parallels to the glory that the Saviour gave to become humanity's Redeemer.

As we sit around the Table of the Lord, remember it cost heaven everything. Heaven, bowed low, burst open and travailed with the first whimpering cries of the infant Christ in Bethlehem. We are here to celebrate Christ's marvellous redemption because He was prepared to leave the throne.

Now Christ has returned to that glory and yet he still mediates for us every time we draw nigh to Him, whether around this table or in our ongoing Christian life. Remember it cost Jesus everything. Don't rush away without sensing the price. Let every one of us turn our lives over to be given wholeheartedly to Him. Let us come off our petty thrones of self-importance and come as His guests, having no more selfish spirit in us, for we have seen the majesty wherewith He has descended from the throne to the table.

Study/Meditation 23

THE TABLE OF SOLOMON – Part 5
The Table Of The Beloved

We shall at a later stage (Studies/Meditations 24 and 25) discuss one of the other guests to the Table of Solomon, namely the Shulamite maid. However, there is certainly a contrast between her attitude at the table and that of The Queen of Sheba that here bears some contemplation. Also, the two tables referred to are quite different. At one table was a shepherdess, vinedresser and commoner, at another table was a queen.

To the natural mind, there would be no comparison as to which would be the most likely to appreciate the Table of Solomon the most. But the truth is simply this. The Queen of Sheba left the Table of Solomon and returned to her own land. The Shulamite maid stayed at the table and became wife to Solomon, and as such could enjoy all the provisions that were his, because she was married to the king.

In a real and spiritual sense, our heart is knit to the King of Kings. We are part of His Bride and one day we will feast with Him because we will be married to Him. There is something more than idle curiosity that has drawn us to Him. It is love. The Queen of the South was drawn by curiosity, criticism and many other factors, but remember she left and returned to her homeland. The Shulamite maid stayed and became part of the royal household that continually fed from the table of the King.

How wonderful it is to find those who have nothing in a real sense of this world's status and wealth. Yet, they enjoy the glorious provision of the Saviour of mankind. I have no rank, title or wealth as this world may measure it. But because I belong to the King of Kings, I now in Him have rank, title and wealth beyond that which human resources can measure. I am an heir and a joint heir with Christ Jesus. I am a child of the King. I am blessed with all riches of blessing in heavenly places in Christ. What a treasured position to be in because I belong to the King.

How wonderful to see men and women come and enjoy the redemption that Christ purchased for them and offers so freely. Yet tragically for some, after a while, they leave following Him and return back to their old and their own behaviour patterns and life. I cannot work it out. Like The Queen of Sheba, they go back, when they could have eternally the provision of the table.

The land of the Sabeans (from where The Queen of Sheba came) was dry, arid land, where its people and The Queen of Sheba lived by trade, which often was extortive and oppressive. They were ruthless, often unethical business people. No, my heart cannot turn back to those pathways where the way is dry and arid, and the affairs of mankind are anything but honest. I have been called to be part of the Bride and indeed that is just where I intend to be.

The name 'Solomon' means 'Beloved' (II Samuel 12:24 & 25). Solomon was called the: "Beloved of the Lord." Let us remember we have a greater than Solomon, one who indeed was beloved of God. He took human flesh as His garment that He may come to redeem you and me. "He brought me into His banqueting table, and His banner over me is love." The Beloved has extended love that embraces me and includes me in the family of the Beloved. Oh what love that it should be multiplied to me and all that are in Christ.

We will not extend ourselves into the negative realm of looking at the polygamy of Solomon, with his seven hundred wives and three hundred concubines, but let us ponder on this concept: The Bride of Christ is a plural identity. And, we each have the privilege of being part of that bride.

No, I am not saying there will be many brides, but the Bride will be made up of many people, of all races, all blood washed and Spirit kept. How wondrous to be so-called.

From near and far we all have been drawn that we may be part of the glorious Bride of Christ. There is plurality in our fellowship as His Bride. We are not drawn from the ranks of any particular denomination or ethnic group.

All may come if they respond to His salvation. Whosoever believes in the Lord Jesus Christ shall be saved. Yet, there needs to be this note of warning. A bride as long as she keeps herself only for her husband remains his bride. You belong to the King of Kings. Don't become a harlot yourself to the world with its gilded toys.

So many came to Solomon's Table. There was no shortage of space. One researcher said up to 15,000 were part of the royal court of Solomon, spread throughout the land and his empire. All were fed to their capacity from the table provisions of Solomon. There is ample room at the Table of the Lord for as many as would become the chosen of the Lord. Be part of His Bride and enjoy the merits of the table.

The bride of Solomon was called to live in his house. "I will dwell in the house of the Lord forevermore." Some, in these last days, regard the church as no longer important in their life. Attendance for them is based sadly on whether they have anything better to do.

The Word is clear: "Forget not the assembling of yourselves together as the manner of some is, but so much more as you see that day appearing," (Hebrews 10: 25). Frequent the house of God. Support your local church, but remember that sinners are still in the world and it is our responsibility to win them for Christ. You have to go out and get them. In your day-to-day activities reach people for Christ. Bring them into the church where they can be properly fed and nurtured and then and in turn be sent out to reach others to bring them in.

The Bible regularly supports consolidated Word-centred gatherings we call churches. It actively supports aggressive evangelism out in the streets, workplaces, and the marketplace places of life amongst the unsaved. Let us get a balanced view of both the need for church attendance and evangelism out in the world.

We are part of that glorious house that the Lord is constructing. From the many quarries in the hills and dales, precious rocks and squared stones were hewn to size and then brought to Solomon's house.

"Look to the rock *from which* you were hewn, And to the hole of the pit *from which* you were dug," (Isaiah 51: 1). You are precious stones and are erected into a holy house. "You also, as living stones, are being built up a spiritual house, a holy priesthood, to offer up spiritual sacrifices acceptable to God through Jesus Christ," (I Peter 2: 5).

Into this 'House Of The Lord,' a table of provision and salvation's reminder has been established. It is part of the church's beauty, and it is part of its continuing worshipful remembrance of the work of Calvary. We have been hewn and dug from a pit. Every one of us has been brought from the mud and mire of life and has been set in His holy house that we may be to His praise and glory.

We are called His 'beloved,' and we are called to His table. There He sups with us personally, yet collectively. Around that table, there is the song of the redeemed, the new song of salvation. "Oh sing unto the Lord a new song, for He hath done marvellous things." Solomon was a great builder, ruler and wise judge. He also was very musical and poetic. He wrote three thousand proverbs and one thousand and five songs, as well as other writings, under the guidance of the Holy Spirit.

The works of Song of Solomon, Ecclesiastes and Proverbs as well as certain Psalms are accredited, in part or whole, to Solomon (I Kings 4: 32). It was custom in the East that the serving of the main meal was accompanied by music and song. This was the lifestyle of the wealthy. Can you imagine the fineness of the court of Solomon being entertained by the most excellent musical presentations, performances and songs of the king himself?

The court of Solomon was charmed not only by his provision but that the 'beloved' had scripted fine musical presentations. He had learned well from his father. David used a choir of all women called the Alamoth. This was extremely rare, as nearly all Biblical choirs were male. This choir was still present in Hezekiah's day, so it could have been that Solomon continued to use the finest of female voices to sing the high crescendos of praise and worship that Solomon wrote to His God. Male voices and accompanying choir would have joined in lifting their strains of praise to the king and their God.

How glibly we often raise our voices to the King of Kings in praise and worship around the Table of the Lord, or at other times of worship. Song is something that is in the very heart of humans and spiritual worship. You may not have the voice of an angel, but every angel will stop what they are doing and listen enraptured to your voice when it freely lifted in heartfelt praise and worship to your Lord and Saviour.

Around the table, those sacred melodies that are lifted up from human voices need to really praise the Lord from deep within the heart and not the mere refinements of the throat. Let praise flow in worshipful adoration from the heart, and not merely from the tongue. I cannot help but feel admiration for many hymn writers. So many of them seem to have captured and crystallised just what I want to say to my Lord and Saviour.

Take Fanny Crosby for instance. Tragically blind, yet she could see more with her eyes of faith than many sighted people. She scripted such magnificent hymns that leave those of us with the gift of sight staggered and almost embarrassed at her insight. Let the heart lift in pure worship to your beloved Lord as you truly worship Him around the table.

All that Solomon was, and had, spoke of the magnitude of his table provision. All that Jesus has done is prefigured in the sacred emblems before us in the Lord's Table. Don't partake idly. Reverence every moment. I would imagine that if you were invited to dine with a king you would spend a long time making sure that you were absolutely ready. Everything would be in place.

Then as we draw near to His table make sure everything is ready. Everything should be right. Everything should be straight in your life and if it is not put it straight at the table. Don't come in condemnation.

Christ is our 'beloved.' He has come and provided a table, especially for His own. Let us come with a new song in our hearts and enter into sweet fellowship at the table of the 'beloved.'

Can you cast your mind back to when you were courting the love of your life? Many happy moments were spent dining together, sharing sweet conversations around the table. You were never in a hurry to move away from that romantic setting. Many homes would do good to introduce a little more of the same romantic inclination and practice after the wedding, as indeed was present before it.

You were happy at the table because your 'beloved' was there and you had their sole attention. How we need to sense the presence of the King. Our 'beloved,' the darling of our heart has called us to sup with Him. Let us fall afresh in love with Jesus, so that the entire world may see the romance and reality of what the table means to His bride.

Study/Meditation 24

THE SHULAMITE'S TABLE – Part 1
The Circular Table

The setting for the next two meditations comes from The Song of Solomon chapter one. We want to highlight verse twelve which says:

"While the king sits at his table, my spikenard sends forth its smell."

This romantic poetry is believed from the pen of the great king Solomon. There is a divergence of opinions as to the implications and characters within the story of The Song of Solomon. But, this controversy is not our emphasis. There is only one desire and that is to extract from the verse above something of the majesty that centres on the Table of the Lord. We will use the passage as a springboard for our thoughts.

I am firm in the opinion that the king referred to was Solomon, and the woman referred to was his bride. She is simply known as the Shulamite maid.

One interesting and honest comment from 'Got Questions,' (www.gotquestions.org) on the Shulamite maiden says: "Solomon uses passionate language to describe his bride and their love (Song of Solomon 4:1–15). Solomon clearly loved the Shulamite—and he admired her character as well as her beauty (Song of Solomon 6:9).

Everything about the Song of Solomon betrays the fact that this bride and groom were passionately in love and that there was mutual respect and friendship, as well (Song of Solomon 8:6–7). This points to the fact that the Song of Solomon is the story of Solomon's first marriage before he sinned by adding many other wives (1 Kings 11:3). Whomever the Shulamite was, she was Solomon's first and truest love."

We know Song of Solomon shows originally the Shulamite was a hard-working vineyard worker who was maintaining and running a vineyard because her brothers were not pulling their weight in farm work. Most probably because of certain references in the Song of Solomon she also tended sheep. From this point of view, certain comments arise. But, they do not alter the context of truth we are aiming at, or extracting from the passage. With these brief introductory comments let us open our hearts to the study/meditation on the 'circular' nature of the table.

..oOo..

Imagine if we could steal a look inside the chamber where Solomon and his bride were feasting. You couldn't help but be impressed with the grandeur of the scene. This reference to the table is not Solomon's grand table of his palace court, referred to elsewhere in the previous study/meditations 19 to 23. This is a private table in the inner sanctum of the bridal or wedding chamber.

Rich embroidery seemed to just cascade in ceaseless folds from the tapestries and curtains embellishing the walls. The richness of the cedar beams, enhanced by ornate carvings and workmanship, stood out from the rafters and supports of this inner chamber.

With the setting so typically Eastern, the guests at this special table were comfortably half lounging semi-across the table on the finest of cushions, equally as delicately embroider as the curtaining. The floor shone with attention. The standing and status of the servants that were given restricted limited access to this inner chamber stood out from ordinary household servants. Wealth was the order of the lavish display and there seemed no end to it.

Centred right in the middle of this refined spectacle of eastern wealth and culture was a table, unlike anything we may have today. It was curved and circular. Curved in such a way that the king and often his bride could enter and sit within the centre. Then, those privileged enough to be invited would sit on the outer rim facing inwards.

The finest setting on the table enhanced the refinement of the table's design. It was typical of many of the eastern royal courts a bygone era. Yet, it fires our minds with inspiration for this meditation. The king and his bride were at the very centre of the table. All others just sat in an arch around them.

Some suggest that no others, except the bride and groom, were allowed into this inner chamber. It was reserved exclusively for the bride and the groom alone. I personally feel this is the case most of the time, but am not dogmatic about it.

The king was noble, regal and powerful. The bride was beautiful, soft and blushing. It had hardly sunk into her that she, a mere commoner, was now marrying a king. All before her was so new, so magnificent. She had only known the meagre existence of the life of a shepherdess and as keeper of the vineyard, where they first met. Now she enjoyed the delicacies of a queen.

Her garments were no longer the garments of a commoner. Hours had been spent on her refinement, by those skilled in fine needlework. They had produced a garment fit for a queen. She touched her wedding dress and ran her fingers down the finesse of its quality. It may also be possible that the bride had been preparing for months, being bathed in various exotic oils – see the Book of Esther as an example (Esther 2: 12).

The king saw her and she became conscious of his gaze and blushed. He smiled and ordered the feast to begin. It was the bride that spoke the words in verse twelve: "While the king *is* at his table, My spikenard sends forth its fragrance." She sensed her glorious position. She was conscious of the change in her status and standing and poured out her love and devotion to the one she loved. It was more a proclamation than a statement. It rang throughout the feasting chamber. Later they would be alone. Then love and adoration would pour forth from her life and heart just to the king of her life.

The scene we have shared is a frail attempt to express how glorious that inner chamber and private trysting place would be. Such wealth for such a tender moment. We can, unfortunately, take this for granted when we read the Word too quickly. Yet, the setting is rich with colour and setting.

The table was circular. We know this as a fact. That may seem presumptuous, but in fact, it is not. If you have access to a good concordance, which shows you the Hebrew, roots of the word being studied in the Old Testament, you will be able to pick up our reasoning. The word in Song of Solomon 1: 12 is the only place in the Word of God where the Hebrew word *'mesab'* is used as *'table.'* The word literally means: 'A circle, round table.' It only occurs here and in its sole reference provides an inspiring insight into our privileged position.

History tells us only two classes of people could enter this inner chamber and be invited to the 'mesab,' the circular table. These were first, the bride (as in the picture, Scriptural setting before us). And secondly, the great generals of war who came to plan battle strategies in deep secret. In either case, we can see ourselves as part of the 'Bride Of Christ,' yet at the same time being part of a 'Warrior Class.'

How often do we feel others are closer to the Lord than we are? Or, even worse, how often do we feel some have more rights or privileges to be closer to the Lord than we have? One dear very elderly gentleman, giving sound advice, who used to be in my congregation many years ago used to say in an aging croaky voice: "If you're not as close to God as you once were, don't ask God who moved." God remains the same. He wants to draw us into the intimate circle of His love and be seated with us. If only we would open up to His embrace.

So often in the past people have created in their minds a pyramid structure relating to access to God. At the top they feel are the apostles, the evangelists and important speakers. Next comes the ministers. Then come the large group of workers and finally the bottom group comprising Mr and Mrs Average – the congregational members. Nothing is more damaging or further from the truth.

This unusual table before us represents an interesting aspect of truth that has personal relevance for us all. We are co-equally seated around the table. The table was circular hence no single individual has greater access, or is closer to the Lord, who is the very centre of its attraction. Christ is the centre of our worship and adoration. We are equally accessible around Him, and so all have the same opportunities for fellowship. None of us has exclusive rights over His attention.

As we draw around the Table of the Lord we all have the same opportunities. Remember the Queen of Sheba left the table of Solomon, though we're not implying she had access to the 'Mesab.' No one forced her to leave. Nobody will force you out of your relationship with Christ. You leave it yourself on your own misguided terms. We are potentially equidistant from Christ. He is the centre, the very hub. We are on an equidistant rim of fellowship because the Saviour desires fellowship with each of His new creation, whilst at the table.

The Table of the Lord is a common table. Not common as in ordinary, average or of little worth. It is common in its accessibility to all of us. It brings all of us back to a common denominator. Your access at the Table of the Lord rests in your own mind. Seek to press in and gain for yourself as much as you can from the Lord. Because we all have the same opportunity.

There had been a rich and meaningful experience of love between the couple before the king had brought his bride to this feasting chamber; this intimate private chamber reserved for a privileged few. Let love flow from each of our hearts continually to the Lord. Let us not be guilty of rushing into His presence and to the Lord's Table, unmoved by His great love and wondrous salvation. Let the cords of our heart be stirred from within so that the overtures of love truly might flow to Him who is the lover of our soul.

The bride speaks softly, gently, and sweetly, yet her voice carries throughout the entire chamber.

"While the King sits at His table…" remember, the King attends His table. No longer a Nazarene. He is the King. If a mortal king were to attend our 'communion service' how attentive we would be to 'put' the best foot forward? Remember the King of Kings, the King of all ages is always at His table. King Jesus is here. The presence and consciousness that the King is present should captivate our entire being. Jesus is here with us around the table.

How it would smarten out attitudes and attention around the table if He literally appeared in the communion service. But, He is here nonetheless. The King, not just a commoner is here. The King, not just a servant attends the table. The King, not even an important official, desires our fellowship. Yes, the King of Kings is at His table. Will we take note that it is 'His' table that we are coming to?

Jesus owns it. He instituted it. He waits to draw us into its hallowed relationship. The King is here and all glory is due to Him. How tragic we so often fail to appreciate Him.

Many times we fuss around in the Christian life, but note the king is seated. There is tranquility and calm in this scene. He is not rushing about, attending to the table's provisions. It is a finished work. Calvary is a finished work. No longer do we need to be restless. Rest with the King in the finished work. With careful study of John 4: 34, John 17: 4 and John 19: 30 we can see how Jesus, whilst here on earth, considered the importance of finishing the work committed to Him.

Now the King sits. Now the work is complete. Now is salvation wrought in a manner that never needs duplication again. "It is finished." Those immortal telling words shattered earthly space, ears and time. Angels bowed low when those words were uttered. Demons shook with terrifying pain as the Saviour finished His work on Calvary with those victorious words. This finished work is spoken of and outlived in the glory of the Lord's Table, which we celebrate together.

The king is resplendent in glory. His garments, status and surroundings marked Solomon as the earth's greatest ruler at that time. Indeed so is the King of Kings. This reference to the king sitting is immensely important in expanding the concept of the finished work of Calvary. To be seated implies the work of the day is done. The relaxed position shows us that the king has completed his obligations and now he is relaxing.

Two passages that deal with the splendour of the Son of God in His eternal glory are Daniel 10: 5 & 6 in conjunction with

Revelation 1: 13 to 16. The passages speak of that majesty and have most things in common. One speaks of His glory before He came as the Babe of Bethlehem the other of His glory after the work of Calvary is complete.

Despite the similarities in the passages there is one fundamental difference that is important to note. Carefully examine where the position of the 'girdle' is to be found.

The reference in Daniel says it is about His loins ('reign' being 'loin' in Hebrew). In Revelation, however, the girdle is definitely in another position. Here we find it around the 'paps' or breast/chest area of the Saviour. Why the change? What is the importance? Simply it is that the girdle was a piece of garment that had a specific use.

Whilst a man worked, primarily in hard labour work such as farming, he wrapped the girdle around the hips, and loins so that it would support his actions, movement and working efforts, bracing him. When the work of the day was over and the workingman returned home the girdle was removed from the loins and placed around the chest. It allowed the garments worn to hang loose. It gave freedom to rest and relaxation. The two positions of the girdle imply both a working and a relaxing position. This should speak volumes to our hearts.

Daniel shows the Saviour before Calvary, ready for the work and task of redemption. He is able for the task ahead. John in Revelation shows the Saviour relaxed and rested with the work of Calvary completed. The King is resting and relaxed in victory, just like the image in the Song of Solomon.

My Saviour has completed the glorious work of Calvary for me. It 'is' finished and He calls me to rest also in the finished work. Jesus has wrought glorious salvation in perfect righteousness and faithfulness to the eternal plan.

Isaiah catches these concepts when he writes in chapter eleven and verse five. "And righteousness shall be the girdle of His loins, and faithfulness the girdle of His reins." Indeed the great work of salvation was prepared before that horrific day when the Saviour willingly died for the sins of the world.

Indeed the Saviour has wrought a mighty work on Calvary and remember: "It is finished."

What a privilege that we have, to come with the King to His table. The King is there in all His glory. The King has completed the finished work. When we gather around the Table of the Lord remember that the work is done. This should create a heart of overflowing praise and adoration.

Our King is seated with us. He brings that completed work and sits right down with us so that we might enjoy the fullness of His provision. But, as we conclude, note that we are seated with Him. We're not running around in a 'stew.' We should be rested, relaxed, loved and loving the great King of Kings that has called us to the great table of intimate love.

Indeed the Lord has "drawn us" (Song of Solomon 1: 4). We feel the pull of His love to "come apart and rest awhile." Jesus calls us to rest in the finished work. The table calls us to rest. Learn to join your Saviour in the centre of the circular table. Make your Christian life an eternal romance born in heaven and enjoyed here on earth.

Study/Meditation 25

THE SHULAMITE'S TABLE – Part 2
The Response That Flowed

So many people have picked up the Song of Solomon to read and have somewhat got lost in its poetic form. Some have rather indifferently laid it aside with some thought, after reading it in modern text or translations, that it is far too amorous for sacred Scripture. Yet, it is one of the most precious books in my own personal devotional life, for the depth of relationship that it brings out concerning the Saviour and myself, let alone its inspiring beautiful references to the true love of a husband and wife.

Within this study/meditation we will be considering the response of the Shulamite maiden (refer to Song of Solomon 1: 13). What was her response to the king and how should it stimulate our own heart, especially around the Table of The Lord, to flow in ceaseless adoration towards the one who has done so much for us all?

Let us go back into that inner dining chamber of the king with the Shulamite maiden at his side. I am convinced the feast before us is the 'private' wedding feast of just the couple. It is not the one with all the guests, but just the two lovers alone in the inner chamber with the food of love.

Certain intimate liberties in action and words occur after verse twelve that from a Christian context are only permitted after marriage. I am not alone in this conviction, many Biblical commentators strongly take this position. We should sense the sacred sweetness of this book, relating to married lovers, rather than anything unseemly or sordid.

.o0o.

The guests had left the formal wedding banquet. The couple had retired to the inner chamber where the 'Mesab' was central to the room. The maiden turned her eyes enraptured with her beloved. Her dress was the finest in the land. Her grace was something regal, though she had come from common ranks. She was not born a princess or even of aristocratic birth.

She was with the king and that was all that concerned her. If you had been permitted within those nuptial walls, you would have noticed the most glorious of odours. Distinctly there were two, yet they blended into a rare fragrance of its own that filled the wedded chamber.

The young maiden had prepared before her wedding day both herself and the fragrance she would wear. Her body had been laced with exotic spices. Spikenard, which was of immense value, and more than often kept until the wedding day, hung in a wafting sweet fragrance, like a vapour of love.

It was custom then, and I understand still is in selected parts of the Eastern world, that a sprig, or even a crushed form, of spikenard, was placed, tucked into the bosom of the bride. The mere heat of her body slowly melted its form and the accompanying aroma filled the wedding chamber and followed her wherever she went.

It is important to continually remind ourselves that the bride had made herself ready. Time and space do not permit us to develop the glories of the romance as the couple developed their relationship from verse 1 of Song of Solomon chapter 1 to verse 12. It would take a book to itemise the development of their love. Here we just touch on aspects of that love development to give a meagre, limited view:

- *Desire* is expressed in Vr. 2 – just for him.
- *Drawing* love has captivated her in Vr. 4.
- *Discovery* of the majesty of the king comes to her in Vr. 4.
- *Devastation* at the revelation of her unworthiness is shown in Vr. 5.
- *Dependence* upon just the king is shown in Vr. 7.
- *Dining* with the king in love in the inner chamber is seen in Vr. 12.

- *Demonstrated,* consummated love is shown in Vr. 13.

The maiden grew in love till the king took her as his own. An ordinary woman metamorphosed from commoner to princess before our eyes. There was still so much change necessary in her life, as the rest of the Book of Song of Solomon shows. Such is the lot of any married couple. But, her life was his and she desired only him.

The language of the passage often sets many people back. I can't imagine many wives or sweethearts enjoying hearing the following in a sweet moment of passionate love:

"I have compared you, my love, to my horse/filly among Pharaoh's chariots." (Vr. 9)

I'm sure they would rather hear:

"You have dove's eyes…" (Vr. 15)

But all of the comparisons and expressions of love used by the king are very distinct and intentional. The horses of the chariots of the Pharaoh of Egypt were regarded at that point in history as the finest horses in all the world. So at the time of Solomon's statement, he was referring to the finest in the world. Later he would become a powerful king and his stables, horses and fame would be of world renown. But, we're seeing Solomon as a young prince here.

The noble horses in Pharaoh's ownership stood perfectly still. Though everything around them was moving, they responded to only one thing. The voice of the charioteer, or the rider, or the slightest flinch of his grip on the reigns, spoke volumes to these horses. They were totally disciplined to the desires of the master.

Are we so in love with Jesus that just a word from Him sends us obediently after the delights of His heart for us? When we feel Him softly pulling on the reigns of our life we sense His direction and obediently follow. This is a total picture of disciplined love. We should be obedient to every desire of the master who directs and guides our lives.

The spikenard of the maiden rose and emanated from her body as an expression of her love for her beloved. She sought to glorify and love him in every way possible. Do we seek to magnify the Lord at His table, or do we sit quietly back and let the whole 'performance' go quietly on, whilst we sit non-participating in the greatest overtures of love that lie in emblem form before us in the Lord's Table?

Spikenard is only found in the inaccessible snow-clad heights of mountains. The Himalayas today in Tibet have most of the supplies. In Solomon's day, most of the snow-clad peaks of the Lebanon and Anti-Lebanon mountains may also have nurtured spikenard. The little rose pink to purple flowers of nard, with their little spikes so rich in fragrance lay dormant in the cool of the snow. Yet the plant was yielding its perfume, spreading its fragrance throughout the entire area around them. The plant grew to around a metre high and was characterised by its pretty bell-shaped flowers, called nard.

> [For the botanist inclined: spikenard is derived from Nardostachys grandiflora (or N. Jatamansi) – a plant of the family Valerianaceae (Valerian family). The purest spikenard is extracted from the highly fragrant rhizomes (underground stems). These were crushed and distilled.]

Often when life and experience are coldest and things don't seem so good that's when we can exhibit beauty the best. When those chilly winds of adversity blow and it feels like snow in our soul, then let the spikenard be gathered. Let its fragrance flow. Let King Jesus be glorified in the midst of the battle.

It is often easiest to praise God when all is going well. But pure worship is collected off snow-clad peaks. When all is cold and indifferent, and you can still exhibit a fragrant love to the Saviour then indeed you have something of rare beauty. The world can only stand back and envy and stand in awe of what life we choose to live.

Jesus draws close to us consistently. Does this Song of Solomon passage of His presence stimulate you so that your whole being quickens, warms and a fragrance of worship and praise ascends from your life to His? Around the table do you quicken in love? Does your praise waft heavenward like the sweet smell of spikenard? I like the translation of Moffatt of II Corinthians 2: 15 which says:

"I live for God as the fragrance of Christ."

J.B. Phillips puts verses 14 and 15 like this: "Thanks be to God who leads us, wherever we are, on His own triumphant way and makes our knowledge of Him spread throughout the world like a lovely perfume. We Christians have the unmistakable 'scent' of Christ."

Can you consciously say that every time you come around the Lord's Table, or in fact any time in your life as a Christian, your life is a sweet fragrance of praise and worship to the Lord? The odour of worship is something that pleases the nostrils of Almighty God. That spikenard was something that the Shulamite woman had deliberately used for the desired effect. She made herself ready. History shows poorer, farm-working girls would save their entire life for sufficient spikenard to adorn their bodies on their wedding night.

Is the 'Bride Of Christ' deliberately making herself ready to be received by the Lord? From our life is there the flow of endless praise and honour to a matchless Christ?

The children of Israel had little knowledge of modern perfumes outside of those provided by nature. True praise and worship are not to be manufactured. It is natural. It flows from the soul and spirit like liquid love. The spikenard was used either as essence from the crushed roots of the plant or as small sprigs of slices from the roots. Both were very valuable and highly aromatic.

The spikenard was used only on very rare occasions, usually on the wedding day and wedding nights. Here in the Song of Solomon 1: 12 the little maiden has her body adorned with it and most likely tucked in her bosom was that sprig or spike of nard that body heat would energise like melting its fragrant release that sent its fragrance wafting throughout the room.

This worship is a form of thanksgiving. She is so thankful for what the king has done for her that she responds to him in every way. Are we so insensitive to what Christ has done that we do not react and respond to Him on every occasion? Open up towards your Lord and feel the spikenard of praise and worship begin to melt within you and send an aroma of fragrance to the one that has redeemed you.

But we must remind ourselves that there was more than one fragrance in that wedding chamber. There was the unmistakable sweetness of Myrrh. It seemed to stand out on its own and yet mix with the spikenard to form an indescribable united fragrance. We see from the formation of verse 13 that it is the groom or the king, that is wearing or endowed with the fragrance of Myrrh. He is injecting something himself into the romance and situation that will ever speak of the redemptive work.

No doubt you are fully aware that in Scripture Myrrh speaks of suffering, it was often an anointing oil for those that had died, and particularly relates to the sacrificial work of Christ on Calvary. Consider then that it was used in the feasts and sacrifices of the Old Testament as these feasts stood as shadows and types of the wonder-working purchase of the cross of Calvary.

We can remember also that Myrrh was amongst the gifts that the Wise Men or Magi of the East brought, as they came to honour Christ as the infant child. Gold was given to Him because He was king. Frankincense was given because He was a priest. Yet, Myrrh was given because He was a man and would die as a man.

As stated myrrh was the most common of the anointing spices used upon the dead. It was also mixed into liquid drug form and given to dull pain. Christ was offered such but He turned away from drinking this pain-killing draught, whilst on the cross. Christ's body was anointed with myrrh after death.

His entire humanity and sacrifice are represented in Myrrh. It speaks of what He has accomplished on the cross. It still is a reminder of His redemptive love. The Myrrh of remembrance wafts above and around us at the Table of the Lord. It lingers seeking participation in its message. Its lingering fragrance always reminds us of what He has accomplished for us on the cross.

The two fragrances of spikenard and myrrh move through the chamber of love and centre around the table. The king and his bride sit/lounge across the table in an oriental fashion. We cannot divorce the work of the cross (the myrrh) from the praise and worship (the spikenard) in any one of us. The Apostle Paul considered it so highly that in Galatians he said:

"But God forbid that I should boast except in the cross of our Lord Jesus Christ, by whom the world has been crucified to me, and I to the world," (Gal. 6: 14).

If there is anything that should stir our life to praise it should be that we are redeemed. Christ has completed the work and we are called to be seated with Him in heavenly places to enjoy the work that is complete. Is it so strange to see individuals break down and weep as a dawning revelation sweeps across them of their salvation during the communion service? 'Strange' I suggest because it is so rare. Many would think such individuals are beside themself. Perhaps we need to let go of our sacred defences and fronts and let the heart reach out to magnify the Lord freely around the table.

All that the table stands for is to be outlived by the believer. At no time should this Table of the Lord be allowed to slip into the area of a religious remembrance where wise platitudes are expressed and pious ideals are mentioned in theological terms that few if any can understand, let alone emulate. This Table of the Lord should indeed stir the very depths of the soul till all that it stands for is living expression in all of our lives.

As a minister, I would consider myself fortunate if instead of a lot of intelligent faces smiling at me, on any particular Sunday, I was confronted with tear-stained faces, sobbing and smiles that came from within from men and women who were falling afresh in love with Jesus. Let us not fall into the trap of the Church of Ephesus in losing our 'first love.' Always keep soft and sweet in His presence.

As we leave the hallowed and romantic precincts of the Shulamite maiden that became a princess and her kingly lover, let it relate to all of us. As we tiptoe out to leave them to their nuptial rights, cast a glance backwards. Even if you were blind and couldn't see the love, there would be the lingering fragrance that would speak volumes to your senses for many a day to come. Their love is fulfilled around the table.

In conclusion, consider this old story from rural England: There was in one of the quiet beauty-bound villages of rural England a perfume factory. It employed most of the young ladies of that area. Just prior to lunch the village green, where most of the girls would sit and eat their lunch, was just a normal green. White swans quietly swam on the pond at its centre. Brilliant daffodils surrounded the trees and popped out of grass of emerald green.

The quaint shops were sleepy and almost still. But, when the factory lunch break occurred there was a drastic change. Everywhere the girls went they left behind the most fragrant of perfumed aromas.

The little cake shop, tearooms and sandwich shop were filled with wondrous perfume. The whole village green and surrounding streets became charged with fragrances.

None of the girls carrying the fragrance was conscious of the perfume that they had dropped like dew from their entire person. Because they always worked in the entire surroundings and helped produce the perfumes it saturated their clothes, hair and bodies with its fragrance. They carried it wherever they went as ambassadors of the perfume factory. No matter what their background, culture or creed they were immersed in the effect of their job. They carried the perfume as a trademark of whom they worked for.

What does this story illustrate? When we are immersed in the perfumes of praise, worship and adoring love for our Saviour then indeed Christ can come forth as a fragrance of life to those around us. Let it flow. Let Christ come forth naturally. Enter into new plains of praise and worship for what He has done for you. Indeed let the spikenard send forth the fragrance thereof, as the king sits at His table. May we each develop a fresh intimate relationship with our Saviour.

May this table meditation stir romance in your heart towards the King of Kings. As He emanates His myrrh, emit your spikenard. Let Him know you love Him. Let Him really know that your romance with Him is still very much alive.

Study/Meditation 26

JEZEBEL'S TABLE

It is always best to major on the positive and to bring encouragement in the scriptural examples that breed faith, as we read or listen to the Word of God. However, this is not to say that the negative should always be avoided. In actual fact, those with photographic inclinations will readily accept the principle that in pre-digital photographs you always needed a negative to create a positive print or photograph. You had to let the light pass through the negative to get a positive. So too in life. Similarly, within the scriptural sphere, there is a need to examine in its context the negative so that we may fully appreciate the positive.

Where we need to be cautious is that our lives ought not be constantly focused on the negative and by this behaviour begin to appreciate little of the glorious positive responses and illustrations that bathe the Word of God. With this in mind, it is now important to turn to a study/meditation of the table, and its owner, who is entirely at the other extreme of all the positive forces of Calvary. By doing so it will help us appreciate a little better the sublime majesty of the salvation we have been called to enjoy.

Jezebel is the butt of many clichés and comments. She's the harlot of spiritual faith within Israel. She evidences such a contrast in the concept that because of her table of evil, and debauched wickedness, we can better appreciate the spotless purity of the Table of the Lord.

Within the Word of God (I Kings 18: 19) we are told that her table accommodated a most disreputable group in the light of spiritual values. Four hundred and fifty prophets of Baal and four hundred prophets of the grove put their god-forsaken feet under Jezebel's table. What an immense contrast to those that gather every time we celebrate Jesus and His salvation around the Table of the Lord and are called to be spotless and clean through the blood of Christ. They are servants of the Most High God, rather than servants of the devil.

'Baal' means 'possessor,' 'lord-over' or 'master of.' Such high-minded and godless attitudes are not welcome at the Table of the Lord. We approach the table with a subjective humility full well knowing it is by His grace alone that we are privileged to even sit at the supper of His grace. That ungodly company of eight hundred and fifty heathens sat at the table of the queen of iniquity.

We sit at the table of the King of Kings. It was common back in the era we are looking at that leading religious identities and dignitaries would feast with the king and queen. The provision would be made at the king's table. Previously (study/meditations 19 to 23) we noticed how great a company was provided with an unbelievable daily provision at the table of Solomon. We need not worry, there is always provision at the Table of the Lord for those that love Him. Have no doubts Satan will always feed those that choose his godless table to put their crooked feet under.

Before this time period around Jezebel, the northern tribes referred to as Israel had just passed through a period of expansion and great conquest under king Omri of Israel. When Ahab, his son, came to the throne ten of the tribes of Israel may have been at one of the peaks in its expansive glory. Ahab sought to reinforce his father's principles.

Omri had built Samaria into a huge centre and capital city. Ahab sought to further invest in the city's growth, but in a godless direction to the spiritual detriment of the children of Israel.

Today archaeologists have unearthed the palace of Ahab and it shows the splendour of this period of Israel's history. Samaria was a city unparalleled, except by Jerusalem, and from its leaders came perverted judgements. It does not matter how grand the buildings are, and what the outward appearances may be, it is what is on the inside that really counts. Samaria blossomed as the booming city of the north, yet in terms of spiritual values, it stank of the filth of the cesspools of heathen idolatry. Keep in mind that the tribes of Israel identifying with Samaria were committed to its godless worship.

Commercial trade was reaching untold heights, yet the souls of men were being traded for the temporary excellence of advancement and prosperity under Ahab and his wife, the wicked Jezebel. It is not important whether the outward appearance shows great wealth. The crux is, whom are we joined to on the inside?

Ahab's glorious palace did not alter the fact that he was aligned and joined to the wickedness of Jezebel's lifestyle and beliefs. No doubt we are aware of those passages that seek a total abandonment of ourselves to God's ways. There are pertinent passages that instruct us not to be aligned with those of this world (I John 2: 15). But we have to often remind ourselves around the Lord's Table to watch whom we are actually associating with.

There seems to be no doubt from Scripture that queen Jezebel was the main perpetrator of the vile wickedness that crept throughout Israel. The Word declares that the evil Jezebel stirred Ahab to wickedness (I Kings 21: 25). From her table evolved some of the most diabolical atrocities that Israel had seen for years. Deceit, hatred, lies, murder and idolatry all flowed from Jezebel's table.

In the Table of the Lord deceit, hatred, lies, murder and idolatry have all been swept away by the all-atoning death of Jesus Christ. From Jezebel's table, the deceit, hatred and murder of righteous Naboth were conceived and executed. From her demonic wiles came the near-total destruction of all of Israel's prophets (I Kings 18: 4).

The cancer of vile worship of Baal was spawned from Jezebel's heart, mind and spirit. Baal worship spread like an incurable disease throughout the land. From her table, hatched like a viper on its nest, evil reigned. Jezebel plotted great evils against godly Elijah. This all emphasises the malignant wickedness of Satan. So how can any of this have a spiritual lesson?

We all understand that Christ took upon himself the total hatred of mankind, which was unleashed, like some ravaging mad animal. He took upon Himself the deceits and false accusations that speared Him to death's door. That eventful day of Calvary is certainly to be seen as the murder of the just for the unjust. Christ accepted it personally for each and every one of us. The idolatry of that day, in that man, worshipped the creature more than the creator forced the inevitable sacrifice of the spotless Lamb of God.

The Table of the Lord speaks of the submissive acceptance by the Lamb of God of all the deceits, hatreds, murders, lies and idolatries, with the evil of the world, in one all-atoning sacrifice by our Saviour.

Jezebel sat at her table conniving deep-dyed evil in deceit, hatred, lies, murder and idolatry. That which was so negative only further reinforces the divine positive when brought under the divine exposure of the developing light of Almighty God.

There will always be 'Jezebels' in life to attempt to pollute and drag down the work of God to such an incredibly vile depth that it continually remains as a foil under the graciousness of Almighty God. Their deeds are so black that the glorious gospel shines beautifully as a sparkling jewel against its blackness.

Even within the New Testament church the attitudes of 'Jezebel' started to rise and pollute the sacred work of God. Revelation 2: 20 shows a modern form of Jezebel being very active in the church of Thyatira. We make no comment on her actual or metaphorical meaning in that reference, but sufficient to say those vile negative attitudes and ways are ever present and lurking to inflict their evil influence. They are ready at any time to abort a work of God and debase the household of faith with her vile seductions.

I Kings tells us Jezebel was the daughter of Ethbaal, king of the Zidonians. God's men and women should know better than marrying outside the family of God. Zidon, like so many other places in Palestine, was the home of Baal worship and the accompanying perversions it brought with it. Some authorities suggest that as a daughter to the king Jezebel was therefore the high priestess of this vile form of worship. How low had Israel sunk that her kings could be joined directly to and directed by such evil forces? We look around society today and at government levels and sadly see the same godlessness and perpetuation of ungodliness.

This woman Jezebel reeks of worldliness and godless sensuality. Her artificial looks as described in II Kings 9: 30 reveal something of the worldly proverb that she has become. I can imagine at this fresh height in the culture and glory of Israel that her dress would have staggered the eyes in both wealth and sensuality. Priceless fabrics from afar, laced with the wealth of a hundred trading nations hung in sensual folds, purposefully barely hiding her body. Remember that Baal worship fully imbibed sexual perversion. Baal's high priestess would have reflected this in her demeanour, and no doubt she entered into the debauched practises of Baal.

Exotic fabrics and jewelled beauty displayed in an erotic sensual manner would have been Jezebel's continual garb. Gold and silver beat as fine as paper and others moulded as thick as weight would allow, hung from her amid costly jewels and an over-exposed body. Jezebel's painted face, for which she is famous (or is it infamous), is given special scriptural reference. Her entire deportment and presentation were seductive and provocative, to say the least. What a vile, soul-destroying image she would have made at her table.

But every time the pure Bride of Christ gathers around the Lord's Table, as pure chaste virgins unto the Lord, they come arrayed in white linen symbolising their purity. We are clean through the blood of the Lamb. We do not have to compete. Who can compete with the perfection of the Bride of Christ?

There will always be a Jezebel trying to influence the church. Note I didn't use the term 'Bride.' She will constantly seek to erect her godless table of wickedness and try to gather to herself base fellows and worldly women who: "Having a form of godliness, yet deny the power thereof: from such turn away," (I Timothy 3: 5).

Some may come to the table breeding the infestation of evil and debauched iniquity that the evil Jezebels of every age seek to perpetuate. They will always be there. Choose to look upon and be part of the purity of the Bride of Christ, not the ever-present antichrist.

In closing let me share that because we live in the world that is no excuse for worldliness. A careful note of Scripture will show us that in I Kings 17: 9 Elijah had to flee Jezebel and hide in Zarephath for a season. He was preserved by the graciousness of God through a little widow woman.

Now Zarephath was in Zidon, the very original home of Jezebel. This evil woman had come from the very place and land in which Elijah is now hiding. Why then was Elijah not affected by the evil degradation of Zidon's Baal worship? Simply this, it doesn't matter where you are (there are reservations in this statement). But it matters very much who you are with when you are where you are!

Elijah may have been in Zidon, but nothing of Zidon was in Elijah. We may be in the world but nothing of the world should be us (John 17: Vrs. 11, 14 to 17).

We can see the horror, evil and Satanic manifestation that was on the table of Jezebel. This is still abroad today. Yet, we sense the glorious comparison and realities in the Table of the Lord, and all it stands for. All that is of the world and its ways have been consumed in His love in dying on the cross for us. We can feed at His Table in restful repose at any time.

Study/Meditation 27

THE TABLE OF ELISHA

The great Elisha sat quietly contemplating, musing on the things of the Lord. His servant was away on an errand that left the prophet alone with his thoughts and his God. By this stage in his life, he was nearly completely bald and his aging frame showed the marks of a man who had known how to work the plough in his younger days, in the heat of the day, or tread countless miles in his journey following the commands of the voice of God.

He stood quietly by his window breathing deeply in prayerful aspiration over the country that was so rebellious towards God. Turning around he sat quietly again at his table and softly touched its simple lines and his mind wandered to the tender love that had been displayed to him by the Shunammite woman and her husband.

With them consciously in his thinking, he reminisced over the incredible events that had transpired in their lives. Out of sheer kindness for a tired traveller, the woman had first offered the tired Elisha a place of rest and the hospitality of their table and its provisions, as he passed by their home. That bond of friendship had grown over time to such depths that Elisha stayed with them for a meal whenever he passed through that area. He knew there was always a warm heart and a ready meal in the loving home of the Shunammite woman and her husband.

Being stirred from his thoughts by a call to dinner he purposefully moved to the door. Turning he looked at his little room. Elisha recalled that after stopping with the couple many times on his travels to enjoy their hospitality in a meal they had purposefully built this room on the roof, especially for Elisha and his servant. Elisha could now stay the evening, enjoy their hospitality and meals, and fully rest.

Elisha stood for a moment silhouetted in the doorway against a crimson sky where the sun was melting its last ounce of energy and light as the tired workers of the field made their way back to their homes. He viewed the splendour of the setting sun and the homely comfort of his little room. The sight of the tired workers of the field reminded the prophet of the day the Shunammite woman had brought the lifeless body of her only son to his room, laying him gently on the prophet's bed.

The child had been born as a direct result of a miracle. From that room, the little lad, who had just been raised from the dead, had run to greet his near-collapsing mother, who had last seen her son in the unyielding grip of death.

Another call from the house below brought Elisha's thoughts back to the evening meal he was being called to. He headed down the stairs and into the house. He found his servant helping the Shunammite woman with the final preparation of the evening meal.

He exchanged a playful jostle with the son of the Shunammite woman, as he entered the house. He knew within himself the gratitude they all had towards the Lord for the strength of this fine growing boy. Sharing conversation with the husband they made their way together to the dinner table.

The meal was plain, typical of rural farmers, and yet a further expression of the love the couple had for the man of God. He had over time become a dear friend to them. As the night hours crept on the sun's red and gold had exchanged their glorious coloured hew for satin indigo and velvet black, studded with a shimmering array of diamond stars.

The prophet was found sitting and teaching the eager-faced youth at his feet. The Shunammite woman and her husband sat close by listening. With a glowing candle or tapper in his hand, he slipped from the home with his servant, excusing himself and entered his little room upstairs to rest before tomorrow's long walk.

Stooping over his candlestick he shared the illumination of the flame till his room was alive with shadow-casting candlelight. He looked around again at the kind provisions of his hosts. The furniture was very simple but comfortable. As he lay on his bed on one side of the room he viewed the two stools and the table with the candlestick upon it. The flame was dancing with light at every draft of air.

Worship rose from Elisha to his God above and after a time of quiet meditation he extinguished the candle flame and lay down to sleep with the heavens blinking down the silent acceptance that they shadowed a man of God.

Simplicity marked the dwelling of Elisha and his servant. There was a bed for the prophet and most probably one for his servant. A table, two stools and a candlestick completed the room. Simple, yet sufficient – country, rural hospitality. Not pretentious, yet very precious to the aging prophet. Many Evangelists would probably scorn it today. They are often more concerned not by the genuineness of the hospitality gift, and the purity of the stars above the room but with how many stars on the motel's rating.

Christians today have often amassed around them a barricade of 'things' that are of little use. All the prophet lay claim to was a bed, a stool, a candlestick and a table. And, he knew that when he left in the morning he had to leave these things behind.

So many Christians live as if they are taking what is theirs to glory with them when they depart this life.

Possessions can become one of Satan's 'fifth columns' that have intertwined themselves around our priorities in a life-and-death struggle. It's a subtle hold, but it can detract from life's and God's calling.

The little bed spoke of the rest of the Lord that the prophet both enjoyed and lived in. His candlestick was a constant reminder of what he was – a light in a darkened, sin-blackened world, as well as the light of God's truth and Word that shone through the prophet. The little stool speaks of the state of being seated in heavenly places. Finally, the table spoke of God's continuing remembrance and grace.

Elisha was the circuit preacher. He didn't have a big congregation but no man or woman would dare badmouth this great man of God as experience had shown (II Kings 2: 23 to

25). He never had a plush salary for his work but was continually fed by God's providing table.

Note in II Kings 4: 8 & 9 that it was Elisha's conduct at the family table of the Shunammite, when he first ate with them, that led them to realise he was a man of God. Our actions do speak louder than our words. He didn't force his way or his view but he had flowing out from his life the unmistakable scent of a Man of God (II Cor. 2: 14 to 16).

The old cliché says: "Manners make a man." When we come around the Table of the Lord perhaps that is certainly true in the sense that our manners and approach to the table are vitally important to the sweet relationship that Christ is wishing to form within us.

The kind lady of the II Kings 4 passage is only called the Shunammite woman. 'Shunam' means 'uneven.' Today the area is called 'Salem,' which means summit. Certainly from a life of uneven purposes, God caused this little family to reach the heights of spiritual happiness in their provision and care of the man of God.

The table in Elisha's room was a table for his personal provision. Often he would eat alone, yet at other times he would enjoy a meal with the family at their table. The two tables are important in significance.

Firstly, at the Table of the Lord, there is the personalised aspect that illustrates the sacred love that flows between Christ and His new creation, His redeemed one by one. This is symbolised in the personal table in Elisha's room. In these times the illuminating candle of the Word searches deeply into the very recesses of the life of the believer while we sit alone in His presence. At the Table of the Lord, there is a vital need within us to draw apart privately and personally communicate with our God.

Families should be aware of this need for private time as much as possible. Mothers, when children are small, working alone on meals, often have a difficult time fully concentrating on the preciousness of the table. It would be good for both parents to share the responsibility of the evening meal so that both may appreciate the meal together. Both of their minds can also be on the children's needs. We need to consider each other's need to touch God personally.

Secondly, Elisha spent several of his meals with the family itself. There is a sense that we corporately can come together in Jesus' Name at His table. At that time we come as a family to the Lord in His presence.

Both the individual and the family attitude are important around the table to develop a fully balanced healthy growth within the work of God. Collectively we feed together, but individually we digest what has been committed to us as a family.

As we leave Elisha and his tables we leave a man who gives us a pattern of simple things. No great fuss and glamour in his little room. Only functionality and practicality are seen. So let our lives be marked by simplicity and practicality as a Christian expression, especially when we gather around the Table of the Lord.

Study/Meditation 28

THE RESTORED TABLE OF HEZEKIAH

The air was filled with thick clouds of choking dust that swirled around hardly showing the place where it had left. Priests, discernible only by the style of their garments, not by the colour of them, stood at the entrance of the door of the House of the Lord. They were gasping for breath before they returned back within the cloud of dust to tackle the removal of more heaps of rubbish.

Outside the temple piles of rubbish and broken items lay, while other priests filled waiting carts with the debris. Slowly the carts with portions of rubbish lumbered down the hillside of Zion towards the valley and River Kidron. In the first few days of this rubbish removal farmers in distant fields looked up at the strange sight of the filthy state of the priests and loads of rubbish. Countless hours of work only made them dirtier, but slowly the rubbish was being removed.

Young king Hezekiah had commissioned the work and removal of the rubbish. The once spotless white garments of the priests became hardly recognisable by the end of the day. Yet the next day here they were back again in a pristine pure white garment ready to start again whilst yesterday's garment was thoroughly washed and returned to its former glory.

Inside the palace, Hezekiah attended to matters of State. With the death of his godless father, the running of matters of State had fallen to the young prince, now king. Within the first passing months of Hezekiah's ascension to the throne, he had issued a directive from the depths of his heart concerning the cleansing of the House of God, ready to reopen it again for worship.

With regret, he remembered it had been his father who had ordered the closure of the House of the Lord. It seemed since now closed to worship to have been used as a rubbish dump, probably of useless surplus items. The massive doors of Solomon's Temple had creaked shut never to be opened again for priestly worship till the godly Hezekiah took the throne.

When those doors shut fast the colossal now aging structure of the Temple of Solomon stood as a mute testimony that God was dead in the hearts of Israel's leaders. Godless worship was conducted elsewhere in groves and on hilltops around the nation. This worship was not to Jehovah God, but to satanically inspired gods of heathen background.

Smoke from a hundred heathen altars curled their way into the heavens in the early morning sunshine as priests of unrighteousness ruled over Israel. Imagine the impact that Hezekiah had when he ordered the opening of the House of God, the cleansing of the temple, the sanctifying of the priests and the reintroduction of godly worship in Israel. In II Chronicles 29, we find this restoration described at the hands of a godly Hezekiah. Eventually, he would outlaw heathen worship.

Days before the court of the king's palace had been filled with priests. Each nervously discussed the reason for their summons to the king's domain. Some may have speculated that the son of the wicked Ahaz would certainly put an end to them, even as his father had put an end to true worship in the temple. Other priests, with faith still flickering as an indistinguishable flame deep within their hearts, born out of a hardly discernible glimmer of faith, had hoped that this new king would be godly. They yearned to see right worship established again.

When finally they were ushered into the presence of the king what joy and relief it was to find that his decree was to restore the House of God and true worship. Hezekiah specifically names fourteen priests to accomplish the task or oversee it, as Scripture implies a much larger workforce was committed to the cleaning task. It says: "They gathered their brethren." Levites, all Levites came to the call. No stranger was given the sacred task.

Sons of rightful worship were commissioned as holy vessels to cleanse the temple. The cleaning was not committed to women. This cleaning was men's work. God wanted his men to establish the right order from the House of God clear through to every one of their own homes. It is important to note Hezekiah the king, not the high priest or a leading Levi, is giving the instructions. God had raised up a young man in the midst of a godless idolatrous home so he could turn the nation around when his day came in coming to the throne.

To our way of thinking Hezekiah's instructions just didn't seem to make sense. In verses 5 and 15 he specially instructs the priests to go home and sanctify themselves for the task of cleansing the temple. We don't have time to itemise the lengthy and ceremonial process necessary for priestly sanctification but believe me, it was humbling and time-consuming.

But as they came ready for work they were clean, cleansed and sanctified. They stood in beautifully clean priestly garments. They were ready to go out and get filthy dirty cleansing the House of God. It doesn't make sense to us. It may seem more than strange to many of us. Why not just use old clothes if you're going to get so dirty? Why not pull on some old Levis (sorry about the pun)?

But to God, every task, no matter how menial, relating to honouring Him requires the full sanctification of the believer. They had to carry filthiness out of the House of God. This was their instruction. Can we understand the mess, the dirt, and the accumulated filth? Heaps of rubbish lay within the House of God in the various courts and even within the outer court of the temple.

Some commentators suggest, that especially the outer court had become a dumping ground for the city's garbage. What a shame when God's House tolerates garbage, rather than keeping it totally clean. The Blood of Jesus Christ washes whiter than snow and there is no need for garbage to accumulate or be tolerated in the temple of the Holy Ghost.

For eight long weary days, the priests worked to cleanse just the temple portion of the House of God. Can we imagine what a mess that must have represented? It took well over fourteen grown men with wagons to shift the accumulated filth to cleanse the temple. Piles of rubbish were carried away in their arms and dumped into waiting wagons. Hour after hour the procession of dirt, rubbish and filth on the move filed past the unbelieving eyes of Jerusalem's dwellers.

Some may have joked at the filthy state and appearance of the priests. Others wept for the debauched state of the House of God. Cast your mind now into what it would have been like as a priest returns home just before dusk after a hard day of removing rubbish. He stands in the doorway. Two dust-filled eyes blink white through a blackened face of sweat and dust. His wife looked on not knowing whether to laugh or cry at the beard of her husband that issued clouds of dust when brushed. His beautiful priestly sanctified garments were unrecognisable for grime and filth.

For several days he would return home equally as filthy from the work. But towards the end of the eight days dust gave way to softer grime as they lovingly cleaned every aspect of the temple. The job was drawing to a conclusion.

It took eight full days to cleanse the temple just to the temple porch. It took another eight days to cleanse from the porch through to the outer court and the temple enclosure. After the total cleansing, each item of temple furniture was lovingly cleansed, restored and replaced ready for the reintroduction of worship again.

Verse 18 specifically refers to the restoration of the table/s. It is given special mention in the restoration process. For years the temple had laid waste. There had been a broken law. Exodus 25: 30 emphatically indicated that the shewbread would be before the Lord always. But such had not happened. The law lay broken and God offended.

Can we imagine the holy awe in the hearts of the priests when they took those sacred ingredients and mixed them again to make the shewbread to lie before the Lord perpetually for His glory? Remember, this was Solomon's temple that was being restored, in which there were ten tables of shewbread, not just one. So, the restoration was immense.

In this act of cleansing, God's Word only specifically mentions the restoration of two items of the temple, though every item would have been meticulously restored. One was the table/s of shewbread and the other was the altar of burnt offerings. At one, the altar, the atonement of sin was made. At the other, the table, remembrance of that atonement was perpetuated.

Whenever God has restored Himself to His people throughout the eons of history I find these two things present. Firstly there is a fresh consciousness of the blood of Christ, reactivating the atoning value of Calvary. Secondly, continual remembrance of that atonement comes alive, helping us confront sinfulness and waywardness as on ongoing principle, as the value of the Lord's Table freshly lives again.

The altar stood before the temple. The table was inside the holy place. Before we can come into the temple or be part of it we must come by way of the altar. We must have an encounter with the shed blood. Before one can fully appreciate, assimilate and outlive the splendour of the reality of the Table of the Lord they must come within the Holy Place.

Hezekiah came into the temple when it was clean and sanctified. His name means 'Jah/Jehovah is Strength.' Before the King of Kings can come into His temple it must be clean. As priests of the Lord in what the New Testament calls a holy priesthood that is created by the shedding of His dear blood let us rise up and cleanse the temple. Keep the Church of Jesus Christ clean and pure, spotlessly clean and without blemish.

God laid the blame for the state of the temple where it rightly deserved to be, with the fathers of Israel. Then He committed the task of repair and restoration to their sons. "Be not negligent," was God's command through Hezekiah to the young priests.

When the House Of God was dedicated and opened again what a celebration it was. Seventy bullocks, one hundred rams, two hundred lambs, six hundred oxen and three thousand sheep were sacrificed in an offering for the dedication of the House of the Lord. It was restored back to

Jehovah's glory again. That whole day is crystallised in this one statement: "So the service of the house of the Lord was set in order."

Despite the joyous celebration of the day how tragic that so few got to enjoy it. Remember this was the time of the divided kingdom. Hezekiah was king over Judah and could only bring his small kingdom into line with God's purposes at the temple. The other tribes, to the north, referred to as Israel, were lost to captivity in Assyria, because of their sinful lifestyle that mainly excluded God.

Many claim to be of the household of faith, yet so few take much time to cleanse their own house or life within and keep it clean for the Lord. The table/s was again raised but it now stood proudly in a clean house before clean people.

The priesthood that would every Sabbath partake of the shewbread off the table/s, replaced it with fresh shewbread. They were clean priests, with garments pure and white.

The army of priests had gone through the ceremonial body cleansing to stand before God as sanctified priests. They stood cleansed and ready to serve. These fine men had known the filth of the temple. They had removed it through hard work. They seemingly had almost become men of low degree (garbage removers), so that they may be resident priests to an Almighty God.

Keep in mind that the glory of God had not yet departed from the House of God. Such departure is described by Ezekiel and occurs many years later. God still abode Himself in the House of God. He fully restored His glory when they fully restored the temple.

The table worship was specifically reintroduced by the instruction of the Lord through Hezekiah. May God cause to rise, across the face of our land, righteous men and women who will stand to affirm the importance of our sacred responsibility to cleanse the house and come again to His table in purity.

As we gather around the Table of the Lord, remember we can only do so free from the filth of life. As we draw near to time around the table we can often sense personal garbage of this world that needs to be taken out to the Kidron valley and river and dumped.

Kidron means 'turbid' or 'muddy – not clear.' Indeed each of us has been brought out of the mud and the mire. Let's leave it at Kidron. Don't drag anything of unholy character before the Lord and before the table. God wants our lives cleaned up and the rubbish carted away, back to the cesspools of the world.

The world is filthy because its overlord is the devil. We are children of light and are cleansed by the blood of Christ. So let none of the old life come before the Table of the Lord. God grant us a thousand Hezekiah's who will restore a holy table again that His name may be glorified in each of us.

Study/Meditation 29

THE TABLE OF NEHEMIAH

They moved amongst the workers as they toiled rebuilding the wall. One was stately and well-dressed having almost the regal marks of royalty. The other was of noble background, but in a different manner, as if a holy presence accompanied his every movement.

Nehemiah, the governor, and Ezra the priest moved amongst the workers in encouragement and help. A worker frail in health, but determined to be part of the rebuilding of the wall of Jerusalem struggled to place a large squared-off rock into place in the wall. Nehemiah stopped walking and talking with Ezra and quickly stepped over and helped the man, patting him on the back and commending his effort when they finished the task together.

Other workers stopped their tasks to see the leadership of this man destined to change the face of Jerusalem. A short distance off, and just below the wall top, a group of workers stood armed, not with tools of the trade for building, but with weapons of warfare. Many neighbouring people all around Jerusalem had exhibited mean hostility and hatred toward the process of rebuilding the wall of Jerusalem. Protection was needed as sporadic attacks had commenced against the wall rebuilding.

Bending to help another aged man Nehemiah lifted another stone into place and remained till the task was complete. Then, with a fatherly, or was it kingly dignity hugged the man across his aging shoulders and chatted to him about his son and grandsons working on another area of the wall just a short distance away. Then Nehemiah moved off to inspect another area of the wall.

Ezra was seated with a group of eager-eyed children around him as he reminisced with them how great a city Jerusalem had been. He described to the amusement of the children the magnificent temple of Solomon that had once graced the crest of Mt. Moriah.

The aging priest himself was of rare descent. In his lineage had been the famed priest Hilkiah who had been responsible for the revival in the days of Josiah.

It was nearly one hundred years since the first Jews had returned to Jerusalem and regained Jewish soil for Jewish interests. Ezra had been in Jerusalem for thirteen years before Nehemiah arrived. He had personally injected a high level of faith and spiritual hope within the people. Yet, the walls were still in ruins. With the rebuilding of the wall, the surrounding enemies initiated attacks on the workers on the wall to stop the progress of reconstruction. It was sport to them.

Ezra was a priest and to this end, he was sovereignly used to raise the spiritual tone of the people who had come back from exile. Nehemiah had been made governor of the land by the decree of Artaxerxes. For twelve years he brought his outstanding organisational abilities together with the spiritual leadership of Ezra. They made a good team instilling new hope in the fledging renewed city of Jerusalem.

It took a while for people to accept Nehemiah as governor. Previous governors had bled the people dry of their wealth, resources and their enthusiasm. Nehemiah 5: 14 to 19 shows the deep dedication that Nehemiah had for his task. He refused to take any costs for his service from the people of Jerusalem whilst he was amongst them. As governor, he served in this sacrificial capacity throughout his entire time of service in the city and region of Judaea. He laid no costs at the feet of his people, bearing it all personally.

Christ also is not one that laid on us the cost or charge of our own redemption. Willingly He accepted it all Himself whilst He rebuilt the wall of relationship again between God and mankind, keeping out the enemy of our souls.

From the formative chapters in Nehemiah, we learn that Nehemiah held a high position in the court of Artaxerxes. Being the king's cupbearer was no menial task. Once Nehemiah heard of the condition of his people back in

Jerusalem, and the state of the walls, he was deeply stirred (Nehemiah 1: 4). For four months (Cp. Nehemiah 1: 1 with 2: 1), his heart was stirred and moved with a holy purpose to see his people set free and the city wall rebuilt.

Some individuals can be easily stirred in a moment and act upon an impulse, not the genuine quickening of the Spirit. Wise is the man/woman who finds the will of God through using or understanding time passage as God's direction becomes a stirring, growing burden in their hearts. Then, they act on it.

I have discovered if an issue is the will of God, over time its emphasis on your spirit and thinking will be reinforced, grow and expand in both your mind and spirit. It becomes engrained, part of who we are. It grows in attention.

If it is a momentary impulse of the flesh, even if a good thought or concept, perhaps moving on quickly stirred emotions, it will likewise pass away with the passage of days. It doesn't mean it wasn't a good or even noble idea; it just wasn't exclusively 'The Will Of God.' God lives in the human non-existent commodity of time. Don't think that He moves with as quick a breath as every passing thought of man.

For four months this conscious burden about the state of Jerusalem and its walls bruised and crushed the very soul of Nehemiah. It wouldn't leave him alone on a daily basis. Like hot needles, it seemed to drive deeper into the very recesses of his thinking. He cried out for God to meet its need. God did this by using Nehemiah himself.

We know the account well of Nehemiah's call to rebuild the wall, as recorded in Nehemiah 2: 1 to 8. It was God's sovereign appointment of Nehemiah, through the king, to make Nehemiah governor of Palestine. "So I prayed to the God of heaven." These words in Nehemiah 2: 4 seem to thunder out of the deep prayer life of this man of God. Although he may have been a government instrument in the hand of God, certainly God knew he needed a man of high ethical integrity as well as rank to accomplish the job.

The personal financial loss to Nehemiah whilst in the land of Palestine cannot be overlooked. He extracted no tribute or support from the people. He expected none of them to keep him. Instead, he provided them with deliverance and a table of provisions.

Nehemiah 5: 17 beautifully details the daily provisions of the table of Nehemiah. Every day he had a table spread with provisions that would have cost him personally a great amount. The Word declares that there were daily around one hundred and fifty Jews that sat at his table as well as rulers and strangers. Every day in excess of one hundred and fifty people were fed from his table, by a benevolent ruler. Daily Nehemiah provided one ox, six sheep and numberless fowls as provision. The personal cost to Nehemiah would have been enormous.

Not only did Nehemiah bring deliverance from the enemy and victory over them but also he did it amidst spreading a table of provision on a daily basis. None at the table was accountable for any of the costs. All of the provision was met by Nehemiah's personal love and devotion to their liberation. How like our Saviour Nehemiah was.

Our Saviour has brought victory to his people, and all who come under His deliverance and emancipation from the onslaught of the enemy. As good as the system of religion was or was not, it took Christ to bring deliverance to all mankind. Then, as if that were not enough, He spread the table before us and invites us to come freely and share in His continuing provisions.

The characters around Nehemiah's table are interesting. They were Jews, rulers and strangers. It embraced so many. Our salvation has been provided for more than a select group. He is the mighty Saviour to the Jew and the Gentile, the rich and the poor, the noble and those of common heritage. All can come on a common footing to a common table with the Table of the Lord. You might be Jewish you may be Gentile. But you are all invited and drawn to His table because He has invited you there.

From a table of limitless provision and description, such as Nehemiah would have enjoyed in the court of Artaxerxes, to the smaller personally invited guest list, this was the destiny of Nehemiah. Can any of us conceive the majesty, splendour and glory that would be Christ's within His eternal glory? Yet, He left it all to come and redeem His people to set them free.

God used Nehemiah to unite and rebuild the wall. Notice Nehemiah's strategy. He got every man or family to work on a specific part of the wall and complete just that assigned task. Within a staggering fifty-two days, the wall was complete, because the people had a mind to work (Nehemiah 4: 6).

After the third night of arriving in Jerusalem Nehemiah went out in the night to view the state of the wall, with its incredibly damaged status. He declared by faith it finished as he saw into the future the plan God had given him to finish the task. Christ went out into the night of sin and after the third day rose triumphantly to declare the enemy vanquished.

Never was life valued as so low as at Calvary. Heckles, jeers and insults accompanied the Saviour's death. They did the same to Nehemiah as he rebuilt the wall.

Time has a strange way of turning back on itself. Daresay many of Nehemiah's hecklers would have been standing upon the very crest we call Calvary in their jeering across the valley to the walls now being rebuilt in reconstruction.

From those same walls, years later passed a sad jeering procession with the Son of Life lumbered with a cross. He was crucified and jeered at from that very same spot. But He rose triumphant and through His sacrifice and resurrection rebuilt the walls of relationship back to God. None can smash it down again. And within those walls stands the table of provision for every believer.

Imagine the great feast of thanksgiving that Nehemiah would have had, once the wall was rebuilt. If over one hundred and fifty ate daily from his table in 'normal' provision imagine the standard of his celebration once the wall was finally finished. Hezekiah's table is a token of a finished work. Is our Lord's Table any less?

Unite around the table that is prepared for Him and paid for by Him. It is an enduring expression of His love and provision. It is spread daily or as oft as you eat it – Till He Come!

Study/Meditation 30

MALACHI'S TABLE

The governor's kitchen was a hive of activity as the staff prepared the main meal of the day. The smells were exotic. The animals waited quietly. They were unwittingly aware that this was their last day alive. Cap in hand Jacob stood by the door as the head of the governor's staff checked over each animal he had brought to see that it was an absolutely perfect beast, fit for the governor's table. With the price agreed on Jacob left happy, with money in his purse to continue his cycle of daily responsibilities in shepherding.

Early that morning had come the instruction to select out three of his best sheep for the governor's table. With an eagle eye for quality, he had selected the very best to take to the house of the governor. This was an important order. He could not afford to lose their favour as he was being approached for the first time. Only a week before Eliab down the road, who was the usual supplier of meat, had taken sheep that had been rejected because they were not the first class, or adequate quality. One had a disfigured leg and was immediately dismissed. Only the very best graced the table of the governor in Malachi's day.

Back within the palace food preparation was in full swing. The sheep had drawn their last breath. They had been bled and now lay on the kitchen table having been carefully dissected. Their bodies were still slightly warm, and an occasional muscle involuntarily twitched as the cold steel of the knives sliced through their layers of meat.

Only the best cuts were taken. The choicest of meat was demanded from one who expected the very best. The staff knew the high standard and stress on quality and work expected. Their jobs depended upon their being skilled and efficient at their respective trade.

Not far away from the walls of the governor's elaborate dwelling came the bleat of a little lamb. Its owner led it down the road to the House of God to make atonement for himself and his family. The trespass offering walked its last few steps bleating.

The journey was slow because of the lameness in the right foot of the poor-looking creature. It was a sorry sight. When very young it had snapped its leg whilst frolicking around. A fall into a hidden foxhole in the fields had fractured the leg. Since then it lacked size and condition and hobbled on three good legs, rarely letting the injured leg touch the ground. Its health could never be counted on.

This sad little lamb often fell or stumbled over rocks by the wayside, yet its owner was pulling it along mercilessly to its fate. Once at the House of God it was received with customary indifference to the sacredness of the ceremony. Though a ram was the required offering the priest was indifferent about receiving the injured lamb, even though it was male. It seemed to one standing afar off observing the ceremony that the only sincere one in the ceremony was the lamb.

The knife was raised. The deed was done. The lamb silenced. Blood quickly flowed. The priest was ritualistic and unmoved by the symbolism of repentance imbibed in the ceremony. The person offering this sacrificial lamb was there only because it was the thing to do.

Aside from the whole event had stood a silent figure, powerful, brooding, silent yet fuming. He had just been in the House of God pouring out his heart to the Lord. The burning passion within his soul was the state of his nation and their indifference to the Lord God Almighty.

Malachi stood and wept as he beheld the scene of the death of the little lamb in the distance. Unashamedly pouring out his heart to God he bowed and intercession poured like a warm running healing balm from his soul. As he observed the callous scene his meditations continued. The prophet stepped forward and strode with holy fervour into the end of the ceremony. All heaven and nature seemed stilled as the voice of the great prophet boomed out across the face of the nation:

"You offer defiled food on My altar, but say, 'In what way have we defiled You?' By saying, 'The table of the Lord is contemptible.' And when you offer the blind as a sacrifice, *is it* not evil? And when you offer the lame and sick, *is it* not evil? Offer it then to your governor! Would he be pleased with you? Would he accept you favourably?' Says the Lord of hosts," (Malachi 1: 7, 8).

The man making the sacrifice look bewildered at the priest, and then they both burst out laughing and walked away to their day's pursuits. The prophet's words were falling upon the ears of a deaf nation. Indeed they may laugh, but they couldn't laugh to scorn the words of the man of God. As dogs retreating with tails between their legs the priest and the man slunk off the scene smarting with the words of the Lord from the prophet.

It confounded the giver of the sacrifice. It incensed the priest. Often the mighty prophet Malachi would rise to challenge the nation's spirituality and the spiritual apathy of God's people, which lay as a gaping wound festering with decay. It seemed to many that his words were as salt in the wound of the nation. They squirmed under Malachi's smarting assault, yet their souls were numb to change and repentance.

The Spirit of God was stirring the prophet. He turned being moved in the depths of his soul for his nation and its sin. He strode into Jerusalem's trading centre and the crowd gathered to hear him as he proclaimed:

"But you profane it, in that you say, 'The table of the Lord is defiled; and its fruit, its food, *is* contemptible.' You also say, 'Oh, what a weariness!' And you sneer at it,' says the Lord of hosts. 'And you bring the stolen, the lame, and the sick; thus you bring an offering! Should I accept this from your hand?' Says the Lord," (Malachi 1: 12, 13).

The crowd shuffled with uneasiness. Some wiped the words of the prophet off as the ramblings of a fanatic. Others were stirred in their souls.

The nation however was not brought to its knees in repentance. They resisted the words of God's prophet. So the iron hand of oppressing nations gripped Israel so hard that she was numb to the Spirit of God's direction, even in the hope of the coming of the Messiah.

Some years later Syria would capture Israel and enslave her. Then, no sooner had the Maccabean revolt freed Israel from the Syrian's domination than Rome lengthened its conquering arm to take hold of Israel by her throat till she choked her life into dispersion in 70AD with the destruction of Jerusalem.

The Book of Malachi stands as a convicting book to both Israel and the Church. Haven't certain sectors of the church, or individual Christians, lapsed into the same careless state? Isn't it true that some have the wilful pattern of offering just anything to the Lord, feeling He will blithely accept anything?

The centre of this study/meditation comes from verse 14 of Malachi's first chapter when the prophet boldly proclaims: "But cursed *be* the deceiver who has in his flock a male and takes a vow, but sacrifices to the Lord what is blemished—For I *am* a great King," says the Lord of hosts, "And My name *is to be* feared among the nations." Clearly, Malachi had stated: "The table of the Lord is defiled."

God requires nothing but the best. Consider that man's mess is replaced by the Messiah's best in glorious redemption. Should then He receive anything but the best from us? As we gather around the Table of the Lord, could it be said of us that we have turned it into a 'contemptible table' as Malachi called it? Have we consciously or unconsciously offered or brought into His presence broken or lame lives as an offering that should be bursting with the fullness of life in Christ Jesus?

I do not here suggest that the Lord will not take us 'just as I am,' but to the believer, there is a real need to be living the fullness of Christ, so we can boldly and in the conscience of a pure heart come into His presence. The table is not the place of show, but the seat of sincerity. Truth and Love mingle their immortal qualities together in the work accomplished on Calvary. Surely truth and love should demand a true presentation of ourselves to the Lord.

The children of Israel could not plead ignorance in Malachi's day. The Old Testament displayed a crystal clear pattern for them to follow. Leviticus Chapter 1 clearly defines the condition and sacredness of an acceptable sacrifice. Cursed would be the person who tried to deceive those standards.

We today will not deceive the Lord, only ourselves, to think we can present anything that is less than the perfect sacrifice. We are dealing with the King of Kings. He desires as well as deserves the best. Israel back in Malachi's day was offering anything as an offering, when the Lord required the male, whole and perfect. Let nothing but the best be presented at His table.

Consider the tragic state of Israel in the Book of Malachi. The priests had departed out of the way (Malachi 2: 8); the leadership and all of Israel would not hear the Lord and treated God's things lightly (Malachi 2: 2 also 1: 13). Even marriages within the priesthood, as well as the people, were desecrated (Malachi 2: 11, 14 to 16). And finally, nationally Israel had sinned and stood indicted as a nation before the Lord (Malachi 2: 11 & 3: 5).

It is hard to imagine the 'people/children of God' in such a sorry state. But possibly today a similar list of indicting crimes is to be found nailed to the 'Wittenberg' churches of modern times. Throughout the world, there are men and women who are raising their voices like Malachi and speaking out. They are nailing their objections into the heart of their nation. Often they are tragically treated just the same as Malachi was treated.

With cutting conviction Malachi challenged Israel about the desecration of the Lord's Table. It is not exactly the same table as we celebrate today, but a table of the Lord nevertheless. Is the Table of the Lord precious and soul-stirring to us or do we treat it as common?

'Contemptible' and 'polluted' are the two terms that are used by Malachi about the attitudes in his day about the Table of the Lord back then. Let us guard against making the Table of the Lord anything close to this in our thinking or our actions.

Hold the table in the highest regard, not as something 'contemptible.' Bring holy lives before it, not something that is 'polluted' with the world.

Do we live double lives? Israel did and God stood against it. Our day and age in many ways mirror Malachi's day. Hear the words of that ancient prophet as he stands in the temple and harangues the priests before the people.

"And this is the second thing you do: you cover the altar of the Lord with tears, with weeping and crying; so He does not regard the offering anymore, nor receive *it* with goodwill from your hands." (Malachi 2: 13).

Malachi continues with a smarting admonition against the priests divorcing their wives, crying out: "For the Lord God of Israel says that He hates divorce, for it covers one's garment with violence," Says the Lord of hosts. "Therefore take heed to your spirit, that you do not deal treacherously," (Malachi 2: 16). Some would suggest that 'domestic violence' by some priests towards their wives is inferred.

Leading a life where we are trying to be one thing before the Lord, and yet acting another way before people is sin. Double lives have dire consequences with God. He will not accept them. Our lives around the Table of the Lord need to be straight and clean. We stand in the presence of an Almighty God. Do we stand with holy awe?

Malachi shows Israel is on the verge of spiritual suicide. Today much of the church is on the verge of spiritual suicide. In our world today tragically thousands of suicides occur every day. Many go unreported. Many more are unsuccessful. This world is running hell-bent on destruction. To claim to be one thing before His table and yet live a different life is dangerous.

Wake up. Don't approach the table and indeed our entire Christian life, with the indolence of a sinner and the outward ceremony and smile of a saint.

Don't allow our lives to be 'polluted' and then expect to come before His table with sin and its pollution in our souls. Come for repentance – Yes! But, let not any of our hearts come unchanged to sit at His table.

In conclusion, note the graphic description of the prophet Isaiah in chapter 28 and Verse 8. He affirms the same indolence and indifference that Malachi was standing against: "For all tables are full of vomit *and* filth; no place *is clean.*"

In Christ, there is a clean place. Let us bring our hearts and lives into that clean place. Let clean living approach the Table of the Lord with inner purity. If not, then let us have a consuming determination to put our life right and to be clean in His presence. May our testimony not be the description of Malachi or Isaiah. May Christ's words to us be: "Come and dine the master calls, come and dine…" Till He Come!

Study/Meditation 31

THE CHRISTMAS TABLE

At Christmas time many families are lost in the flurry of activities that often marginalise the true meaning of Christmas. We don't do it deliberately, but it happens. Christmas' true meaning is not totally lost but certainly takes a sad second place to the hectic pace of the season. With a flurry of tinsel, wrapping paper, string and emotion the early morning gifts at Christmas are opened and quite often the lounge room has a fresh carpet of brightly coloured Christmas wrappings.

I know many are concerned about losing the purity of the message of Christmas. Whether we're celebrating it on the right date or not is not the centre of our discussion here. It is 'how' we are celebrating Christmas that should stir our hearts. For all of us in the Christmas Morning Service, there is abundant opportunity to refocus on the pertinence of the Christmas message. In some churches celebrating the Lord's Table has become an integral part of that Christmas service. With this in mind, the following study/mediation has been set aside to energise fresh thought about the Table of the Lord at this special time. Till He Come!

.o0o.

The day had been long and the journey arduous for both Mary and Joseph, but especially for the heavily pregnant Mary. It had been exacting, because of the soon-expected child. For Joseph, because of the concern for his wife, the trip was joyfully nearing its end.

As the sun snuggled into the ridges of the western hills that topped the rim of low hills that led to Bethlehem, already twinkling were the dull reflection of oil lamps in many windows. Through the light of a closing day, the traveller's bodies seemed to glow with the soft brown dust that the sun reflected off them.

But Bethlehem was far from sleepy. In fact, it was bustling with activities and fresh faces all returning to Bethlehem for Ceasar's census. Streets familiar to Joseph were filled with strangers. Customary boarding inns were filled with noisy guests. The late afternoon wore on into the evening and the energies of the two divinely appointed travellers began to wane. Mary kindly urged Joseph to immediately seek shelter as she felt the first twangs of discomfort heralding the imminent birth of her first child.

"No room at the inn," was the all too common greeting or response to Joseph's plea for accommodation. Finally, whether out of pity or being brushed off, we don't know, an innkeeper directed the weary couple to the inn's stable.

There have been many honest and thorough attempts to identify the place and type of shelter Mary and Joseph used. Probably, it was nothing as attractive as so many Christmas cards make it out to be. It is strongly felt it was probably a cave stable that was developed close to the inn with an outward wooden structure to keep the animals inside. Some suggest it was a rough wooden annex to the back of the inn, a place for the guest to stable their steeds. The manger was either a wooden or stone-eating trough of the stable. They have never enjoyed a reputation of being the cleanest of farm utensils to form a crib for a newborn baby.

With birth heavily upon her, young Mary lay in the hay that Joseph had gathered and comfortably arranged for her. We do not know if any others assisted Mary in the birth, save Joseph. But, we do know: "But when the fullness of the time had come, God sent forth His Son, born of a woman, born under the law, to redeem those who were under the law, that we might receive the adoption as sons," (Galatians 4: 4 & 5).

Soft and warm was the cry of a little babe in those first hours after birth. Joseph, I am sure, did all that he could to block out the drafts and gusts of wind from entering the stable. The only Biblical passage that fully describes those moments, even if in sparse detail, is in the Gospel of Luke in the first twenty verses of chapter two of his gospel.

We are not advised how long they spent in such circumstances till Joseph could find more suitable accommodation for his precious family. Minimally it was overnight to accommodate the visit of the shepherds. Much later when Jesus was recorded as being a 'child' they would be found in a 'house' when the Wise Men or Magi came (Matthew 2: 11). Jesus was then anything up to two years old at the time of the visit from the Magi.

But what of the stable hours? They must have been long and uncomfortable in comparison with the expected comfort of an inn or proper accommodation. The shepherd's arrival interrupted the evening hours. Tenderly Joseph doted on the needs of his wife and baby Jesus. Already they had named him Jesus after the solemn instruction of the angel. The night wore on and in the serenity and quiet of those moments, a table was spread.

It was not an elaborate table of beautiful wood with the finest of linen for a cloth, with expensive cutlery. It wasn't bedecked with splendid silverware and expensive China. I can imagine a concerned Joseph smoothing out the straw near his wife and the snuggling infant. Joseph then laid a humble cloth on the straw. He spreads his simple provisions from their belongings or what we had quickly purchased in places close by, especially the inn because of the lateness of the hour.

"Eat, 'honey.' You'll need it for your strength and for the baby." Comforting words from a gentle Joseph. "It's not much dear, but do eat up." The table was very humble, but the beloved King of Kings was there. The most ornate and expensive tables the world can offer can still be without the presence of the King of Kings.

There in that crude, almost repulsive setting the first table was spread with the King of Kings being the central attraction and presence. The table was prepared and spread with the new life, the new birth as its central feature. The table was set with the Saviour as the centre of attention.

Churches can come to the communion service and yet there may not be the slightest hint of 'new birth' in the house.

The implementation of communion is purely a ritual, not a reality for many. The structure of the church may be incredibly wealthy, the building costing millions, yet the pearl of great price is sadly lacking. How much better to have a humble presentation and yet know that the Saviour is alive and present among us? Why build the most austere and ostentatious of surroundings and not have the presence of the Saviour?

Many churches today would put out the door the rough-clad shepherds, as being unsuitable visitors. Yet, they were the first visitors to worship the Lamb of God. They brought praise and worship to the humble table and the presence of the Lord. Where praise and worship are sadly missing, though replaced with piety and properness, the presence of the Saviour is not enhanced.

Shepherds speak of those who care for the flock. In any service that gathers around His Table, the greatest thing we can do as Pastors and Ministers is to bring our own people, our congregations, to worship and adore our Saviour with sincerity.

The surroundings are not as important as the person who is present. The stable and the manger have become immortalised in Christmas memory and tradition, only because of the presence of the Saviour. That simple, humble table on the straw was much richer than words can describe because of the presence of the Son of God. Not that any of us would go out of our way to purposefully create such poor surroundings, but it is the presence of the Son of God that is the all-important factor.

Today the real effective surrounding for the Saviour is our heart. As we sit at the Lord's Table is He really there for us as King of Kings and the Saviour of mankind? Or, is He in attendance as the last thought or religious participation in our celebration of communion?

The ancient cradle was built in a rough manner. That manger would have been made of wood or hallowed stone. The manger is remembered only because of the nestling comfort it gave to baby Jesus. What is the state of our hearts where we invite Jesus to reside? The cradle of Bethlehem was one of love, not money. The cradle of our hearts is to be of love, nothing else, as we come around His Table.

What a meagre meal was eaten from that hurriedly prepared table. Today the emblems of communion may be very meagre and simple, but it is the presence of the King of Kings that ennobles them. He makes the difference. It is the Saviour that turns the unpretentious presentation into something that the noblest of monarchs of this world would be honoured to sit at.

It is not the outward show of the church's communion table that matters, but what the table of our hearts reveals. How have we spread it before the King? Have we invited Him to be the principal guest at its presentation?

So in the midst of Christmas, we can sense the message of the table to be important to every believer. No matter what the age of the participant at the Christmas morning service let them be aware of the true message of the 'Christmas Table.'

Study/Meditation 32

THE TABLE – A PLACE OF MANNERS

In nearly every home the conduct of the children can be best demonstrated by their behaviour at the table. Here I refer to the family table of the home, where the daily meals are shared, or should be shared together. Tragically 75% of USA families take their evening meal around the TV. Don't let this happen in your home! Using this concept of table meals as a springboard for our thoughts it can be useful to share pertinent lessons about the Table of the Lord.

Parental discipline really meets its match with the display of manners or behaviour from the children in the family's mealtime gathering. Especially when visitors are around and are sharing a meal the behaviour patterns of the children really come out – often in family fun to deliberately embarrass their parents.

Then there is bad behaviour. How many times can you think of having guests over where you have had to apologise for some behavioural slip by one or more of the children? "I really don't know what came over them." "They are not really themselves. Please excuse them." Quite often they are 'really themselves.'

I know as parents we all strive to raise our children so they will be a credit to the Lord and to themselves throughout life. Yet the table often brings out those traits that show their manners and training.

So too we find that around the Table of the Lord the manners and training of God's children often come out. Not that our Father is inadequate in His training, but often we are very rebellious children. Many times the head of the house has something of real importance to share with the family and chooses to do it at the table, as it is one of the times when we all get together.

Mealtime is something more than a place for the family to eat together. It is also a place for family devotions, family sharing and sometimes family discipline and correction. As we gather around the Lord's Table perish the thought that it should only be a time of family eating. It is the family of God in devotion and adoration of the Father, the family in conversation with the Father, and the family sharing meaningfully with each other. Sometimes the family may need discipline, which can be gently administered whilst eating together at His Table.

When people in the world observe our manners and the way we conduct ourselves, it should be apparent that Christ shines out in us. Consider carefully the situation of contrast here. It is no use at all putting on the airs and graces at church around the Lord's Table if our conduct before the family at home is something different.

If 'crucified pastor' or any church member has been the diet of the conversation around your meal table, yet you come to the Lord's Table with a holier-than-thou appearance then be really careful. The table calls for us to right wrongs before we come to partake of its emblems. But, worse than our hypocrisy consider the damage you are doing to your family. "If that is Christianity Dad, then you can keep it," says your child as they leave the church for good.

If you are one thing at home and another thing at church then you have a serious problem on your hands. You 'will' lose your child/ren from the kingdom of God, and it will be your fault. Your manners have shown you are a hypocrite. Have you asked yourself why a certain percentage of children from Christian homes turn to the world? Then check the hypocrisy factor.

The gospel *is* a revolutionary process that changes lives. The table is a sacred remembrance of the salvation we embraced, but further a repeating of its claims over our continuing life. The table reminds us that we should constantly be changing to become more like Christ. By a thorough understanding of the table's power that life is attained.

Proverbs 22: 6 says: "Train up a child in the way he should go and when he is old, he will not depart from it." Note it doesn't say the way 'we' want him/her to go, as good as that may be. But it says the way 'he' or 'she' should go. Every child has a destiny. The Holy Spirit wants to perfect our destiny in the things God has planted within each of us.

But how much use will the training and destiny of God be if the philosophy of our behaviour is: "Son/Daughter, do as I say, not as I do." Parents I don't want this study to be a parenting exercise, yet many Christians feed their offspring with nothing but criticism of the Work of God and its minister and workers, then wonder why they have problems.

Some parents nurture their young with half-hearted excuses for not supporting church, its attendance, or its programs, then they wonder why their child is not interested in church. They are crazy. You got what you trained. When you ridicule others whether in a church setting or out you destroy your child's possible walk with God. What we sow, we will reap.

The table can be a pretence or a reality. The choice is yours. The children of Israel were specifically instructed to teach their children about the things of God and The Law. Not only their manners but also their spiritual and social training came from their parents. You as parents have the training responsibility over your child 'not' the school. Education in Biblical days was primarily the duty of the parents (Cp - Exodus 12: 26, 27; Deuteronomy 6: 7; Joshua 4: 21 to 24; Proverbs 22: 6; Ephesians 6: 4; Colossians 3: 21 and II Timothy 3: 15).

Don't be foolish enough to leave the moral, social and spiritual training of your child/ren to school. It is your sacred responsibility. As a qualified high school teacher, I can speak with authority that in over 90% of children, the secular educational system will wipe out trust and belief in spiritual things if the home is not countering this.

Satan is clever and the school with its maddening emphasis on secular education is one of the most powerful tools to break down the moral fibre of Christian training. For goodness sake acquaint yourself with the material that passes through your child's school bag and often their minds. And, when that material is subversive to Christian teaching challenge it with the school authorities.

Teach your children values and the truth of the Word of God. Often this can be done around the table. Also, don't leave the training either just to the Church. They will help, but it's your responsibility as a parent. As good as Youth Groups, Sunday School and Church services may be, still recognise that the responsibility is yours to train up that child in the way he/she should go.

One of the best places for the teaching of manners is the table. Again we emphasise our behaviour at our family table and the Lord's Table must not have a hypocritical comparison. I understand every father and mother knows they make mistakes, like the children. Yet, being honest before the family, and seeking forgiveness is what building strong character is about. It is a redemptive principle. Children seeing parents modelling honesty, forgiveness and openness are far more relaxed about being honest themselves.

How can we tell children not to lie if we lie and they know it? The Table of the Lord should not be a façade of our spirituality, but an exposure of our sincerity in humility and truth. I Corinthians 15: 33 boldly shares: "Evil communication corrupts good manners." Let our conversation around the family table not be evil in malicious criticism, or judgemental attitudes, for it will corrupt good manners. Make it a family principle that we want to nurture not destroy the 'flock' at home.

If something is amiss and needs to be corrected teach the home to deal with it compassionately and to bring it before the Lord in our home devotions and prayer time. Sweetly pray for and leave controversial matters in His hands. Don't allow the family to repeatedly pick up issues, again and again, to chew over. So much of our table conversation needs a touch of love and forgiveness.

Manners are really the customs or habits of a people within an area, within a specific time frame. Rachel (Genesis

31: 35) and Jephthah's daughter (Judges 11: 39) displayed the unique manners of their day. But manners or habits can become bad manners and bad habits. Apparently, the writer of Hebrews was concerned over the indolent way certain of the Hebrew Christians were treating the matter of regular church attendance. So he wrote: "Don't forsake the assembling of ourselves together as the *'manner'* of some is: but exhorting one another; and so much more, as you see the day approaching." (Hebrews 10: 25 – emphasis ours).

In times when we gather together it is good to be able to share and by so doing grow in the Lord. Today is a day of the overthrow of the good. Good traditional customs and manners are being deliberately attacked and overthrown. But as Christians, we should be slow to accept change, just for change's sake. Change should produce the 'better,' not the novelty.

The family altar, respect for elders and authority, respect in the family, a holy fear of God and modesty in how we dress and conduct our lives are sadly lacking as good habits/good manners around many families and their table. Let the Table of the Lord be a challenge that every Christian family itself should have a family table and home manners that are exemplary and will encourage love and not drive individuals away from family, or their God.

This aspect of study/meditation on Table Manners has been a different approach. But 'Till He Come,' God gives our homes great grace to run their life/lives as if we are seated around your table. Prevent us from having two standards.

Study/Meditation 33

THE TABLE OF CRUMBS

The golden sunshine splashed its scintillating reflection off the vivid aquamarine blue of the Mediterranean. The sandy shores washed white with shingle lay lazily basking in the sunshine. Fishing fleets could be seen, some with sails, others sails tied back, as the corks of their nets bobbed up and down with the lap of the tide and swell in the natural coastal harbour. The occasional gull circled, landed, and then took off commencing its senseless shrieking cycle again.

The early morning tranquility was only pierced by the shrill giggle and scampering feet of small children. They were running through the meadows and adjoining sand dunes of the coast. The coastal harbour village was sun-drenched, white-walled and sleepy. Yet amid the utter tranquility of the area, a mother stood breathless and distraught beside the bed of her daughter.

Writhing contortions, with violent spasms of involuntary jerks, that could more correctly be called convulsions, wracked the dear little frame of a tiny child. Her mother bent down wringing her hands as if every drop of emotion and energy were being wrung out. She had been here so many times before. There was nothing she could do till the violent attacks subsided.

She spoke consolingly to the child, smoothing the brow and sweat-drenched hair and head of her daughter. Her husband had left very early for the day's work, probably fishing, and she again faced the indescribable horror of seeing her daughter writhe from the power of unseen forces. Then, just as quickly as it had come, her child relaxed and resume normal composure, but was energy-drained. She would attempt to enjoy the usual delights of a little girl during the day, but sadly often listless.

The noise of the waking village and township increased as the sun climbed higher. Women were making their way back from the village well after their morning chore of mixing both the collecting of water and the pleasure in half an hour's conversation with their many friends at the well. It was the place where 'information' was shared and sometimes created.

Yet, this woman of Syrophenicia was usually more occupied with her sick daughter to be able to go and spend much time in social pursuits. The hum of the passing women developed into loud chatter. Then the mother caring for her daughter froze at one of the comments of one of the women to her friend beside her as they passed her house. Her body went cold as the adrenalin coursed through her. She sensed a chilling shiver pass through her hands as she caressed the throbbing brow of her daughter as she was easing out of the attack.

What was it they had just said? Had they said Jesus of Nazareth was stopping in an adjacent town? She stopped rigid and yet moved at the same time. Never had she covered the distance from the bed to the door in such a short time. Calling out after the woman she breathlessly ran a few paces and enquired as she ran. "Did you say that Jesus of Nazareth actually is coming to the town?" Her ears couldn't believe the joy of the affirmative answer.

With tears streaming down her face she enquired exactly where the Saviour had spent the night. With the same speed that she approached the woman in the street, she was gone, lost in a flurry of dust and emotion through the front door of her home. The women in the street just stood and stared.

After ensuring her recovering child was well supervised she left the house at a faster pace than she was accustomed to walking. Occasionally for short distances, she ran. Eventually, she made her way to the place the woman had said Jesus had resided overnight. It was in a Jewish part of town and in an area that she was not accustomed to frequenting.

Soon she found the place where Jesus was and wondered how she would recognise Him. How could she make herself and her need known? Would she be permitted to see Him at all? There He was. She did not need to ask which one in the crowd he was. The crowd thronged around Him. The look of His eyes, the grace of His stature, and the warmth of His personality all gave Him away.

Before any of the startled crowd and guests, where Jesus was staying, could do anything about the intrusion the Syrophenician woman was across the courtyard, into the opening to the room and bowed at the Saviour's feet. Vibrant conversation instantly stopped at this untoward intrusion.

Before Jesus could utter a word or hardly observe the pitiful sight at His feet she was pouring out her request. Would He come and cast out the devil that was so viciously tormenting her daughter?

For many of us, the interlude in the conversation that is recorded about this episode is hard to understand unless we realise the cultural difference and the problem that seems to be involved. Consider its reporting in Matthew 15: 21 to 28 or Mark 7: 24 to 30.

Jesus was not unsympathetic to the desperate need of the woman or unconcerned about her daughter. The faith in His dialogue stands as an encouragement and example to us all. The woman hanging on in faith eventually received the answer and the desire of her heart.

The crux of our meditation lies in the verse that glistens with the display of the inner faith of the woman. After seeming to be initially rebuffed she says: "Yes Lord; however the dogs under the table eat the children's crumbs," (Mk. 7: 28). Matthew in verse 15 puts it as: "And she said truth Lord, yet the dogs eat the crumbs which fall from their master's table."

Jesus had just referred to the provision of blessing and especially healing, which she desperately wanted, as belonging just to the 'children,' meaning in this instance the children of Israel. She immediately took up the same metaphor and carried it one step further to give foundation to the miracle that was born from the womb of faith.

Something must have told Jesus straight away that she was not Jewish. We too were once far away and outside the provision of God. Yet, He rescued our souls with divine love. Israel could have had the blessing of the provisions that Jesus here alluded to that were rightfully theirs. But, they ultimately rejected them so the door of blessing to all of mankind was opened.

Taking the parable of the prodigal son as an example, Israel here is the elder brother in attitude. He lived amongst the blessing, having full rights and claim to it, yet turned away from it. This woman came and sought the face of the Saviour. Though her prayer and petition were short they were effective. Someone has looked at her prayer and made the following summary: It was determined, short, persevering, humble, worshipful, fervent, respectful, desperate, and yet rational. It was full of faith in Christ. Not a bad pattern for us to duplicate. Through this kind of prayer, she came into a blessing.

So often we have heard the expression: "Healing is the children's bread." It has its basis in this passage or story. Yet, it can still convey elitism. Can we justify the validity of the expression? Was Christ not referring to all the blessings of salvation rather than one specific group of people or issue, such as healing?

Certainly, for this desperate woman, we understand healing was the need in her daughter's life. She reached out to get a touch from the Lord with a level of faith rarely seen in many mature Christians. She didn't ask for the finest of the table because she knew that even the crumbs of Christ's blessings were richer in blessing than anything the world had to offer.

She didn't seek to monopolise the blessing, just to receive from Jesus' hand her personal portion. Her cry was for the full sanity and health of her daughter and freedom from the satanic forces that bound, drove and tormented her. She needed a mighty deliverance.

For this, the table was an appropriate parallel of speech. Love and faith demand the crumbs will fall. So often people feel they have God's blessings cornered in their little world. Yet, others are reaching through to gain the 'crumbs' and their faith rewards them greater than those who didn't take from the table to enjoy the provisions before them. She didn't naturally have a provision or a place at the table, but she took and was satisfied with crumbs nevertheless. Others were shown a full table and took nothing.

The woman cleverly used a very warm and endearing description of the Master's comment. She introduced a colourful picture of the little child feeding the crumbs under the table to the household pet dog/puppy who waited hopefully near the child's legs well under the table. Implications are that the dog got not just the crumbs but also the little extras that the child's love and father's watchful eye would allow.

Can you see it in your own mind's eye? A little child has one eye on the puppy and the other on Daddy. He or she occasionally lets his/her scraps drop, 'accidentally on purpose,' to the floor to their wonderful, loved canine friend. The dog does not mind at all that they are scraps. He doesn't care that it is on the floor. His wagging tail indicates it does not care they are just scraps falling from the table, it's love coming down as well. The woman, though desperate to see her daughter healed, continued to feed faith and trust into the situation by keeping the metaphor alive.

We now enjoy the provisions of the Lord's Table. But let us not be as the Jews of old, having access to the full provisions of a table of blessing, yet making little or no effort to avail themselves of such incredible provisions. Let us treasure every crumb that is falling our way, having these two confidences:

First: We should be feeding upon the full provision of the table whilst we can, as He has made and full and complete provision for each of us. Second: There are countless numbers of others who as yet have not come to the provision of His table. Do not withhold from dropping crumbs/provisions to them that they, in turn, may learn to respond themself to the mighty provisions of Calvary.

This desperate Syrophenician woman came to understand the provisions of the table. She clearly understood that these blessings were initially the inheritance rights of Israel or the Jews. In the story, those chosen by birth were first qualified to attend the table. But, many left empty-handed. Yet, the woman of our story, didn't by birth qualify to eat at the table but made the blessing hers and left with a miracle.

We have the provisions of the blessing of the table because we are creatures of the new birth. Let us do more than praise the provision. Let us partake of that same provision in Christ Jesus. Blessings have become ours because the Jews put them aside as their inheritance rights. So let us now not be guilty ourselves of putting aside the accompanying blessings of the Lord's Table. Don't push it aside. Take hold of its blessings today.

The incredible faith of the woman brought her to the miracle she so desperately needed. She did not return home with a weary defeated tread on her feet. Skipping, running and eagerly she ran home to see tranquility and peace spread right across the face of her daughter. She was resting peacefully on her bed. Her caregiver was sitting near her with tears in her eyes because of the radical transformation that had happened a short time ago, a time they would later realise was exactly when the Saviour issued His word of healing.

Throughout the day her daughter strengthened and she never had any further seizures, which occurrence had been sadly several times a day. As the sun was setting across the hills the red tinges of its rays melted away the last memories of anguish from the mother as she walked with her husband and daughter across the shell-strewn beach to the lapping sea, turning deep turquoise with the approach of night. As they stood quietly musing on the goodness of their creator with unspoken impressions, they knew each other's thoughts that indeed the creator had touched their lives richly that day.

As we gather around the Lord's Table don't allow it to be a meal spoilt by your non-participation. "Come and dine the Master calleth, come and dine. You may feast at Jesus' table at any time. He who fed the multitude, turning water into wine, calleth now to thee, come and dine."

Study/Meditation 34

THE GARMENTS OF THE TABLE

The guest shifted restlessly. Throughout the great banqueting hall there was an air of exhilaration, as well as breathless anticipation. As fresh guests kept pouring in, those that had been there for some time kept their eye on the entrance. Craning their necks they were trying to see if they might catch a glimpse of their benefactor. They gathered in groups where they recognised one another. Many stood admiring the robes of their friends and the hall décor, as they were all in surroundings that were not their normal habitat.

Some of the guests appeared to be very rough men and women, possessing distinguishing tell-tale features on their faces. Yet, their personality seemed unduly subdued, by the grandeur of their dress and the magnificence of the feasting chamber they were in. But most of all they were humbled because they had been asked, personally invited, to this special wedding feast by the king.

"I hear the king is really annoyed with those he first invited," said a woman as she stood talking to an acquaintance she had never expected to find at the wedding feast.

"You know I heard that he has ordered the punishment of all that were invited and then refused to come. How could they refuse such a noble invitation?" answered her companion as she stroked her beautiful wedding feast garment.

"The thing that I cannot fathom out," said a man joining the party, "Was why did they not respond to the invitation when they were first sent their personal invitations. Didn't they realise the honour?"

The custom of the land was that guests were first bidden to the marriage, then at the time of preparation of the wedding feasts the servants of the king would go throughout the length and breadth of the land calling those that had been invited to the feast. "They simply wouldn't come," interrupted a young lad. "My father told me that even some of the king's servants were severely treated and threatened by some of the nobles of our area when they came to escort them to the feast."

"I cannot tell whether it is true or not," commented another "but, I heard it said that some of the king's servants lost their lives in the whole process. No wonder the king is angry. They despised his son and his wedding. And they have shamefully treated his servants."

A fresh contingent of guests spilled into the banqueting hall, all stroking and admiring their new garments as if it was indeed the finest thing they had ever seen – which it was. They mixed quickly and were almost instantly totally absorbed by the large crowd that already milled around in quiet chatter.

"Not two hours ago I saw the king's men ride out with their fresh orders in their hand for the apprehension of all who have trodden underfoot their personal invitation to the wedding of his son." The speaker was a notorious villain, noted for his crimes and disreputable life. Yet, here he was within the banqueting chamber of the king dressed in a refinement that seemed to turn this shady character of darkness into the gracious man that politely stood with his friends. His personality had changed. He turned to see another friend of crime.

"I thought my hour had come," commented the scoundrel that just joined the group. "Here I was blissfully relaxing under an old olive tree when I was suddenly surrounded by the king's men. I thought that I was gone for sure. I thought to myself 'I'm headed for prison.' But instead, I was handed this gorgeous gold-embossed royal invitation." He was waving it in the air. His friends all grinned then reached inside their lavish garments and withdrew similar invitations. They all waved theirs at him. Laughing he continued.

"Well, I must say it nearly knocked me off my feet. With great grace and care, they escorted me back here after I accepted the invitation. And just look at this garment the king's servants gave me to wear as I was ushered into the palace." He had stopped speaking and was slowly turning around so that the amazed group could view him.

"Unbelievable," said a woman noted for being a woman of ill repute from the streets. "Unbelievable." She could speak no more for the tears that ran freely down her cheeks. She stroked her beautiful garment after admiring her friend. She was a common woman no longer. In the robes of the king, she had been transformed into a princess. Her husband held her waist seeing her tears. They both were speechless at the magnificence of their apparel and the fact that they had been invited to the wedding feast personally by the king.

A royal herald stood forward and with a blast from his golden trumpet summoned the attention of the awe-struck, chattering large crowd. He spoke with a loud voice filled with grace and dignity that inspired his listeners. He welcomed them and asked that they move through the veiled curtains that were being drawn apart by other servants, to the table of the king.

As he spoke a huge veil and drape that had separated the area where they now stood and the actual banqueting chamber silently folded back, with the assistance of several servants, to reveal a sight that caused many of the guests to gasp. Before each person was the most magnificently displayed table that they had ever seen. The food for the first course, now being brought in by an army of servants dressed like royalty themselves, was beyond description and the setting of the table was in the words of one guest: "Out of this world."

As they began to be seated another flurry of trumpets announced the coming of the king. Some blushed as he entered. All their life they had stood against his purposes, rule and reign, hating him and his servants. Now by his grace and love, they sat at his table. The room was stilled at his presence. As the king entered another herald announced that the bride and groom would soon arrive.

The king walked through the crowd, welcoming different people as he came to them. Amazingly he knew everyone by name. Here and there men and women burst into tears as he greeted them seeking his forgiveness for a wayward life and pledging unswerving loyalty.

"You were forgiven a long time ago," said the king with a consoling hand upon the shoulder of his new loyal servant, once the town's most accomplished thief. He greeted them all by name and they could scarcely believe that He should know them at all.

The king turned and spoke to many. Then he stood still staring across the room. Pointing a finger at someone across the room he spoke. The love was still in his voice but added to it was an unmistakable authority. He pointed directly at one man. Quietly those around the man stepped back a pace. He was conspicuous by his dress. "Friend, how did you come in here without a wedding garment?"

Everyone was aware of his presence and turned to see the man still dressed in his dirty street clothes and not arrayed with the finest garment that had been given to every guest as they entered the palace. There was no answer. He was speechless. He motioned to speak but the searching eyes of the king, who was now walking towards him, brought muteness to his tongue. The king motioned to his servants.

"Bind him hand and foot and take him away and cast him into outer darkness; where there shall be weeping and gnashing of teeth." The crowd gasped. The servants moved quickly to remove the man. The king turned to speak again to his people and subjects. The first phase and tone of his voice dismissed from their thinking the scene that had just taken place.

"You are warmly welcome today to join the wedding feast of my son and his beautiful bride. Let me say your garments enhance the beauty and fineness of each of you." The hushed crowd blushed with the blush of adoration and love, rather than embarrassment. The king's son and his bride entered to a fanfare of trumpets. The gathered crowd stood and applauded and the feast commenced. The king dined with his people for what to them seemed like an eternity.

Matthew 22: 1 to 14 and Luke 14: 15 to 24 both provide the setting from which we have created the backdrop for this study/meditation. Here Jesus is teaching about the kingdom of heaven by use of a parable. It is the uniqueness of the wedding garment and our right to be at the table that will be our main focus.

Certainly, we can all identify with the great gathering in the parable. Possible few if any of us were of noble spiritual birth that would have merited an invitation to be part of the family of God. But, it isn't a matter of natural birth rights, but 'new birth' rights.

In Jesus' day, the Jewish nation though initially invited to accept their Messiah rejected Him. They despised their right to come to the wedding feast of the Son. Individual Jews may have accepted, but nationally they rejected Jesus. Then the invitation went out to: "Whosoever Will!"

The Word of God takes time to specifically itemise that both the good and the bad were called. And they both responded. Across the church, there is always a cross-section from both good and bad backgrounds. They have immersed their past in Christ's redemptive forgiveness and purposes and are walking now in 'Robes Of Righteousness,' that He has provided for all.

The provision of wedding garments in ancient days was a well-accepted Eastern custom that is still maintained in some areas. People of high rank showed their magnificence by providing their guests with wedding or festive garments. Could any outdo or outrank our God? He condescended to send His Son in the form of sinful flesh, but yet not sinful flesh, for humanity to redeem it. Now His Son has gained a Bride for Himself.

We were all lost in sin on the highways of the world. Whilst we were wayward, right there one of the king's servants came and brought the invitation of God's love to come and dine with Him. We were drawn into fellowship with God, because of His great redeeming love.

It may seem amazing, but there was one at the wedding feast without the graciously provided wedding garment. From our state of being outside of Christ, dressed in filthy rags of sin (Isaiah 64: 6), we have been given the most magnificent of garments. Isaiah 64: 10 speaks of: "Garments of salvation," as well as: "Robes of righteousness." Job puts it another way in 28: 14 when he says: "I put on righteousness and it clothed me." Why then with such heavenly provisions was the man rudely standing in the wedding feast without his appropriate garment gifted by the king? It had been offered, even given, but arrogantly he refused to wear it.

There will always be those who reject God's love and salvation. The 'tares' will always grow up with the 'wheat.' It is God's, not our, prerogative to sift out the one from the other. We can see the outworking of this parable constantly in day-to-day life.

There are people who are in church, but not of it. The guest that didn't think it important enough to wear the wedding garment represents this. He was picked out as the king entered the chamber. I can imagine people standing around him had talked with him urging him many times to put on the provided garment. They knew the etiquette. They understood refusal to obey the wishes of the host was an insult to the invitation and disrespect of the provision of the love demonstrated in the provision of the garment.

The king, not his servants, picked out the man. The king had issued the invitation. It is God's prerogative to sound out those who are true in heart and profession of their faith. There is no hope of hiding from the ever-present eye of God. It wasn't that the man was naked or in extremely filthy rags, but that he violated the honouring of the king's son, his love and grace.

Notice in the Scriptural text he is addressed as: 'Friend.' How that word must have smarted to the depths of his soul. It was his obligation to put on the wedding garment that was freely given to him. The servants are not scolded for allowing in such a man. The onus was on the man to be prepared or otherwise.

It is the man's presumption that he could come anyway he chose into the presence of the king that was acted upon. "How did you come in here like that?" The finger of judgement was resting solely upon him. Accountability penetrates to the depth of the personal question that rests behind the whole revelation of the gospel of our Lord Jesus Christ.

The table must be approached by those whose life is straight and clean. If they are not then they can put straight any issue before they partake of the emblems. The garments of our Christian life need to be pure and clean, those provided by our God. No wonder the finger of God stands against so many when we think we can come to His Table without considering the purity of our garments.

God desires to see purity in our garments on a day-to-day basis. Christianity is not something we put on and off when we feel like it. Is it not true that a replacement garment for our sinful garment (Isaiah 64: 6 already cited) has been provided? Certainly, then why is it that so many refuse to wear the righteousness of Christ? They still wear the grave clothes of the old life.

In John's Gospel, we have the wonderful story of the raising of Lazarus from the dead in John chapter 11. Graveclothes were part of the story. Can we imagine Lazarus returning home, after being raised from the dead, and still retaining those dreadful grave clothes after he had been given new life? No, he would have excused himself, slipped into his own room and found one of his finest garments and put it on. He was alive and so he dressed in the garments of the living. Gathering those old grave clothes up he would have thrown them out to be burned later.

Sin is a fretting plague of leprosy (Leviticus 13: 47 to 59). It remains in the old grave clothes, the garments of self, the flesh and the old life. If we hang onto them they will reinfect the life that has been freed from the power of sin and death. The instruction of Jesus to those around Lazarus was: "Lose him, and let him go" (John 11: 44). Note those surrounding the miracle were not to take the grave clothes right off him, just loosen them. His naked body beneath the grave clothes was the reason they would not be taken right off him. But when he got home and was in the privacy of his bedroom off they came and immediately he was dressed in garments of the living.

In the quiet of our own lives, we can slip off the old grave clothes of the flesh and slip into the glorious provisions of the cross of Calvary. None of us can fully remove the old life from another's life. It must be done by the believer himself or herself. We can imagine standing alongside Mary and Martha and hearing the Master's voice. "Lose him, and let him go." Often we in our labour of love try to free an individual. But like the little chrysalis of the butterfly, the emergence out of its hold and entry into the newly created butterfly must be accomplished by the individual butterfly itself.

I once heard of a man seeing the struggle of a butterfly straining to be free of the chrysalis cocoon eased the sides so it could slip out more easily. After it emerged it sat on a branch. Its wings wouldn't form properly. You see the normal great pressure of struggling free squeezes that new life through every vein of the wings and body till eventually free it rises above. This butterfly couldn't fly will ill-formed wings.

We can help so much in our care of new Christians, but they have to realise it is up to every one of us to struggle free from the old life and kick the trappings of the past aside to be burned as we enter into a living relationship with Him who has saved us.

What a garment we each have. Let us quickly list some of the glorious garments that God's children are referred to as wearing. Throughout Scripture we see:

- Job 29: 14 --- "Righteousness, and it clothed me."
- Psalm 132: 16 --- "Clothed her priests with salvation."
- Isaiah 52: 1 --- "Put on your beautiful garments."
- Zechariah 3: 4 --- "I will clothe you with the change of raiment."

- Isaiah 61: 10 --- "I will greatly rejoice in the Lord, my soul shall be joyful in my God; for He has clothed me with the garments of salvation, he has covered me with the robe of righteousness, as a bridegroom decks himself with ornaments, and as a bride adorns herself with her jewels."

As we approach the Lord's Table together, are we dressed in the fullness of salvation that He has provided for each and every one of us? Remember when the prodigal son returned home and was received by the father? He came in rags but the father reclothed him in the best robes (Luke 15: 22). To the 'overcomers' in Revelation 3: 5 and 18 they were promised a covering or raiment that defies the imagination of the world. Peter addresses clothing as he calls on women to realise that their adornment or dress shouldn't be primarily an outward preoccupation, but a concentration on the inner beauty God has given them (I Peter 3: 4).

When we come to the table become conscious of how we are dressed. Not in the natural outward sense, though for some that could be considered (you are coming into the presence of the King of Kings), but duly consider the inner man's clothing. Give consideration to how we are dressed spiritually.

Some might suggest that this inward reflective mood can lead to personal condemnation. If we realise and live in the power of the blood how can it? Let us continually keep our lives clean and checked. How on earth can we make sure our garments are not spotted with the world (Jude verse 23) if we do not expose our lives to His searching, so we may be spotless before Him? The Psalms create a beautiful backdrop to this study/meditation, with respect to being clothed in God's designer beauty. We will consider and develop this again in Study/Meditation 50. Psalm 45: 13 says:

"The King's daughter is all glorious within:
Her clothing is of wrought gold."

The Bride is making herself ready. She is all glorious. Note it is from 'within' that her beauty is assessed. It is of gold because the work of Calvary is of the highest price. The spun fabrics are exotic. They are made by the Holy Spirit to fit us individually perfectly. I cannot come to the Table of the Lord before I consider how I'm dressed and how I appear in His sight.

May we take a fresh look at how we're spiritually dressed, and how we come to His Table. Christ deserves the very best. He has provided the very best for us to be attired in. Why is it so many are resistant to walking in such purity on a daily basis?

Study/Meditation 35

THE LAST SUPPER TABLE – Part 1
A Table Prepared

We now commence a set of four studies/meditations that are taken from 'The Last Supper' incident. We know that it was at this Last Supper that the Lord's Table, or Communion was instituted. It is therefore important that the setting of the occasion creates an area of meditation for our thinking. You can expand your own thinking on the Last Supper but sufficient here to open the Scriptures for your consideration.

Again as with other series, we feel you are best to read and/or use them sequentially from the first to the fourth. Some of the later material requires an understanding of formative comments. We pray you will be blessed around the Lord's Table because we more fully appreciate The Last Supper.

.o0o.

Peter walked with John away from the rest of the disciples and Jesus. They were quiet for a while as they journeyed towards the heart of Jerusalem.

After walking for a while Peter said: "Did you hear the Master right, John?" enquired Peter as he looked at John with one of those 'half-looks,' sideward glances.

"Do you mean about finding this fellow with a pitcher of water?" answered John with a grin.

"That's just what I mean. We both know the Master knows more than both of us put together, but really John, how does He know…" Peter stopped still in his conversation. His jaw was no longer forming words. It had oddly dropped in sheer amazement at the sight in front of him.

"We should have known better," smiled John, as he gave Peter's dusty coat a tug. They approached the man right in front of them carrying the pitcher of water. Peter followed shaking his head slowly and smiling at John with a broad grin.

When the man reached his destination John began to speak to him exactly what the Saviour had requested and soon they were admitted to a large upper room.

There was quite an amount of preparation to undertake and the two disciples busied themselves. They found the Saviour and other disciples and informed them of the location, though it seemed the Saviour already knew. Back to the Upper Room they concluded preparations. All was in order. Around the table there was seating for thirteen. Jesus was placed in the centre and his disciples flanked either side and possibly across the table. Don't take Leonardo da Vinci's portrayal in 'The Last Supper,' as your understanding of seating arrangements.

We know that John sat immediately to one side of Jesus because of the conversation in the gospels. It seems to have been Peter who was on the other side. That night would be full of many incidents that the gospels would reveal. Each event adds another strain of thought to our meditation. The passages dealing with the incident includes: Matthew 26: 17 to 29; Mark 14: 12 to 25; Luke 22: 7 to 38 and John 13: 1 to 38.

The night air was filled with the singing of thirteen rich baritone male voices. Singing of Dayenu (Hebrew: דַּיֵּנוּ), or its formative primitive form, was part of the normal celebration of the Jewish holiday of Passover. Before the eventful night was over both iniquity and eternity would have their fill.

Each of the gospels reveals variant aspects of truth about the institution of the feast of the Lord's Table. This special Passover celebration occasion created it. Keep in mind it was a prepared table. It wasn't something that just happened, where the disciple arrived and a Passover meal had already been spread for them. It was prepared. It was made ready according to the pattern of the Scriptures and the manner that the Passover should be celebrated.

The death and sacrifice of our Saviour were no accident. It was prepared. It fulfilled the pattern and predictions of Scripture. The Word of God stands as testimony to this process and pattern in His death. From Genesis' opening vibrations of Messianic hope to Revelation's fulfilment of the triumphant

Messiah, the message is just the same. Moses penned those immortal words in Genesis 3: 15 when he declares under the inspiration of the Holy Spirit:

"And I will put enmity between you and the woman, and between your seed and her seed; He shall bruise your head, and you shall bruise His heel."

Thousands of years now roll by. The cup of man's iniquity fills and in the closing days of his life the apostle John contemplates eternal matters. He is now an aged man. He is writing under the power of the Holy Spirit. Revelation 13: 8 tells us:

"...in the book of life of the Lamb slain from the foundation of the world."

The centre of the Lord's Table is not a thought hastily created. No, it was a table prepared and a work accomplished in heaven's planning before the world was flung into orbit and our solar system existed. The work of Calvary was prepared.

The work of the table we celebrate, mostly in a church is prepared. It didn't just happen a few moments ago. Some individuals kindly prepared the emblems. It was also prepared an eternity ago and consummated on Calvary. It was completed and it was finished. Note Jesus and the disciples were not brought to the upper room till the table was prepared. The Saviour likewise does not call us to something that is not prepared, but rather complete in every detail.

As we read the gospel account we see that it was in a 'large' upper room that the table was instituted. Smallness belongs to man. The largeness and the vastness of His love belong to God. The work of the cross was not small. It was completed in such a manner that the blessings came just to a few. It is a large room. There is a banqueting table where the banner over us is love. Salvation is a large room that will hold many who will still answer the call of Redemption.

Salvation is not a 'secret order.' It is something that extends to the 'Whosoever Will.' Paul attacks the idea of the exclusiveness of salvation to just a few:

"For the king (referring to Agrippa) knows of these things before whom also I speak freely: for I am persuaded that none of these things is hidden from him; For this thing was not done in a corner," (Acts 25: 26).

This work of the cross, this redemption is not small, poky, or done secretively in a small corner away from public awareness. Redemption is immense. The world knows that Jesus died for the salvation of mankind. Whether they accept it is another thing. However, it's out there. It's very public.

Salvation is larger than often any denomination or church thinking can comprehend. It can't be contained to a theological library. It's huge and destined for humanity. It's a large upper room, not a small one. No work was ever loftier or higher than the completed work of Calvary. Let us enter afresh into the largeness of His work. It covers every race and creed. It covers every age and dispensation since Calvary. Jesus gave us a large redemptive work higher than anything a man can attain, but ever attainable through His redemptive grace.

The large upper room was furnished. It was not bare but furnished with every good thing. Salvation, healing, restoration, peace and an endless list of blessings are the furnishings of His provision. We are not drawn to something that is meagre, bare. We are drawn to something that is furnished and complete.

The table was prepared. The table was large and the table was furnished. As we sit and partake of the Lord's Table it embraces and keeps alive the concept of the 'prepared,' 'enlarged' and 'finished' work of Calvary. Before His rejection by Israel, perhaps the basis of salvation or redemption may have fallen just to the Jewish nation. But, the table is enlarged. Calvary cut across every culture and conviction of heart. It countered the corruption of sin. It deals with all of life till King Jesus is established as Lord over, and on the throne in our hearts. Truly He has prepared a table in the presence of our enemies that brings glory to His name.

Luke chapter 22 includes an interesting statement that inspires us around the table. He says in verse 7: "Then came the day of unleavened bread, when the Passover must be killed." It 'must' be killed. The Saviour had to die. We cannot understand the justice, or is it injustice, of Christ's death. We can hardly comprehend with human minds the blessing that flowed by the Saviour dying.

Caiaphas the high priest, before Jesus died, captured in his own cynical words the eternal message of redemption. We are sure that he didn't know what he was saying, or that it had any spiritual significance to anyone, but he said it. John 11: 50 records his words: "Now consider that it is expedient for us, that one man should die for the people and that the whole nation perish not."

He had caught hold of insight into the message of the redemptive plan. It was not in his mind that he was referring to the eternal plan; nevertheless, it came out of his mouth. Not only his nation but also all nations of the earth would die and perish in their sins had not the Saviour come and died for all sinful mankind. It was expedient.

The Saviour gave of His love. He gave of His life. He gave His all so that the world's masses need not die unredeemed, but have everlasting life. He must be killed. Now seated on this side of Calvary we thank God for such love. He allowed His Son to suffer as He did.

Jesus knew He was preparing something. He was laying down the foundation for a 'new creation.' Because of the Last Supper feast, and of course, the redemption wrought on Calvary, which it so nobly speaks of, we are ushered into a new era. The Saviour took the cup and lifting it up before all of their sights He boldly announces:

"Drink you all of it; For this is my blood of the New Testament which is shed for many for the remission of sins," (Matthew 26: 27, 28).

A 'New Covenant' was being prepared. A new table was being ushered in. The old tables of the Old Testament would pass away and the Table of the Lord was taking form. Drink all of it, not just part. Drink deep of the provision of the blood of Christ for none can cleanse the heart like Jesus. Here is where the disciples were last together as a group prior to Christ's death. Only the Saviour went alone into the depths of Gethsemane and eventually the cross.

Interesting isn't it that in rising from the dead He often met with His disciples in breaking bread together. The work is complete because it was planned and prepared.

As we conclude let us think about Luke 22: 22. "And truly the Son of Man goes, as it was determined." Calvary's work was no accident. It was the glorious, planned and prepared act of the ages. This Lord's Table is the living reminder of that preparation. May we sense the outstretched love of the Saviour. May we indeed sense the planning of the King. May we come equally prepared to a table that was itself prepared before eternity.

Study/Meditation 36

THE LAST SUPPER TABLE – Part 2
A Table Instituted

Of all of the times of man's celebration, none is so universal as the Lord's Table. Australia Day relate just to Australians. Thanksgiving predominantly is a special North American celebration. Guy Fawkes Night to the British. But the Lord's Table is a universal celebration, and celebrated not just once a year, but Till He Come.

Heroic men accomplish much, as they fight for liberty and justice. They may lay their life down in the ultimate sacrifice for their specific country. Their deeds are glorified in remembrance. But none can compare to the Table of the Lord and the sacrifice of Christ, literally for all of humanity.

In the Lord's Table we have a feast that was instituted in love and will be celebrated throughout the ages 'Till He Come.' This feast was even instituted before the event it remembers. It didn't arise out of the sentiment of an occasion. Jesus commissioned the remembrance of the Lord's Table well before those horrific hours of Gethsemane and Calvary. The table is a deliberately 'instituted' feast.

I know there are some small elements in Christendom that have wiped it aside on the grounds of dispensationalist doctrine, or some other personalised reason. But, my heart is not stirred by their philosophy or words. Jesus said: "Do this in remembrance of me." That's good enough for me.

Time was running out for Jesus. In those last few weeks, the Lord packed so much teaching into His disciples. Most of it would lie latent till after Christ had died. It would then be resurrected in their thinking and be fully appreciated for what it was.

In those years after Christ had ascended to glory, and the infant church was born, those days of Christ's teaching would become crystal clear. They would know. His words were blazoned in their spirit.

It would have been hard for the disciples to have fully comprehended everything Jesus said at the Last Supper. Yet, Jesus left strict instructions to His disciples that the table of remembrance was to continue after His death. From the very early chapters of Acts we can see they were obedient to that calling.

The hour of Christ's ultimate sacrifice was so close, but the disciples didn't know it. Luke says the timing was so close that he uses the phrase: "When the hour was come" (Luke 22: 14). John puts it this way in John 13: 1 – "…When Jesus knew that His hour had come that He should depart out of this world to the Father, having loved His own which were in the world, He loved them unto the end." The time was at hand and nothing should be wasted in establishing a feast of remembrance that has had more celebrations and celebrants than any other single celebration/remembrance in all of earth's history.

Can you imagine the last moments around the Last Supper table? The disciples were quiet and somewhat serene. The Saviour's conversation had been very serious and indeed the Passover feast was a solemn occasion for Jewish born. Yet, this was no ordinary Passover celebration. The teaching and the evening were on two different wavelengths. The Saviour knew He must die and longed to impart something of the lasting value of this feast whilst He was still alive. Certainly, it was a Jewish Passover, but it similarly was the birthing of The Lord's Table.

The disciples discerned none of this dualistic purpose. Nor would they fully understand it till many days later, well after Jesus' death, resurrection and ascension. Their minds were on other things. The Passover, the betrayal that had been mentioned by Christ, prominence in the kingdom and other matters clamoured in their minds. Treachery in Judas left him sulking at the table. Impetuousness in Peter sat at the table. Self-seeking in James and John sat at the table.

However, love and eternal love in Jesus sat also at the table. Jesus spoke and His raised voice quietened the ripples of self-centred conversations. "With desire, I have desired to eat this Passover with you before I suffer," (Luke 22: 15). Something strong was beating urgently and fast in the Saviour's bosom. The King of Kings was aware of the timetable of the next few hours and days.

There was something deep within Christ that yearned to come to this point and unfold and institute this feast. It came from before the very foundations of the universe. From the eternal dimensions of the Saviour rose up a desire to reach out to His disciples in the formation of this new feast. They were on the brink of eternal history and the disciples didn't know it.

It would become the satisfaction of a planned event. It was a desire that had been born before eternity's beginnings and found its expression now amongst His own disciples. This desire would drive Him to complete the work of atonement, fully accomplishing what He was destiny to fulfil.

We cannot really fully understand this desire for we are still mortals. But, the Saviour reached out to begin to put into place the motion, intent and design of the eternal plan. And, the Lord's Table is a vital part of that. It commenced here in the institution of the table and was culminated at the right hand of the Father when Christ was glorified after the ascension.

As long as hearts remain human I don't think we will fully comprehend how the Saviour could look forward to the experience of the cross. It defies our human reasoning that with 'desire' the cup could be taken and its bitter dregs consumed. Our hearts today on this side of Calvary can only look back with thankfulness and reach out to praise the Saviour who, considering not His own well-being, drank this cup for each of us.

Do we with deep desire draw around the Table of the Lord to celebrate the table with Him? Is it really desire that draws us, or is it some form of religious performance, even duty? God forbid that the latter should ever be our motivating attitude. Meditate upon the redemption that you have, before you partake at the table. Then, with desire burning within our hearts, let us draw near with hearts of deep gratitude. His desire was to finish the work committed to Him and to institute the table to keep its remembrance alive. Is our desire so fervent to finish the task of worldwide evangelism, which was His purpose, and to partake with Him around His table?

The Lord's Table was instituted to unite not divide. Jesus united His disciples with His purpose as He sat with them at the Passover. There are churches that have separate cups, there are some that have a common cup for all drink from. Some churches have a common loaf and they break off portions, whilst others have already segregated separate pieces. It is not the exterior pattern or performance that is important, but the attitudes in the inner man/woman that matter. And let's not forget 'Covid-19' has militated 'how' we partake of the elements of communion.

Let's not argue about 'methods' of communion and lose the relevance of what the emblems stand for. I can still remember many years ago a man in our church, that we dearly loved, refusing to take the cup because they were separate glass instead of one cup. His attitude was spoiling his fellowship with others. We did not deny the worth of his comments and indeed his reasoning. However, he couldn't see that when Jesus said that the cup was to be 'divided amongst us' (Luke 22: 17), as the Saviour handed it on that such a comment could at least accommodate the idea of separate cups.

I do not wish to convey that we were opposed to this fellow holding the view he did. Not at all. It was his inflexibility and making mere 'methods' a test of fellowship that was the problem. That's what alienated him. By his own actions (no one else's), he separated himself from fellowship with others.

I cannot believe Jesus instituted a feast to divide us. Let it not become a 'divided cup,' in the sense that it divides us one from the other. Jesus united His church with the table. Can we comprehend all that He meant for us to grasp in the sacred emblems? The Saviour instituted it. Don't get lost in its method of celebration, but the centre of its meaning.

Jesus instituted this love feast as a uniting feast of 'remembrance.' This word is used extensively throughout the several passages relating to the table. Surely if the Holy Spirit was so careful to have it included so many times then we should be sensitive to its meaning. Do we draw near to the table to 'remember' or to dream? In the words of the old hymn: "Lest I forget Gethsemane, lest I forget Thine agony, lest I forget Thy love for me, lead me to Calvary."

How our view of life would have changed if we literally had stood a moment at the foot of the cross. But we cannot do that in reality. But, in drawing to the Table of 'Remembrance' we have a fresh opportunity to revisit the work of the cross.

It is not remembrance in the sense of great sorrow of the dead. Christ is alive. Death holds Him no longer. He holds death answerable. This table stands as a magnificent remembrance of all that 'was' accomplished and that is 'still' being accomplished in the life of every believer. But the point of coming to the table is to claim the current coverage of Christ's atoning work.

The table speaks of life and power. Let us remember it in the same capacity. This remembrance is something potent, not latent. It is something alive, not languishing. It is something worth remembering, not burying in meaningless platitudes. Lord create a pure remembrance of the work and power of Calvary, whilst we are at the table with you.

Matthew 26: 20 indicates: "When it was evening…" they came to celebrate the Passover. It was coming on dark in more ways than one. The total darkness of man's sin was to be accepted by the Saviour. Evening's darkness crept across the land and oil-filled lamps were trimmed and ignited. Homes outside the upper room had natural oil lamps. The upper room had 'the light of the world.' Darkness hung like a wet blanket that night. Evil was going to attempt to have its way. It is worthy of note that when Judas went out it is stated that 'it was night.'

The darkest deed of betrayal was cast as the mould. The dark sins of humanity awaited the spotless Saviour. Darkness spread as the Saviour instituted a feast that would be celebrated forever – Till He Come. It was darkness, but there was light. If any individual comes to the table and feels darkness, they only need to open up to the 'Light of the World' and the darkness will be banished. Christ ushered in the light illuminating grace through Calvary. So let it continually dawn on our soul.

This instituted feast is only 'Till He Come.' Paul advises us, as do the Gospels, that this table has an end. The end will be His coming again. Let us accept with rejoicing that this is a feast of love, graciously given by the Saviour, to be perpetuated throughout the ages. But it foreshadows in its very message that He is coming again. The feast has been instituted not 'institutionalised.' It is something living. May we all ever remember it so.

Study/Meditation 37

THE LAST SUPPER TABLE – Part 3
Table Of Service

The hum of conversation of thirteen men filled the large upper chamber. The meal had been eaten and they generally were engaged in conversation from light-hearted issues to deep serious topics of an eternal nature. Power struggles were beginning. Jesus had often, over the past few days, spoken about His kingdom. Kingdom and placement in the 'kingdom' fascinated the disciples.

Certain of the disciples yearned to be in prominent positions in that kingdom. Across the other side of the room Judas was brooding and only the Saviour knew the intent of his heart. There had been a relaxed attitude amongst the disciples, yet something of Eastern etiquette was missing.

Jesus rose and laid aside His outer garment. He girded Himself with a towel and moved to the corner of the room where a copper basin was placed. Pouring water into it He moved back towards the disciples. Every one of them knew the intent of the Master. There wasn't one of them, with the possible exception of Judas, that didn't flush with embarrassment at what the Saviour was about to do.

Unlatching each sandal He lovingly talked on with His disciples as a group and with them as individuals. He bathed their dusty feet and dried them with the towel. Many of them were so embarrassed that they showed it when the Saviour came and bent low at their feet. The water in the bowl started to colour with the many miles of dust and perspiration that lay upon the soiled feet of His disciples.

Moving through the disciples Jesus eventually came to Simon Peter. Withdrawing his foot from Jesus' grasp Peter commented in an enquiry that initially seemed to question the meaning of the Saviour's gracious act. "Lord, do you wash my feet?" The Saviour answered affirmatively. The disciples may not immediately have understood why Jesus was doing this act of service, but in the coming days after His resurrection they would fully understand.

Peter still withheld his foot and adamantly said: "You shall never wash my feet." The Lord looked up softly and kindly at Peter. Humbly He was kneeling at the feet of this impetuous disciple. With a penetrating voice that Peter had learned to recognise, the Saviour answered the refusal of Peter.

"If I don't wash your feet, you have no part with me."

Flushed, Peter stared at the Saviour. Through stuttering embarrassment he demanded Jesus wash not only his feet but his head and hands also. Jesus smiled at His impetuous friend. He continued to unlatch the shoe that now was willingly before Him. As he began to wash Peter's feet He spoke once more before moving on to the next disciple.

"He that is washed needs nothing more than to wash his feet, but he is clean every bit, and you are clean, but not all." These words seemed to strike Judas to the core of His heart. Did the Saviour know what He planned to do? Rather than meet the eyes of the Saviour, which he expected, Judas turned away as if to busy himself with something else that had occupied his attention.

Even as Judas had his own feet washed it seemed that his feet were hot with anxiety. He had a profound amount of sweat spotting all over him. His entire being was consumed with the concept of betrayal. After Jesus had concluded washing all of the disciple's feet He dispensed with the water and moved back to take up His garment.

He continued speaking to His disciples about serving one another. He reminded them that they called Him Master, and rightly so, yet here He was being their servant in washing their feet. The disciples lived in a legalistic age of Jewish indoctrination perpetuated by heartless Scribes and Pharisees, and the brutality of Roman overlords. They were constantly aware of who was in control. They were forced into service to one regime or another. But, here was a fresh law, a law of love. Serve one another. Forget who is master, don't play the power games, just serve one another in love.

Whether it was before or after the washing of feet we do not know for sure, but John 13 records the episode of the disciples arguing over greatness. The situation must have been so tense that the Saviour not only spoke about the issue but also demonstrated service one to another. It did not escape His attention. He was patient with them, probably far more than we would have been.

Softly He spoke. Every voice was stilled when the Saviour was speaking. He gently referred to man's constant struggle for power. "But you shall not be so," said Jesus referring to the dictatorial ways of many in the world. He continued: "...but he that is greatest let him serve." This teaching was revolutionary. The noise of the night insects could be heard as the Saviour softly spoke, and the ears of all of His disciples were tuned to His teaching.

The greatest of lessons had been imparted to them that night. One lesson was in words. The other lesson was in actions, as He washed feet. This night, indeed this teaching, would stay in their thinking for a very long time and end up recorded in the Gospels.

All of this activity and teaching of service occurred around the Last Supper table. Jesus felt it so important to impart something of eternal truth about serving one another that He left it to the time around the table. In His own actions throughout His life, Jesus taught us much about His own love and condescension. Notice that John 13 verse 4 declares He laid aside His own garment. How this prefigures the act of Him laying aside His divinity to assume humanity.

Man is used to toiling in the hot sun with just his loincloth on. The Saviour laid His garment aside so that He might identify with humanity, with the common man. Certainly, we know that in the heavenly realms He laid aside the glories of eternity to step into the fullness of human form to come and stand by us.

In the words of a very old chorus:
"He laid aside His reputation when He came and
  stood by me.

> *He knew full well my degradation, yet became*
>   *a friend to me.*
> *That's why I love Him, oh yes I love Him.*
> *He laid aside His reputation when He came*
>   *and stood by me."*

As well as laying aside His garment Jesus came and served the disciples at their feet. Most of us know that Eastern etiquette required that the servant or the lowliest of rank in the household should have washed the feet of guests when those guests arrived. Peter and John had made all things ready, except this one courtesy. The basin, ready for water, was there. Its presence commanded attention and service. But none would humble themselves to wait on their fellow disciple.

Jesus finally took not only the towel but also the initiative, the water and an example to the church ministered serving principles. Here we see His ministry to His disciples, as an example to us all, coming also in the encouragement of Paul in Philippians 2: 7 & 8.

"But made Himself of no reputation, taking the form of a bondservant, *and* coming in the likeness of men. And being found in appearance as a man, He humbled Himself and became obedient to *the point of* death, even the death of the cross."

Such condescension. Such outreaching love that the Saviour gave and yet practically illustrated at the Last Supper. When we gather around the Lord's Table are we reminded that there are none more important than another? We are all the same in God's eyes. Peter, through the Holy Spirit, put it this way in Acts 10: 34. "…of a truth, I perceive that God is no respecter of persons."

James 2 verses 1 to 9 thought it so important a topic that whilst writing his epistle, under the direction of the Holy Spirit, James included a stern warning about pompous respect of persons. God has no time for the self-imposed hierarchy of importance. Tragically, we can see it in churches at times. We are one in the bond of love, and it is by love that we should serve one another.

Jesus led by example. Constantly we are reminded that the Lord's Table is a place that is bringing us all back to a single common denominator. We are all sinners saved by grace. Jesus is still the Lord. We are still and ever will be co-equal workers/servants together. The Lord's Table levels us all. It raises up 'servanthood.' It puts down personal arrogance.

On rare occasions, when I was pastoring, I found it a useful exercise to distribute part of the emblems amongst the congregation myself. To wait on them and serve people is a privilege. Often I would do this on the first Sunday of a new year. It just seemed appropriate to pledge our lives together to serve each other for the year ahead. On other occasions rather than having 'helpers' already allocated to distribute the emblems, we have invited 'whoever will' to come and take the emblems and go serve their fellow Christians.

Some might suggest this would tend to disorder. But I would rather have a little 'controlled disorder,' with true values, than tradition creating an insensitive impenetrable barrier. We are called to serve one another. The table stands as the greatest testimony of that fact as instituted by Christ's own example. Now let us demonstrate before the world how much we serve one another in Christian love.

"By this shall all men know that you are my disciples if you have love one towards another" (John 13: 35). Notice this challenging verse is given around the Last Supper setting, where the Lord's Table was instituted. This serving one another is serious business. It is something that should emanate from every heart. Ask yourself: "Can I serve my friends, my fellow Christians? How can I best serve them?"

When we capture this sense of service to each other we release one of the greatest influences for the promotion of the gospel. The philosophy of the world is 'every man for himself.' The household of faith has come to live a different call – 'Every man for one another demonstrating Jesus' love.' Do we see that commonly displayed?

Jesus is the supreme example. There is nothing new in what the table calls us to be. As we serve one another in love, in the service and example of our Saviour, we remember the powerful essence of the table with promise. Luke records in chapter 22, verse 30 that we shall eat of His table in His kingdom. But, before catching up with the eternal rewards, let us put in place the earthly outworking of serving one another. Provoke one another to good works in love. This is an essential element of the table. We are called to fulfil it.

Study/Meditation 38

THE LAST SUPPER TABLE – Part 4
Betrayal At The Table

The air outside the upper room was still. Night had settled over the entire city of Jerusalem. But, it was a night never to be repeated. Before the rays of the sun would warm the earth again betrayal would have led the Saviour into the hands of His enemies. The cross was only hours away.

The betrayer sat quietly listening to the other disciples. He was not as jovial as they were. Much was on his mind and buried deep in his heart and motives. Not many hours before he had been in consultation with the chief priests of the city to deliver Jesus into their hands. They had one purpose, the extermination of the Saviour.

Even as the Saviour talked Judas' mind kept switching back to the events in the temple precincts. The promise of money filled his thinking. At this thought, he reached down to the purse that hung from his belt. As 'treasurer' for the band of disciples, he was entrusted with the care of their ministry funds. He unwittingly fingered the round shapes of the coins through the soft leather of the purse.

Judas had come to love the golden lustre of money. Its possession meant more to him than anything else. But what he failed to realise was that it was money's possession of him that was his problem. The words of the priest rang still in his ears. "Thirty pieces of silver. Just the price of a slave." With a jolt of subconscious recognition that someone else was speaking Judas realised where he was. The Master was moving to the other side of the room to take up the bowl, fill it with water and begin to wash the feet of the disciples.

It was embarrassing enough for the other disciples but when the Saviour took Judas' feet and looked up into his face he turned crimson with sheer conviction. The words that Jesus had spoken to Peter about 'not all being clean' stung. They cut right through the hardness of his heart. He cringed under the smart of their meaning. He looked away from the Saviour's gaze and held conversation with the one next to him as a distraction to his conscience.

The Passover meal was almost over. Conversation hung as a light thread through the air. Every now and then someone would pick up another thread and further develop the night's conversation. Some topics were deep and meaningful. Others were light and just those of men sharing time together. Jesus has also chosen this time to teach important lessons to the disciples. The overall context of the conversations has been woven, to some slight degree, into the four gospels.

Every now and again a serious discussion would start. It seemed to Judas it was all directed at him. He could feel the pricks deep in his soul. Conviction makes an uncomfortable bedfellow. The Saviour raised 'betrayal' issues on three separate occasions. The disciples themselves unsure of the true meaning picked up the conversation, but more in questions.

We can imagine how Judas felt as the disciples aghast with the consciousness that there was one amongst them that would betray the Master. They looked one to another and then to the Saviour. "Is it I?" Who was it that was seated alongside of Judas we do not know. But, as he turned to Judas with the same transparent honesty of the other disciples, Judas asked if it could be him. Hot needles of conviction spread to the very inner recesses of the betrayer.

From the context of the gospels, I would say that Judas was no more than two or three places removed from Jesus in seating, if not directly seated across from Jesus. He had to speak personally to Jesus. He had to also be close enough to have the dipped piece of bread that Jesus would give him, passed personally to him. Judas had reached over to accept it from the Saviour's hand, whilst Jesus still had His hand within the bowl.

Sensing the conversation of the other disciples and not wanting to be conspicuous Judas joined in the appeal. "Is it I?" he asked. "Thou has said," remarked Jesus quietly to his bent ear. Judas recoiled back. Had the other disciples overheard?

He had leant right over to Jesus. Probably the Saviour had leant towards him to hear his question amongst the noise of the room.

Judas looked around again. What had the other disciples heard? Judas' face and neck reddened. He could not face those eyes of Jesus. He knew that He knew. Quickly he turned to catch up conversation with the one alongside him and felt the smartening flush drain from his face. Judas' heart quickened as he heard the Saviour speak of betrayal. He continued talking. It soothed his ears from listening.

John, next to Jesus was leaning on Jesus, in typical Eastern fashion around the table. Peter motioned to him to ask the Saviour who it might be that would betray the Lord. Quietly John whispered into the Saviour's ear. Jesus answered simply. "The one that I give this morsel of bread to after I have dipped it, he is the betrayer." The disciples were finishing the last traces of the meal and the bread was used to dip into the bowl and clean it by taking the last fragments of the meal with it as it wiped the bowl.

Jesus dipped the bread and spoke to Judas. He beckoned for him to receive the bread (sop). Judas leant right across to receive it at the bowl. Something transpired at that moment in the heart of Judas. No longer was he embarrassed. It seemed that hatred rose up like a lurking demon and captivated his every thought, emotion and expression.

Judas sat upright. Jesus had spoken to him: "That which you do, do quickly." No one knew what the Saviour meant. Most thought it related to a financial transaction or matters related to provisions for their Passover feast. Judas rose and began to leave. Nobody paid him much attention with perhaps the eyes of Jesus and John.

Judas stepped into the night air. It was now very dark. The cool of the evening had settled against his cheeks and matched the intent of his heart. The die was cast. The mould was set. Satan ruled complete in the heart of the betrayer. The gospel records: "And Satan entered into his heart."

As he walked swiftly towards the temple where the priests waited for his report he wasn't aware of the complete change to his own demeanour. Satan was now in control and had been so since he had received the dipped bread (sop). He brushed aside any feeling of guilt. All that concerned him now was the glint of gold and profit.

It was night and its inky darkness seemed to hang in so close on that horrific night. Betrayal had sat at the table and betrayal had now moved to put its last evil plans into action. The eternal plan of redemption was to be bought with a high price – the spotless Lamb of God and His shed blood.

Often we look at the actions of Judas and form a biased opinion that he was half monster. Indeed, he was all human. There lies his failing. He opened himself up to the jaws of hell.

Many might have heard that when Leonardo Da Vinci in painting the picture of the Last Supper, was troubled over the face of Judas. He originally painted the face of a man that he felt ill towards. They had fallen out and Da Vinci wanted to immortalise this man as the evil face of Judas. But he couldn't do it. His heart would give him no peace. He went and confessed his fault to the man, seeking forgiveness, then returned to paint the face of an ordinary man, with similarities to no man in particular but probably to everybody in general.

Judas isn't the accumulation or incarnation of evil in our mind or another's estimation. He didn't look evil, he became evil. Judas was an average ordinary person. But he succumbed to evil and evil took hold of him. Judas wears the face of a thousand people.

As we draw around the table are we a Judas? Are we sold out for God and His eternal purposes, or are we sold out to other intentions? Judas could partake of the Last Supper just as easily as any of the other disciples. Each and every one of us can draw near to the Lord's Table with just the same responses as everyone else. But is everything right? Is it real, or just a surface show?

We can leave church on Sunday, after partaking of the Lord's Table, and go our own way and be highly thought of in the eyes of the church and the community. But how are we in the eyes of the Saviour? It is His gaze that pierces the very depths of our being. It is His penetrating search that we need to remember is the only thing that counts. Idleness around the table carries a severe price. These are sacred moments. Let's not be a Judas at His Table.

Keep in mind that if we leave the table and our heart is not right with God that we go out, and: "It is night." There is a great difference between betrayal and denial. Peter also came in for the searching eyes of Jesus (See Luke 22: 31 to 34). Peter turned his denials into a devotion to Jesus. Judas failed.

Peter was exposed as the one who would deny his Lord three times. Yet, it was not the same motive that stirred the heart of Judas. Peter's three-times denial was out of terrifying fear and was later countered by his three-times affirmation of faith (See John 21: 15 to 17).

Although Peter had much to learn, he was prepared to be broken himself in the process and before His Lord. After Peter let the Lord down Matthew records that he went out and wept bitterly (Matt. 26: 75). Often we let the Lord down. But, never let us be a Judas that sells Him out.

In the rashness of fear Peter denied. In the cold determination of hell, Judas sold Jesus out. Peter sought forgiveness. We haven't time to elaborate on that. Judas was a pawn from hell.

There is not one of us that sits around the Table of the Lord that hasn't suffered times when we have felt ill with the heartache that we have let the Lord down. Our hearts have been sorrowful, but we have taken time to put it right with God again.

The table allows us that special time when we can search our hearts to ensure there is no betrayal there. Root out everything that is holding you back from God. It seems to be implied in Scripture that Peter had a personal time with the Lord where he put everything right. Seek in the privacy of your own time with the Lord to right wrongs and come to the table clean.

If the Lord convicts you of things whilst at His Table then that is good. That is daily, healthy Christianity. Put those issues right, there and then. Don't partake of the emblems still having areas of conviction still within you that have not been dealt with, submitted to Him in repentance and forgiven by His enduring love.

Betrayal is a strong word. However, there are many who are selling Jesus out for some cheap image. He is Lord, not some religious celebration. He does not fit our infantile human concepts. Our concepts need to be fitted to His directions. God would have us enlarge our concepts of Him to accommodate the vastness of His Son and the priceless salvation that He has wrought for us all.

Don't betray the Lord in word, deed or action. Hold Him up as higher than anything in life, even life itself. This table before us demands purity of purpose and heart. If there has been a moment of weakness come quietly to Jesus and He will grant you the renewed cleansing of His blood deep within.

May God grant that there is never any betrayal at His Table.

Study/Meditation 39

THE TABLE OF EMMAUS

The sun was already climbing high into the sky as the little Jewish man made his way down one of the side streets of Jerusalem. Dust curled from his tread every time he put his leather-sandled foot down. He almost missed his neighbour's polite greeting, as he was deep in thought. Presently he arrived at his destination and gave a sharp knock on the door. Cleopas answered and they both went into the cool of the courtyard.

After sitting for some time, discussing matters in what could only be termed far from a cheerful manner, Cleopas' wife appeared. "I think you had better get going dear. You know you must both be at Emmaus by night." With that last bit of encouragement both of the men readied themselves for their journey. The journey was just over seven miles (a little over eleven kilometres), and with the rays of the sun warming and tiring their every step they set out. It would take them most if not all of the afternoon.

They left the house and moved through the city, deliberately picking the shady side of the street as they journeyed. Soon they were crossing the last rise that blocked Jerusalem's walls and gate from their sight. There were relatively few travellers on the road that day and their conversation had turned quickly to issues that totally consumed their thinking and spirit.

They had followed the Lord in a distant sort of way. They were not part of the inner circle of disciples but they had found a new zest for living in the words and presence of the Master. Now all seemed shattered.

Jesus had been crucified and to confuse things His body was missing from the grave. This was bad enough, but some of the women were adamant they had seen the Lord. The two on the road to Emmaus put this sighting of the Lord down to a vision or the possibility of a hysterically grief-affected reaction. All seemed lost.

So engrossed were they in their conversation that they initially didn't notice a man walking behind them at a distance. His stature was stately, his countenance familiar, yet different. The conversation and heaviness of the hearts of the two disciples slowed their walking and the stranger quickly caught pace. As he drew alongside Cleopas became aware of the presence of another. They stopped their conversation. After all, some would regard it as dangerous talk, even seditious to Roman rule and Jewish intolerance.

In typical Eastern fashion they exchanged greetings and the two now became three that were headed in the same direction. What the eyes of the two from Jerusalem failed to recognise was this third man was the risen Saviour. He had just joined them for the encounter of their life. The conversation cautiously continued with Jesus enquiring of the two why they were so obviously sad and that their conversation obviously reflected sorrow.

At this Cleopas was aghast. He turned towards the stranger with incredulous disbelief. "Are you a stranger in Jerusalem that you have not heard of the things that have happened in the past few days?" His voice quivered and there was a strange mixture of anxiety and urgency. Tears were obvious in his eyes and he exhibited tightness in his throat.

The Saviour smiled and looking ahead towards their destination replied: "What things?" This was really more than Cleopas' companion could bear. Not just from his lips, but also from the depths of his being he poured out a description of the death and crucifixion of Jesus. He spoke at length of the wonder of Jesus of Nazareth, the miracles and His authority. He shared the hatred of the Scribes, Pharisees and the Jewish religious system all had for Jesus. Slowly, carefully watching the stranger, he ventured that many had hoped that Jesus might have been the Messiah.

Cleopas was eager to butt in wherever he could to enlighten something his companion had said. They shared everything of the death of Christ and the alleged resurrection, which they did not understand. But in the light of a missing body they were confused. To both of them their dream was now all finished. Their hope was gone.

When it appeared that the two forlorn travellers had aired their souls the Saviour spoke. His first words set the travellers back. "O fools and slow of heart to believe all that the prophets have spoken." Then with wisdom, grace and love the Saviour showed the travellers, quoting from the Scripture itself, how it was necessary for Christ to die the way He did. He articulated the fact of the resurrection from Scripture and drew them back to what God's Word had to say prophetically about the Saviour.

Cleverly Jesus dealt with Christ's coming to earth and living amongst men. He skillfully shared Old Testament passages about His crucifixion and death as a sacrifice for all mankind. Finally, He verified the resurrection from Scripture. From the works of Moses to Malachi the Saviour expounded the great redemptive plan of God through Christ. The minds of the two travellers were quickened and their spirit's lifted again.

So engrossed were they in their discussions and listening to Jesus that they quickly traversed the seven miles. The sun was just setting in their face as they were basically walking towards the west. They suddenly began to come across the farmlands surrounding Emmaus. The dust spun in endless circles above their heads, in little eddies of wind movement. It seemed to play in those last shafts of light oozing from the sun. It had been a long day and walk, but now the journey was over.

As they drew alongside the house of their destination the Saviour made as if He was going on further. The two disciples pleaded with Him to stay with them the night as the day was already far spent. "Please stay and share our table together, and rest the night, before you travel on." Jesus agreed. As they sat down together for an evening meal the Saviour continued to talk, further unfolding the plan of God in salvation through Christ. Something was breeding in the hearts of Cleopas and his companion.

The Saviour reached out and took some bread. As He broke it He blessed it and began to pass it to them. It seemed that all heaven broke loose from the other side of the table. Cleopas was on his feet and moving towards the Saviour.

"Jesus, Jesus," he was calling from sobs that came deep within him. His companion was speechless and motionless, though the same revelation had come to him. Rivers of water cascaded down his cheeks as he sobbed, deep and long.

Their eyes had been opened to the fact that it was Jesus whom they had walked and talked with. Now in the breaking of bread at the table He was made known to them. The eyes of their understanding as well as their natural eyes had been opened.

Cleopas stopped still. The Saviour that he had moved towards was gone. His companion for a minute second was so lost in tearful rejoicing that he could hardly see through the tears to notice. Jesus had vanished from the room and their sight. They were alone except for the warmth of the revelation that had dawned on their souls.

They could hardly converse with each other because of their emotion. Finally, one of them said with broken tear-filed words what they both deeply felt: "Indeed did not our hearts burn within us, while He talked with us by the way, and while He opened to us the Scriptures," (Luke 24: 32). Luke further identifies in Verse 35 the importance of the table: "…how he was known of them in breaking of bread." Mutually agreeing that such a revelation of the fact that the Saviour had indeed risen should be shared back with the apostles they hurried all the way back to Jerusalem.

The sun had set, but indeed the Son had risen. Hearts that once heavily trod those miles to Emmaus nearly flew back across those same seven miles. Who knows, possibly an hour was saved on the return trip than coming to Emmaus. They hurried back, occasionally breaking into a slow trot overtaken with joy, giggling and excitement.

Late at night, breathless, they found the apostles. Many others had also gathered, but the basic group they sought out were the apostles, especially Peter and John. They regained their breath and spurted out their story. Even as they were sharing about their encounter with the Saviour, Jesus appeared presenting Himself in their midst. They were all speechless. Jesus was alive and all the earth would indeed know it from that day on.

It is only Luke in his chapter 24: 13 to 36 passage that includes this episode of the two disciples on the road to Emmaus. It is probably one of the most graphic accounts of the post-resurrection appearances of the Saviour. Here two men in the pit of despondency are raised to jubilant heights of rejoicing and revelation because they had met the Saviour. As previous identified Verse 35 says:

"And they told what things were done in the way, and how He was made known to them in the breaking of bread."

Jesus revealed Himself around the table. The response of the Saviour, the actions of the Master, awakened in their hearts the reality of who He was. May every heart, as it comes to the table, have a personal encounter with the Saviour. Let King Jesus reveal Himself to you as you walk with Him in the ways of life. And, let the Saviour become so real to you, in a new and fresh way, as you are seated around the Table of the Lord.

Often, it is all too easy to approach the table with no more sense of His presence and revealed love than the wood the table is made of. But, let something awaken in us as to whom it is that sits at the table with us. Christ is present. See Him afresh. Get a new view of your salvation. What a revelation for those on the road to Emmaus.

As we journey along the way of life we can sense the Saviour with us. Are we sharing with Him from His Word? Do we invite Him home to spend time to just be with us? Have we had our eyes opened whilst at the table? Indeed if we have not then we ought to have such a revelation. Men/Women are not the same when they meet the Lord.

How long has it been since 'your heart burned within you' for fellowship with Jesus? My desire is daily He would open the Scriptures to my heart. My desire is as often as I come around the Table of the Lord, the Saviour would become so very real to me. I need a fresh revelation of Jesus. No, I'm not off on some 'bless-me-now, revelation jaunt.' But, I desire to see the Lord, powerfully present with me as I draw around His Table.

So often the wells of salvation in our life get clogged up. We get cold and indifferent. And, the waters run cold through our life. As far as we know the background to the name "Emmaus" means "Hot Springs." There at Emmaus that coolness of the two that travelled the road to that city was transformed to hot springs bubbling up in their souls. Let us each have a draught of life-giving waters bubbling up hot in our bones and being.

Jeremiah was once disappointed and despondent, probably with God and the calling on his life. From a downcast attitude he said he wasn't going to speak any more in God's name. But note his further words. "But His Word was in my heart as burning fire shut up in my bones, and I was weary of withholding, and I could not be quiet" (Jeremiah 20: 9). Let us get so burning hot with our love for God that it would bubble out of our life in glorious excitement.

The Saviour was made known to Cleopas and his friend in the breaking of bread. Don't let then the opportunity slip by to see your own life deepen as the Saviour is made real to you at the table. He is risen. Let us proclaim it with joy before the whole world.

Study/Meditation 40

THE TABLE OF THE EARLY CHURCH

Throughout the early chapters of the Book of Acts, there exists an interesting study or meditation concerning the Table of the Lord. I feel that the early church had a much deeper appreciation of the table's meaning than many of us today. There are two basic facets of the table that we will share and will differentiate them in the two ideas below.

1. The Daily Table:

When reading the last seven verses of Acts 2 we are confronted with the frequency and devotion of the Table of the Lord with the early church. It possibly has few parallels today. Verse 42 lists four things that were responsible for the incredible growth of the early church, or more correctly its retention rate of new converts. Features that are worth duplicating assisted the early church in retaining their converts that had come to Christ. It would be helpful to see these same four elements actively present in churches today. It may assist their conversion retention rate.

Verse 42 shows that the early church continued steadfastly (note that emphasis) in the following vital four practices/elements:

1. Apostles Doctrine = The Word of God
2. Fellowship = Requires Church Attendance
3. Breaking Of Bread = Communion
4. Prayers = Life of Prayer

May we see an effective resurrection of each of these. Many today will not come under the authority of the Word or the Pastor. Many put aside the need for fellowship, attending church only when there's nothing better on their Sunday agenda. The Lord's Table doesn't rank as a necessity for some. Prayers often seem abandoned.

Announce that there is a singing group at church and the place is packed. Announce a special prayer meeting and you're lucky to get a crowd. People are strangely absent from church with the weirdest and most wonderful excuses. God give us churches that want to come back to a wholehearted acceptance of these four church growth principles. In so doing we shall 'continue steadfastly' in our walk of faith and growth.

No doubt you have noted that one of the four 'necessities' was the breaking of bread in the Lord's Table. Verse 46 continues the comment: "So continuing daily with one accord in the temple, and breaking bread from house to house, they ate their food with gladness and simplicity of heart." Verse 47 continues: "Praising God, and having favour with all the people. And the Lord added to the church daily such as should be saved."

Churches geared to these principles can't help but flow in God's blessing. As we examine those early chapters of Acts we begin to understand that there was a huge congregation to be cared for. By the end of chapter 2, it was well in excess of 3,120 souls that were both saved and turning Jerusalem upside down. By chapter 4 verse 4 either their numbers have swollen to 5,000, or an extra 5,000 were added to the original 3,120. With such a large body of believers, we can understand the difficulty of gathering together, especially to celebrate communion every day, when there we no official church building.

So daily they gathered in various houses, or more probably their courtyards, and shared together the four elements of growth, inclusive of the Lord's Table. Difficulties posed challenges, not insurmountable odds to give up on. Necessity is and always has been the mother of invention. Often today tragically challenges create a spirit of defeatism in believers and they give up.

The early church rose to the challenge of meeting together and a two-fold thrust was commenced. There were large gatherings in the temple precincts, probably in the outer court. Secondly, the division into house groups helped administer some of the day-to-day issues relative to church life. This is how they established a daily faith and daily Lord's Table celebration.

Christ had directly taught the disciples the spiritual and communal value of the table. They in turn taught the new converts. Would we be so keen? If our churches grew to such a size that it became difficult to house them in one venue would we personally ensure that the table was available to every believer?

Create a program throughout the week that embraces daily celebration of the Lord's Table and some churches would think you fanatical. Yet, the early church considered it so important that they held services daily so they could share the good things of the Lord.

Do we so earnestly love the table so much that we would not let any week/month go by without meeting around His table? I am convinced this is an important pattern in Scripture. One of the four cardinal ways to ensure the church is continuing steadfastly is to actively include the Lord's Table in its operation, alongside the other three facets. May we also have as high a regard for it as the early church?

2. The Church's Table Of Provision:

As well as the table of the Lord being prepared and celebrated, note they also had a table of provision for the needy. Acts 6 deals with a specific episode detailing the provision of food to the widows of the early church. Christianity should have as one of its hallmarks the fact that it meets the needs of the spiritually needy and the materially needy.

In most cases, no one could complain about the meeting of spiritual needs today. Yet, often the church has lacked concern in meeting the needs in the material area of those of the household of faith and the community. It is all very well to say we have a good government social service or welfare system that cares for those needs. The church should stand out in its concern for others – firstly towards its own and then secondly, for the community.

Some would contend that the table referred to in Acts 6 is inferring attendance on tables where collections of food were received and then distributed to the needy. Food they claim is not specifically mentioned, and it could have been a financial administration only. However, the majority of translations and commentaries accredit the situation with having to do with actual food served at a communal table by the early church.

My main conviction is the Greek word used here for 'table' is the same one always used for 'dining.' We are not here looking at the problem of why some are food deficit, we are here concerned with the church's response. The gospel brings grace and the meeting of needs. The early church took its responsibility seriously.

All was provided in the table of provision in the early church (Acts 6), yet disruptions still occurred, because some felt they were not as well provided for as others. Typical self-interest comes to the surface, especially amongst the poor and the hungry. Peter and the other disciples called the church together to advise them that the table of provision for the poor, and its service and administration, was co-equally their (the church's) concern and responsibility, not just the leaders.

So often the church leans all too heavily on its leaders to be everything and do everything. The Word spoken by Peter was directional for all of their attention. The table was for all believers. But the responsibility to serve one another falls to all of us. The Lord's Table has glorious application concerning the body and blood of the Saviour to all mankind. Often the apostles or key leaders would officiate at the Lord's Table. But in the table of provision for the widows Peter is saying we all have to take responsibility to serve. But, in that service we should look out servants of honourable godly character.

Participation at the widow's table was free, provided one was a believer. Yet some felt left out, or others were treated preferentially. Perhaps that single emotion of feeling left out in life has plagued more people than anything else in church life. But the provision of the table is still there.

It is up to us to rise up and reach out and take for ourselves provision from His precious table. Once we are a believer we have a right and a privilege to be at the table. The early church opened its table up firstly to its believers. We should be careful not to lower our standards to anything less. The price of the provision has already been paid. Calvary saw the supreme price laid down in blood.

Certainly in the midst of the finest provision contentions can arise about the equality of that provision. But, be assured Christ has more than ably provided for all of His children. None need lack, but many do because they fail to press in to obtain from Him. Don't let upset alienate you at the table. There is more than enough for all of us. When the time of sharing around the table comes, none need feel that another has greater access to the Lord, or provisions from His table than they. Move in to reach out and touch the Lord afresh and gain your provision from His Table.

The dispute of Acts 6 had to be straightened out. Out of problems comes growth and church order. Don't allow personal attacks to dictate an inability to receive from the Lord. May it create a heart that will reach out and cause growth to occur out of need. Disputes can be settled around the table. Indeed allow the sacredness of the table to settle every qualm and ruffled heart.

Let, in the smooth surface of your heart, the pure reflection of the Saviour be seen. It only takes one stone cast into the mirrored surface of a lake to disturb and distort the picture. Let all the little stones be sunk in the sea of His forgetfulness and let us mirror His beauty again. The table is a beautiful place to bring discord and upset to die on the altar of God's grace and forgiveness. Put it right and leave the table knowing that the peace of God rules everything.

We should be careful in church life of inter-related disputes. The widows that brought the complaint could have themselves privately approached those they thought were offending. After all, this is Scriptural order (Matt. 18: 15 to 17). But no they chose, like sadly often is the case, to make it a public issue. Around the table is no place for friction and factions to test their strength. It is a place for individuals to flow in the right relationship.

The early church did solve their problem over the table provisions. May the attitude of the early church teach us much in our attitudes around the Table of the Lord. Let the table of the early church, in its meeting of the spiritual and material needs of its congregation, inspire our churches – Till He Come.

Study/Meditation 41

TABLES OF THE HEART

When Paul was in correspondence with the Corinthian church he had cause to remind them that the soft working of the Holy Spirit had superseded the old order of laws and codes, written on hard tablets of stone. The Spirit now inscribes the very throb of God's purposes deep into the "fleshy tablets of the heart." II Corinthians 3: 3 defines it this way:

"Clearly *you are* an epistle of Christ, ministered by us, written not with ink but by the Spirit of the living God, not on tablets of stone but on tablets of flesh, *that is,* of the heart."

We understand the 'tablets' referred to here are not writing boards, which of old carried inscriptions to be kept as a permanent record. Tablets and tables are used here interchangeably. But its reference triggered in my thinking the question what has been written on the tablets/table of our heart?

This thought of writing on tables triggered in my thinking about a table my son had created. It had wonderful motivational sayings all inscribed, acid-burned, into the face of the grass table-top. Water cascaded through it between two sealed layers. It ran out the end in a magnificent waterfall. A table with writing. As life-giving water flowed out of the end, messages were seen on the table top level of glass. The question is what messages are our lives displaying? May we re-examine our hearts afresh around His Table and ask what the table of our heart conveys?

What do we have – stony tablets/tables of the heart or fleshy ones where God can inscribe His directions? In its Greek origin the word 'tablets/tables' literally means 'a broad flat slab or table.' Onto them were inscribed the words, which were to stir the immortal cords of the heart of a nation whenever they were read. Yet, mere words recorded in print can be as coldly indifferent as the lost souls of men.

God has replaced that old order by bringing in a new and living way, where the sacred throb of His heart is now inscribed in living tissue of human hearts. He, Christ, was the Word and He became flesh. Now God has ordered that His Word become living flesh in the life of every believer.

We can approach the table with variant responses. We can approach His presence softly, with hearts melted, sweetly responding to the Lord in every way. Then also we can approach indolently feeling that the table is mere religious performance. To us, it may be an institution of old given to us and religiously carried on. The ceremony that is carried on around the table may have a form of godliness but it may deny the true power of its purpose. The key issue is what will you choose?

The heart can respond in a wide parameter of responses. Let's swing away from the external performance of the table to understanding God's desire to communicate with every believer, heart to heart. Tables of flesh, not stone. The old stone tables, the natural tables of wood stand for external memorials. Often they lose their relevance.

But around human tables sit as living tables, the fleshly hearts that God can personally write/engrave His love deeply into. It is so sad that often people can sit around external tables in churches and be content with all the external show of the church, and yet be unmoved in the fleshy table of the heart. The heart is offered as a cold offering, a pretence at participation, instead of soft, warm and responsive to God desiring to inscribe His love.

We are not stone tablets. Neither is our involvement around the Lord's Table to be stone cold, hard in response to God. We are warm fleshy tablets into which God can scribe His love and meet us afresh in the hallowed ground around His Table. The flesh here speaks not of the old life but of softness and openness to God. How God desires to come and meet us at that level. It is so easy to be self-sufficient, self-reliant and capable. To some degree the world requires it and as such, it can hang on our spirit as a death shroud.

Women are often excused for yielding to the softness of their emotions. It is worthy of note also that women can more easily respond to God than men because they are already in the feminine response mode that the Bride Of Christ defines us as. Women are called by Scripture to be in submission, in the same way, the Bride Of Christ is called to submission to Christ. It would be beneficial for every Christian to let themselves go a little and discover their softer, God-responding side in their devotions and in their walk with God.

As a minister I have observed this interesting fact. The men who can unashamedly break and be broken before the Lord in public, and is soft to the touch of the Master generally make a much better husband. For in their capacity of yielding to God he is exercising the same level of love display that God wants him to display to his wife. There are exceptions yet I have found it overall to be true.

In the softness of the human heart, not in the hardness of stony hearts does the Lord desire to lay down His loving precepts and guidance. The table speaks of the symbolic meaning of the Lord's death and glorious resurrection and salvation. Tablets record, as historical fact, some aspect or another. The Table of the Lord is a living table, not a stone-hard 'tablet' affair. God forbid that we should approach its sacred celebration just with any hint that it is merely a historical remembrance.

This is holy ground we are standing on. Shoes of self-direction should be slipped off our feet as we seek the direction and guidance of God. As He visits us heart to heart, in a burning bush experience, slip off your direction and put on His. Softness is a godly commodity. Stony tablets are usually reserved for 'headstones' and 'epitaphs' in this day and age.

Let the table of our hearts be a place where the good things of God can not only be written but also spread to be fed upon. As we are quiet before His Table we can allow the soft inscribing of our heart with His purposes by His Spirit Till He Come. The letters and wording of a natural epitaph can often be cold, sterile and indifferent a few short months after one has been laid to rest. But hearts are living things.

Breathing and pulsating life issues flow from the heart, but never from a stone. God doesn't desire a monument, but a movement of hearts – soft, warm and pliable hearts ready to receive His living inscriptions. The inscriptions of God are living words. Penned by the Holy Spirit they speak and continue to speak whilst ever that heart is soft. It will then bring healthy remembrance. Letters of stone kill. Matters of the Spirit live on in the lives of men.

The Table of the Lord is primarily a heart matter, not exclusively a head matter, emotion matter or anything else. Not that God is wanting you to neglect the due process of mind and emotions. It is so easy to approach the table with a rush and bustle. Minds wander.

"Have we got enough prepared for dinner now that the Joneses' are coming for lunch?" Mother thinks about this as the emblems are passed around. Meanwhile, father smiles at the pastor, and watches him, yet he is miles away reeling in that marvellous catch at yesterday's family fishing outing.

Perhaps our imagination has got away with us in the above illustrations, yet the point is so valid. Watch your attitude at the table. It's no mere performance. It is a real heart matter. Fleshy tables of the heart should be empty of their own demands and poised waiting for the finger of God to touch their being, to feel Him inscribe His immortal purposes.

We are not here suggesting that our faith and worship should be a passive thing engendering no response. Yet, we put forward the reality: "Be still and know that I am God" (Psalm 46: 10). That stillness does not in the slightest imply noise stillness. The Hebrew catches the meaning of: "desist from your own efforts and know that He is God."

Give us tablets; give us hearts that are written with the finger of God. The Table of the Lord should sense the hand of God upon the process and the finger of God in the fleshy tablets of our hearts.

Sinai was a barren place when the finger of God wrote on stone tablets of old. On its mount was scribed the Ten Commandments. Dry often are the passageways of human existence. But the touch of His finger turns a mountain ablaze with His presence. Whatever the cold stone of the Ten Commandments was made of, it could not but yield to God's finger scribing the law. How much more His finger, not now on stone-hardened hearts, but flesh soft vessels, scores a mark that can be read and known of all men.

Give us fleshy hearts with your finger marks still fresh, softly imprinted in them.

Our heart itself becomes a literal table. Do we spread before the Lord an ample table and then invite Him to gaze upon it, write upon it, then to fellowship with us? Could any of us say we have only ever spread a table that is totally acceptable to Him? Hardly! Often selfishness, pride and sin have been spread on the table of the heart. Often we are too embarrassed to invite the Lord to sup with us. What do we spread before our Lord? What sort of a welcome does He have and how long would He stay?

Searching questions demand searching answers. May we meditate long and honestly whilst before His Table, so that the fleshy tables of our heart may feel that quickening impulse daily to make Him king of all.

"Not in tables/tablets of stone, but in the fleshy tables of the heart." Lord let us have such a heart for you. Till He Come.

Study/Meditation 42

THE LORD'S TABLE

The sun was shining intermittently through a very scattered cover of light soft clouds. When it pierced the ground it was warm and the air was still and pleasant. People were making their way up the pathway of the church from the parking lot and exchanging customary greetings as they met various friends.

Like pre-programmed machines, they sat in the same seats they had occupied last week and for years. The deacon at the door had backed up to the sun-drenched window as he welcomed people into the service. His back slowly warmed and it seemed to melt away any trace of the fact that he had been engaged in very sharp, unkind and ill-tempered words with his wife prior to coming to the service. His children had sat sullenly in their seats in the back of the car very cross with the way their father had spoken to their mother.

A new vehicle pulled up in the parking lot and received a rather cold stare as he began to park, from another driver, who seemed to have the stare of: "Hey buddy, that's always my parking space." The new person walked inside the church, exchanged a warm greeting with the deacon, who still preferred the warmth of the windowpane to the draft of the doorway. The visitor moved inside without the deacon moving an inch. No handshake!

The man sat down. Presently a hand politely tapped him on the shoulder. "Excuse me, sir," whispered one of the ushers. "That's Mrs Jones' seat you're in. Would you move down three rows? Thank you." He moved quietly and chatted with a friendly couple that he found himself next to.

The service was a blessing and then it came time for the communion service. The emblems were distributed and purposefully he was avoided. The usher bypassed him not offering him the emblems. He had begun to reach but sensed it was being deliberately moved passed him, so he withdrew his hand. Already the man was getting the feeling of a lack of real fellowship.

As he was leaving the service the pastor met the visitor on the porch. "God bless you brother. Nice to have had you with us. Do come again." The visitor was going to speak because there really was something he desired to share, but the minister had already moved off with another plastic welcome to those behind him.

I don't know whether you have ever read the book: "In His Steps," by Charles Monroe Sheldon (first published in 1896 that has sold over 30 million copies), but you cannot but be concerned about how churches can desire growth and yet extend themselves so little to others, especially new people. There is not the slightest trace of 'anti-church' in me to have created the scenario above. It just happens. It literally happened to our own family whilst we were on holiday years ago.

The stress of our study/meditation in this chapter is that it is the 'Lord's Table,' and not of a particular creed or church. Certainly, we must ensure, to the best of our non-invasive ability, that every individual who partakes is solemnly aware of its responsibility and meaning, but do we have a right to exclude individuals on the basis of individual church membership? Nor do I want to enter into a controversy of who should and who shouldn't partake at the table. Because a list of rules as long as your arm will always have exceptions. The depth of this meditation is that it is the Lord's Table.

The Lord has purchased and provided the provisions of the table. He instituted it and commissioned it. Christ sits to embrace fellowship with us as we partake together. If the table was the church's then why does the Scripture take such pains as to single it out as being "The Lord's Table"? I Corinthians 10: 21 refers to: "Partakers of the Lord's Table." Not only is the redemptive purpose of God seen and enjoyed at this table, but also the ownership and Lordship of Jesus are involved. It is the Table of the Lord.

Think about this as you come into the presence of the Lord, the creator of the universe. The Lord of all of eternity has provided this table for his royal creation. To partake, not only recognises His redemptive work, but also His Lordship.

Many individuals have the most difficulty recognising His Lordship. This is a day of independence. On every hand men and women are vaunting themselves against their employers, their spouses, the law/police, the community, the government, the church and so the list goes on endlessly. Women's liberation has risen from the murky pit of confusion to challenge God's ordained family stability. And that in 'no way' ratifies men as legalistic, autocratic dictators of the home, with their word unchallenged. Such is also 'not' God's pattern. The single most liberated woman in all the world should be a Christian woman as she and her husband respond in a Biblical way to God's direction concerning women.

This is not the place to enter into teaching on family order, though very dear to my heart, but to indicate we are being carried along with all strains of independent thinking that want to challenge the Lordship of Christ. Few want to be submissive. "Submitting yourselves one to another in the fear of God," (Ephesians 5: 21), is a threat to many.

The Lordship of Jesus is definitely involved in the table. He is Lord. Revolution in the home, school, society, church and the mind better be put right under the Lordship of Christ before you partake of this Table of the Lord. This day and age need a renewal of the principles of His Lordship.

Are we totally subject to the Lordship of Jesus? Only you can answer for yourself. His Lordship covers all of our life, as well as His redemptive purposes as we know them and have responded to them.

What one has purchased remains theirs till one dispose of it in one way or another. But, here is the mystery. He gives to each of us the wonder of salvation He has purchased for us. Yet, He still holds the table as His to fully administrate its power and efficacy for each and every one of us.

Christ indeed has purchased redemption through His own blood, yet administrates that redemption Himself, through of course the agency of the Holy Spirit. Be open to His ministration in your life and an encounter with the full realm of His Lordship.

As I approach the table, as often as we remember it, I am approaching a personal relationship with Him, my Saviour and my redeemer. The church may be the channel through which we can share together around His table, yet the table is the Lord's and He would meet us at it.

Christ is, if we can put it so irreverently, 'very possessive.' What is His, is His. The possessive apostrophe in the word 'Lord's' means that table is very much His. The fact is what Christ has done becomes ours, as we enter into a relationship of being an heir and joint heir with and in Him. The Lord jealously guards His own, both people and possession.

My life is bound by what I term the power of 'The Rule Of The Possessive Case.' Let me explain further. I Corinthians 3: 23 details: "As you are Christ's; and Christ is God's." When this dawned on my thinking several years ago it made a huge difference in my thinking. I'm ruled by that possessive case in the text. I'm Christ's. I belong to the King. My conduct and attitudes, my behaviours and all I am must be only ever what He wants, for I am His.

I'm ruled by the possessive case. My attitudes need to change from saying: "My beloved is mine" (Song Of Solomon 2: 16). That verse shows a conceited claim of ownership. The maiden is claiming her ownership and possessive rights over her beloved. Her self-interest is the driving force, not her submission to her beloved. Later she would learn to change. In chapter 7 verse 10 she had learned to put it another way: "I am my beloved's and his desire is towards me." See now that her spouse's interests are being put first. She has learned co-equal submission. This is something important for all of us to learn in marriage and life.

The maiden has switched the tense of her possession from herself possessing him, as lovely as that might be, to the fact that his possession of her is the all-important thing. When she came to that position she had learned that all that was his, he was prepared to bestow on her. But she had to get the possession issue right first.

Some Christians claim everything that is in their thinking is theirs. I again stress there is a correct aspect to this. But, they rarely realise we are ruled by the divine possessive. In maturity, it is His possession over us that counts. And because (and when) we are His, then His desire will flow to each and every one of us. This is being ruled by the divine possessive.

We stress the issue above because of the reference to 'The Lord's Table.' It is written in that same possessive case. It is His Table. The demands we make are negligible. Because it is His, His desire will flow towards us. It will flow. Divine ministration will flow when we realise that we are at the table because of His grace, at His invitation, and because He alone is worthy. Is your life ruled by the divine possessive? Or, are you still at the 'give me, give me' stage. Rest in Him, for you are His after all.

When you next come to communion remember you are His. Remember it is His Table, not ours to do with as we personally please. Enter into a place where being His is the thrill of your life. In that unique place His desire is towards you. As you grow in maturity the less you demand, the more you get. The less you insist on your rights the more that flows to you.

Study/Meditation 43

COMMUNION OF THE BODY AND BLOOD OF CHRIST

Satan is a master at making inroads to the purposes of God. If he cannot defeat the church outright he will create a 'fifth column' action and make inroads into the work of God, from subtle inward destructive actions. The proverb: "United we stand, divided we fall," has greater spiritual truth than we often care to acknowledge.

In fact, if it is one thing that Satan works overtime on its division within the church. Breaking the church up into self-ingratiating groups is his aim. Set sector against sector. Create generation gaps, spiritual gaps, and gaps between ministry and laity. Satan seeks to create division in many ways. Concerning the Body of Christ I Corinthians 12: 25 declares: "That there should be no schism in the body."

How the cohorts of hell must snigger when they see the havoc they have caused in a division, in what should be a 'division-less' church. We are here referring not just to divisions in a single church, but in denominations and trans-denominationally across the face of all the Body of Christ. Whether Baptist, Anglican, Methodist, Pentecostal or whatever, there should be no schism. How the Father must suffer in His heart to see such friction.

The Table of The Lord is one of the most levelling, harmonising factors that the church can experience. Levelling, because whether prince or pauper they are both welcome at the table and receive the same emblems. They both need to come to the same Saviour and Redeemer. With God, there is no respect for persons. It is harmonising because that is the very root of the table reconciling us back to God. Let us detail this further.

I Corinthians 10: 16 says: "The cup of blessing which we bless, isn't it the communion of the blood of Christ? The bread which we break, isn't it the communion of the Body of Christ?"

The verse contains two direct questions. They require direct answers. We are challenged to consider them. They're not there for nothing. Can we positively answer 'yes' to each. Do we actually assert that the body and blood of Christ that is remembered at the Lord's Table do in fact constitute a unifying and common union between all the households of faith? This is a serious question.

There is obviously a two-fold communion referred to here. Those being first, communion with Christ and secondly, communion with the Body of Christ. So to partake at the table we confess ourselves to be His redeemed and a 'peculiar' people by the purchase of His blood. Also, this association is in line with all true Christians, with whom we have communion also in this ordinance.

Paul establishes this concept when in verse 18 he aligns it by referring to Jewish worship and customs. Those who were admitted to eating the offerings were reckoned to partake of the sacrifice itself. By his reference to communion, Paul draws all Christians into the same accord. In the original language, the word actually implies: "An act of using a thing in common, a partnership and fellowship." We are sharing both the realisation and the effect of the shedding of Christ's blood.

Is there a common union through the blood, or is the Body of Christ still divided as ever? This study/meditation seeks to accelerate the principle of communion that is constantly and actively at work today. We hear so much about the Ecumenical movement. But we stress that the only basis of cooperative fellowship that is declared in the Word of God, not the precepts of man, is in a unified communion acceptance.

Paul refers to this oneness in verse 17: "For we being many are one bread and one body: for we are all partakers of that one bread." What a unification of fellowship. Metaphorically, one loaf is divided into many parts to feed all. Though we are spread throughout the world and express our worship slightly differently, we are called one. We are the Body of Christ.

We are many and we are varied, yet we are one. The unity that we have is greater by far than the narrowness that Satan causes us to hold in our minds. Consider that no single person or denomination can have absolute rights or a monopoly on truth. Throughout the succession of church history, since the reformation onwards there have been various aspects of truth awakened in various groups that created the denominations they are defined by.

Throughout time a progressive Body has emerged. We should see the glory of Christ within a 'brother' or 'sister' from another denomination, rather than our prejudiced and perceived 'shortcomings' of their respective denomination (in our limited and biased opinion). The table should be something that creates unity, not engenders any further division.

Communion of the blood of Christ should be something precious to every believer. By the power of the blood, and only by the power of His blood, is any individual saved. This is irrespective of whatever background, denomination or creed we may be. "Knowing that you were not redeemed with corruptible things, *like* silver or gold, from your aimless conduct *received* by tradition from your fathers, but with the precious blood of Christ, as of a lamb without blemish and without spot," (I Peter 1: 18, 19). What power that blood has. We can have cooperative fellowship with it and through it with Christ and the rest of the Body of Christ.

Peter thought it so important that he referred to it as the 'precious blood.' Indeed could a finer definition be found anywhere for it? Precious by virtue of its rare price, power and pertinence. The table highlights the communion we have with the blood and through it with one another.

The apostle John takes up the same theme in I John 1: 7 when he declares: "But if we walk in the light as He is in the light, we have fellowship one with another and the blood of Jesus Christ His Son cleanses us from all sin." We can pass over such verses all too quickly. We can quickly skim over them thinking: "Oh, isn't that nice," or some other platitude, rather than allowing the significance to melt our hearts to tears and producing a softer love for the Lord and His people.

What I John 1: 7 is implying is that we can only have fellowship one with another as we are walking in the light. Others have gone a step further to suggest that if we are not walking in the light and walking in harmony with each other as Christians then the blood of Jesus will not be cleansing our life from sin. I'm not sure I'd go that far, but consider the gravity of the passage.

How can we claim to be walking in the light if there is a break in harmony or fellowship between us? Throughout the world on any given Sunday (and Saturday for some), there must be millions who are partaking of the cup of blessing. "For this is my blood of the New Testament, which is shed for many for the remission of sins," (Matthew 26: 28). Many feel they have exclusive rights on spiritual things, or solely command God's attention upon their particular denomination. This is not possible. No. God is not as small as the framework of our minds, or the smallness of any denomination.

God delights that all of His new creation can enjoy the merits of the shed blood. He delights to know that they can also cooperatively appreciate the power of the blood in the lives of others, even those they may not agree with. The table should unify us, not drive us apart.

The precious blood has been shed once and for all (Hebrews 7: 27, 9: 28). Let none of us, that are in the household of faith, fight over who has rights to it. It unites, not divides. It is communion, not disunion. The table should mediate between each of us. It is an outward symbol again of the ongoing power of the blood and the extent of the family of God that enjoys such a privilege.

When thinking about the communion of the Body of Christ we come across several pertinent Scriptures. Romans 12: 5 says: "So we being many are one Body in Christ, and every one members one of another." Constantly the Scriptures are pointing out the uniqueness of diversity in the setting of unity.

I Corinthians 10: 16 was also speaking about it. The redeemed are many and yet we are one through the blood.

Paul's continuing comment in I Corinthians 12: 25 to 27 is important: "That there should be no schism in the body, but *that* the members should have the same care for one another. And if one member suffers, all the members suffer with *it*; or if one member is honoured, all the members rejoice with *it*. Now you are the body of Christ, and members individually."

The thing Paul was saying relative to communion here is what he saying again to the Corinthian church. Note there is no schism! This is a sad difference from the way many see things today. Learn to love the Body of Christ. The table demands our cooperative love of all in the household of faith. There is a communion of the Body of Christ that is a pure melody to the Father's ears.

Mainly in this study we have been considering the impact of I Corinthians 10: 16 comment about the Body of Christ and the power of the blood. But, don't lose sight of the fact that there is another view. And that is Christ's efficacious blood availing for the sins of mankind in the world. We have communion because of that all-embracing sacrifice. But never let us lose sight of reaching a dying world for Christ.

There is a concord between the sacrifice of Calvary and the individual believer. It calls us to an equal surrender. What a communion our fellowship should be with each other, based on our relationship with the blood of Christ. The table makes us acutely aware of these demands. And, in responding to them we draw near to the table that has less to do with religious performance and everything to do with reality.

May our times around the table unite us deeply with both a heightened love for the Lord and those others He has graciously saved that are equally part of the Body of Christ, no matter their difference from us. Lord make us aware more and more of the communion of the body and blood of the Lamb of God, slain from the foundation of the world.

Study/Meditation 44

THE CUP OF BLESSING

The cup as a vessel is almost as old as man himself. He has created and devised them from his earliest existence. The graves of the ancients have often held cups of exquisite design and shape. It is the aspect of the cup that captivates our thinking in this study/meditation.

The apostle Paul, when in correspondence with the Corinthian church, shares in I Corinthians 10: 16 something about the uniqueness of the communion cup. "The cup of blessing which we bless." The apostle shares a thought that can quickly be passed over as we hastily read unless we stop and spend some time on the depth of meaning that is buried there.

Obviously, the cup referred to relates to The Lord's Table and the fullness of what Christ has done for every believer. It is very interesting to note that it is already stated as a cup of blessing. Yet, it is something that 'we bless.' The wording means: 'To speak well of.' It is derived from the Greek word from which today we get our word 'eulogy.'

Indeed the cup of the Lord and the Table of the Lord is something we speak well of. We in turn praise and glorify God in His provisions of the cup. Or do we? Does the opportunity of gathering around the Table of the Lord send thrills through our souls? Are we a people who consistently praise and glorify God before fellow Christians and the world, because of what God has shared with us in Christ?

The first thing we notice is that it is a cup of 'blessing.' All of the wondrous work of the cross is remembered in the cup at communion time. We are not just living this life of salvation amongst ourselves as some secret society. This salvation is meant to be lived and demonstrated before the world.

The greatest thrill for any of us should be to see fellow Christians living their Christian life powerfully in everyday living. This is our calling. So by coming 'as often as you can' we revitalise this consciousness as to our high calling.

It is a 'cup of blessing,' not a curse. This blessing is to be remembered. Have you ever noted the beginning and ending themes of mankind in the New and Old Testament record? They speak volumes of what we are sharing here. Calvary ushered in 'blessing' to be lived continually.

When you turn to the first horrific tragedy in mankind in Genesis you see it is associated with a curse (Genesis 3: 17). That soil, once so rich and productive, took a turn for the worst. Perhaps the entire chemical and nutritional value of the earth changed that day to breed the emerging choking, ground-dictating weeds, and noxious insects that changed the very existence of much from harmony and usefulness to disharmony and a threat to mankind.

Barrenness filled the earth. The curse had taken hold. Work, toil and sweat were now man's inheritance as he laboured under the ever-present hold of sin. The curse had entered like creeping cancer. It ate its way into the very fibre of not only mankind but also creation and nature. Throughout the Old Testament man struggled with the curse.

Occasionally a man would rise above it to lead others to plains of victory, but the root of the curse was never far away, waiting to take hold. The very last thing found in the Old Testament is the word 'curse' (Malachi 4: 6). The end of an era ends with a curse, just as it had begun in Adam's day.

But, as we turn to the pages of the New Testament what a different scene is before our eyes. In Matthew, after the listing of the genealogy of Jesus is listed we find the New Testament days are ushered in with a blessing. "You will call His name Jesus: for He shall save His people from their sins" (Matthew 1: 21). No wonder the angelic host proclaimed with a flurry of dazzling brilliance: "Glory to God in the highest, and on earth peace, goodwill towards man."

A blessing was ushered in with the coming of the Saviour. Salvation and redemption were now available to all mankind. When the New Testament closes, the very last verse

(Revelation 22: 21) ends with a note of heaven's blessing. "The grace of our Lord Jesus Christ be with you all. Amen." Grace has been defined as <u>G</u>od's <u>R</u>iches <u>A</u>t <u>C</u>hrist's <u>E</u>xpense ... GRACE.

The Old Testament started and finished with man's relationship to God involved with a curse, because of man's wilful sinful actions. The New Testament started and finished man's relationship with God with blessing. Blessings arrived because Christ accepted and paid for the curse. "Christ has redeemed us from the curse of the law, having become a curse for us (for it is written, *"Cursed is everyone who hangs on a tree"*) that the blessing of Abraham might come upon the Gentiles in Christ Jesus, that we might receive the promise of the Spirit through faith," (Galatians 3: 13 and 14).

Christ accepted the curse of the law and the curse of our sins and sicknesses. He fully accepted this state of being so blessings would flow to hopeless humanity. Is it any wonder that the apostle Paul says to the Corinthians: "The cup of blessing." Blessing indeed. It is for all of us because of what Christ has done for each of us if we would avail ourselves of His sacrifice on our behalf.

Man's soul has been in famine for so long. Why is that so when Christ provides so richly for us? Not only does He feed us at His table, but also He provides the finest of provision. Like the story of old, He has put His cup in our sack.

Genesis 44: 2 tells the story how Joseph did this very thing (placing the cup in the sack of one of his brothers), to his sinful brothers. He not only provided the finest of wheat, but he gave them his cup. Today, a greater than Joseph has brought us out of famine. He has satisfied our every longing and then placed His cup of blessing within our sack as we journey on our way. He does this so we have a continual reminder of what He has done and what He has provided.

No wonder the Psalmist cried out: "My cup runs over," (Psalm 23: 5). The overflowing joy and jubilation, the ecstatic rejoicing and thanksgiving and the blessing that no mere mortal can contain comes bubbling out of our soul. What a redemption we have. We are caused to live it continually in His blessing, not just when we come around the table. It is a continual Cup of Blessing.

Throughout Scripture, three types of cups appear. There is firstly the cup of wrath. Then secondly a cup of suffering is spoken of. Finally, the cup of blessing is referred to. I am sure you can see an association yourself in these three cups. The cup of wrath is what man has filled through his godlessness throughout the ages. Psalm 75: 8 indicates: "For in the hand of the Lord there is a cup, and the wine is red; it is fully mixed, and He pours it out; surely its dregs shall all the wicked of the earth drain *and* drink down."

Graphically portrayed is the cup of wrath and the state of the sinfulness of mankind. Revelation 14: 10 and 16: 19 are also worthy of reading describing the cup of wrath and the coming and impending judgement. This cup will one day be filled as the winepress of the fierceness and wrath of Almighty God is trodden out (Revelation 19: 15). Elsewhere (Study 51) we have written about the Great Table of God's Wrath. Its cup is being slowly filled with the evil of the world.

But there is also a cup of suffering that Jesus Himself has partaken from. Space does not permit the full inclusion of each text, but reading of Matthew 20: 22; 26: 39 and John 18: 11 will show you what a bitter cup that the Saviour prayed might possibly pass from Him. We can scarcely understand the horror of this cup. Sufficient to say that Christ just didn't only accept our sins upon the cross. The Word clearly says He became sin for each and every one of us (II Corinthians 5: 21). So the Father could not behold the seething identity of sin on the cross. Christ personally drank the bitter cup of suffering.

This now only leaves the cup of blessing. This cup has been left to each and every one of us that accepts and fully lives out the salvation that the Lord has purchased for us all through His blood.

Can we see and understand that it was the cup of wrath that was rightly ours? Humanity filled it with our evil. Yet, Christ willingly drank of the cup of suffering accepting the cup of wrath to pass on the cup of blessing. As we gather around the Lord's Table it is this cup of blessing that we celebrate. We did not deserve the redemption that we now enjoy. Indeed we deserved the cup of wrath, as our sins were very much part of its dreadful draft.

However, we are privileged to hold and partake of the cup of blessing, all because of Calvary. Thank you Jesus that you have so loved as to take the cup of suffering on my behalf, and place my hands on the cup of blessing.

All the world offers is death and corruption. Their cup is like the pot described in the Old Testament in II Kings 4: 40. "There is death in the pot." There is death in the cup of the world, yet life and victory are in the cup of blessing placed before us all. The world offers death, filth, fallacy, delusion and damnation in its cup. Thank God we have the cup of blessing.

Finally, Psalm 116: 13 inspires us. "I will take the cup of salvation and call upon the name of the Lord." The Psalmist had searched his heart, as we often do – or should. The throb of all within him cried: "What can I render to the Lord for all His benefits towards me?" (Verse 12). What could he do, or say or be that would be a perfect thanksgiving to the Lord, for all the goodness of God in his life? God's answer is marvellously simple. Verse 13 simply says to take the cup of salvation and partake of it. God's greatest reward and satisfaction are to see His new creation enjoying the full provisions of His Son. Micah 6: 7 and 8 share the fact that it is not 'things' that God requires of us, but a state of heart that is living in the dimension of redeeming grace.

For those with an Australian heritage, the referred to Psalm 116 passage is of special significance. It was the passage used by the Reverend Richard Johnson in the first public Christian worship service in Australian history. It occurred on Sunday, February 3, 1788, under a "great tree" near the edge of the water. His congregation was hardened criminals and even harder guards. But, the passage was the first ministry proclamation in the nation.

Let us take the cup of salvation and let us call upon the Lord. Enjoy salvation that has been provided for you as you take the cup of blessing, as often as you celebrate communion. Jesus took the cup and gave thanks. Indeed Jesus did fully take the cup and delivered salvation. Redemption flowed to you and I. Now we have the cup of blessing. Let us take it and live it – Till He Come.

Study/Meditation 45

A TABLE OF COMPARISON

"Rather, that the things which the Gentiles sacrifice they sacrifice to demons and not to God, and I do not want you to have fellowship with demons. You cannot drink the cup of the Lord and the cup of demons; you cannot partake of the Lord's Table and of the table of demons." I Corinthians 10: 20. Compare two points of view in the following two scripts:

The statue of Diana stood towering above the tables at one end of the feasting room. The guests were all of the priestly extraction, many dedicated to the name and honour of this hideous god.	The sporting emblems were raised on a pedestal at one end of the well-kept community hall. The guests were all fanatics of the sport, giving all their time and energy to their passion. It came first in their lives.
Demetrius, the influential silversmith rose to speak after they had gorged themselves on food. His garment had taken on the purple of the Romans and gold embroidery was etched into the fabric, figuring the splendour of Diana.	David, the town's noted jeweller rose to speak after they had all eaten the 6-course banquet. He was the president of the club. His royal blue blazer with gold braiding and club pocket spoke admirably of their dedication to the world of sport.
"Much time has passed since the Christians first opposed themselves to our purposes." He said this with a sneer in his voice. "Now seated with us are certain of their number that realises that we too seek to serve the unseen force. We have now learned to live in peace." He sat with a leer on his face that spoke of the evil that lay within his heart towards the Christian message.	"Much time had passed since the church had opposed Sunday Sport, and our efforts to better our recreations," he said with satire in his voice. "It is pleasing to see church teams amongst us tonight who realise, that we like them, are dedicated to the betterment of mankind. We have come to work together. None of us are opposed to each other." He sat with a smug smile on his face.

Throughout the years since Paul had left Ephesus, certain of the church had entered into dialogue and eventual truce with the heathen priests. Now they were sitting in a feast to the gods, which had been called to celebrate the greatness of their city and its ways. They were a trophy to Diana. It was hard to pick out those representatives of the church. Their identity seemed lost in the crowd and all raised their goblets together to worship their respective gods. Diana stood still overlooking the entire scene. [The Acts Of The Apostates – figuratively presented post Acts 19]	Throughout the years since the church opposed Sunday Sport, certain of its ranks had entered into dialogue. Over time Christian sporting groups joined the sporting league, but determined not to play on Sundays. But that lasted only a short time, before many of their catch-up games were on Sundays. It was hard to pick out those representatives of the church from all those gathered. Their identity seemed lost in the crowd, that all raised their glasses to toast the sporting and cultural success of their club. The sports banner overlooked the entire scene. [The Acts Of The Apostates - figuratively presented 2023]

    I know some will take issue and offence, with my presentation above, even finding it intimidating. I expect such. I'm meaning to confront an issue head-on and get your attention. But, in both cases illustrated in the scenarios above the church lost out. What difference is there really to the gods being served if they are drawing people away from enthusiastically serving Christ? If the fellowship of the righteous with the unrighteous, trying to please the world, has so weakened the very fibre of Christian testimony, that it is virtually impossible to tell the church apart from the world, how relevant is the life of the believer?

    Satan quickly realised that in the life of the early church direct persecution only strengthened the work of God. But subtle intrusions of his ways and philosophies brought the cancer of the world and sin into the lives of many Christians and the church.

This is not a day of forthright opinion concerning standards of the work of God. And, I need to categorically say that I oppose legalism in the church and am 'not' trying to introduce it here. Rather I'm appealing to Christians to be and act different from the world. We are supposed to be light and salt. It seems that often more time is spent preaching about freedom of expression, and don't preach rigid standards (which have their place), that will eventually blind the work of God than ever is spent preaching uplifting high and holy standards.

The church has to almost be apologetic for holding views that the world considers strict, and labels us as conservative fanatics. They can cry buckets of tears, and get really emotional when their sporting team wins or scores a goal, but for Christian to show emotion – that's just weird. I am aware that some may not like my approach here with the dual comparison of the goddess Diana and today's god of sport. Some will try to build on what they think I'm implying, rather than knowing exactly what is at the back of this unusual approach. I love fresh air and exercise. Sporting activities are grand within the framework of the fellowship of the work of God, as long as it doesn't supersede the spiritual program. I'll be in for a game of tennis or whatever with the worst of you. So much for my style and abilities.

The implication and motivational force behind the graphical introduction is to confrontationally raise the comparison of how subtly Satan has brought to bear conformity pressures on the church. I believe the church should be the most outspoken force in all the world. Jesus came to set men and women free in every area. But black is black so let's not accept the sly compromises of the devil.

So often we wipe away in our thinking the implication of Satan's influence as revealed in the quoted Corinthian passage. But it related to Paul's generation and so it does to ours. Certainly, as far as we know, Diana is no longer actively worshipped as a major identity or goddess. Maybe in isolated groups, there is still reverence for her. A thousand gods/goddesses have replaced the heathen gods of the early church era.

The New Testament writers stood firmly against the idolatry of their age. They preached against it. They lived godly lives protesting against it and even died rather than accept it. They warned Christians about an all-out attempt to abort the fullness of God's purposes by the subtleties of insidious forms of idolatry.

Today the gods wear different colours and clothes, yet are still very active and still worshipped in various ways. Sport, Worldly entertainment, Rock groups majoring in immoral themes, Materialism, Clubs and Money form but a few if not just the tip of the iceberg of present day idolatry. These can be the subtle intentions of evil that attempt to slowly exercise control over the population.

Let us stand firm against what causes us to be drawn away from full Christian commitment, but not in a sense of being 'anti-everything.' No! I don't care to march in placard-carrying demonstrations against any of the issues I've raised or a thousand others. I'm saying live so close to Christ, be on fire so much with His purposes, that these things have no distracting influence. Be so passionate about Christ that you are a 'First-Priority' Christian. Christ absolutely comes first. Then, other legitimate things take their correct place and the illegitimate things we reject.

As you think about that startling Corinthian passage you don't get the impression that the early church were being directly subverted to worship demons. They weren't being directly drawn off to worship at a literal table of devils.

If you have an Amplified Bible you would be helped by reading from verses 20 to 22 of this I Corinthian 10 passage. It will help your overall understanding? Make no mistake about it demonic forces are ardently actively at work to create anything from morally and socially acceptable programs and interests that draw people away from Christ, to totally depraved agendas to keep you away from your worship of the Lord.

Satan takes no holidays, works overtime and pays penalty rates. It costs to be involved with the world and its ways. Paul was saying that those who ate of such sacrifices, even if unwittingly, were deemed to have partaken in the sacrifice to such heathen/demon gods. The one offering the sacrifice was one with the sacrifice in the worship of an unseen force. An idol is actually nothing in actual fact. It is not a real god at all. What is sacrificed to such gods is nothing. But it is what lies behind it that binds. Eating of it was regarded as partaking with them in the idolatry, and by virtue of that fact renouncing one's Christian faith.

Listen to II Corinthians 6: 14 to 18. If you can memorise it do so. We quote from the Amplified Bible.

"Do not be unequally yoked with unbelievers – do not make mismatched alliances with them, or come under a different yoke with them, inconsistent with your faith. For what partnership have right living and right standing with God, with iniquity and lawlessness. Or, how can light fellowship with darkness.

What harmony can there be between Christ and Belial, the devil? Or, what has a believer in common with the unbeliever? What agreement can there be between a temple of God and idols? For we are the temple of the living God; even as God said, I will be their God, and they shall be My people. (Exodus 25: 8; 29: 45. Leviticus 26: 12. Ezekiel 37: 27. Jeremiah 31: 1)

So, come out from among unbelievers, and separate, sever yourselves from them, says the Lord, and touch not the unclean thing; then I will receive you kindly and treat you with favour (Isaiah 52: 11).

And I will be a Father to you, and you shall be My sons and daughters, says the Lord Almighty (Hosea 1: 10. Isaiah 43: 6)." What a powerful though extended passage.

What we are endeavouring to share is that we are called out to be different. How can we approach the Lord's Table to sup with Him, with the cup of blessing, if our life is tied up with so much of the world? Such challenges our rights at His

Table. Cut loose all of the world's controlling ways. We may be in the world, but we don't have to be of it. Christ has redeemed us from the power of its grasp. The table speaks of the work of Calvary. The cross must be answered to. Galatians 6: 14 challenges us in this way: "But God forbid that I should boast except in the cross of our Lord Jesus Christ, by whom the world has been crucified to me, and I to the world."

Whether young or old, in ministry or not, we are all called to be careful. We cannot (and the Word emphasised it twice), partake of two tables. Decide which camp we are in and serve the Lord out of purity. I am not going to itemise any one thing that can hold you captive. You know what it is in your life. Deal with it and come to His table liberated.

There is really no comparison between the tables. Satan is subtle. He will sway and persuade with enticing words of compromise. People may mock you, but if you don't stand up for something, you'll fall for anything. Some put it this way: we have to be a fool for Christ's sake, but that sure beats being a fool for the devil's.

In concluding I know some will view this particular study/meditation as excessively harsh and restrictive in liberty, even legalistic. Then they don't know my heart. I'm concerned with us being hard on ourselves, not me being hard on you or anyone else. Self-discipline is the highest form of disciple. Deal with your own life in the light of the greatest sacrifice of all time.

Study/Meditation 46

PAUL'S TABLE TEACHING – Part 1
A Table Received

Paul was deeply worried. He paced the floor and quietly prayed. His spirit had been unsettled for a good many weeks since he had left Corinth. Spending a good while there it seemed that much had been accomplished. Certainly, as with any new church, there was much to straighten out, especially when the city had been so soaked with heathen worship, often accompanied by vile sexual perversions, such as in Corinth.

The Corinthian Christians loved to meet around the table in fellowship in what we now understand as their 'Agape Love Feast.' However, it was the intermixing and the subtle transition from this communal feast to the Table of the Lord that bothered the spirit of Paul. The more he prayed the deeper the resurgent waves of revelation began to gather within his thinking. Finally he stopped and began to look for his script and quill.

His mind was beating fast with the freshness of revealed truth. Simply the words flowed as the Holy Spirit energised his heart and thinking. He sensed what was now becoming Holy Scripture was from the Lord. So he etched it onto the scroll in primitive ink as a preface. "For I have received from the Lord, that which I delivered unto you…" (I Corinthians 11: 23).

God was imparting something to humanity, through humanity, for the good of humanity. Mortal hands were writing immortal things and teaching. The weakening eyes of Paul looked at the script that would succeed him by many generations. His Spirit-directed words would become part of our Bible.

The more he wrote the quicker the holy pulsations surged through his being. This was definitely something being motivated from above. Order and direction were necessary around the Table of the Lord. Time seemed to stand quietly by whilst inspiration from the Holy Spirit made a personal contribution to the authority of the Word of God.

The Spirit filled Paul's mind with meaning and relevance. He became pregnant with holy purposes. Theme after theme ran freely from his quill as the Spirit of the Lord directed him. Instructions as to the protocol of and purpose concerning the Lord's Table were the central theme in Paul's spirit. The aged fingers of Paul wrote strongly. These were important matters.

The table is not something instituted by man, and then continued as some man-made tradition. The Table of the Lord was 'received of the Lord,' but initially created by Christ. Now it was reinforced directly into the heart of the apostle Paul. Jesus Himself had left instructions concerning it at the Last Supper. The early church had indeed been celebrating and remembering it as often as they could. But, nothing had been written on it, outside the gospel references to Jesus' instructions, to lay a clear foundation for future generations.

The reception of this outstanding portion of Scripture must have stayed in the mind of the apostle for hours. He sensed he had received something of God. Continuing his comment of receiving it direct from the Lord he says: "That which I delivered unto you." The divine purposes of God are given from above so that we might share, not hoard them. Paul shared what God had given him with the church at Corinth. And, through that process it came to the world at large.

The letter written so carefully by hand finally proceeded to the printing presses of a hundred or more languages, as the Word of God spread to all mankind. You too can receive of the Lord as you partake at the table. You can personally sense the immortal things of the Spirit coursing through your being as you fellowship with the Lord at His Table.

Remember this, God was so concerned that the table should be given to us that he moved the hands and spirit of an apostle to write it. God wanted you to know about the table. God desired to impart eternal things about this feast of love and remembrance. Now if God desired so much to share this with you, then understand the privilege we have to deliver it to others, both in living proof of a life fulfilling the work of the cross and in participating at the table.

Paul found it necessary to refresh in the minds of his Corinthian readers the background of the table. None in Corinth had been at the Last Supper. They more than likely had not seen any written Scripture or gospels at this early stage of New Testament church life. So too we were not there at the Last Supper and must depend on the gospel accounts to initially inform us. This important table instruction of Paul the becomes also informative to us.

It is not just the introduction of dogma or doctrine, but also the resurrection of the Master's specific instructions at the Last Supper. We are reminded of the Saviour Himself and all He has done for us. Our relationship with Him is crystallised in this table remembrance.

The shedding of Christ's blood is the vital issue revealing a new covenant. The New Testament, or will, has been written through Christ's sacrifice. It was how man's salvation was secured. And, we get to not only enjoy it, but also keep it alive through the table. There is a new agreement with mankind. All the provision has been made by the Godhead. All creation has to do is avail itself of the provision and become the new creation.

Consider this for a moment. Before Calvary there was no opportunity or hope for you or me. After Calvary there flowed eternal benefits from and through Christ to all humanity. It was indeed a New Testament or a new will. It had not been the mere passing of time that made the difference. It was accomplished at the cross. This table stands as a living symbol of that accomplishment, not as a bygone heritage, but a living reality.

How often do well-intended remembrances become aborted distortions of what they stood for? Think of Christmas. Here we have something that probably started as a well-meaning celebration of Christ's birth. Now, however, it has lost its true meaning for multiplied millions through the trimmings, the trappings and the commercialism.

The table remains unspoilt. Why? Perhaps because it was created by the Saviour Himself. All of heaven stands behind the merits of the table. Be aware all of hell also will do what it can to destroy its presence and power. If the hordes of demonic forces can nullify or water down the efficacious value of the table, then it will work overtime to do so.

This is a new agreement we have before us. In the world of trade, agreements continually are updated to reflect the current market or operating conditions. But the table agreement remains the same. The currency has not changed. Christ's blood is still as powerful as the day it was shed. The cost has not changed. The Saviour gave His life for the sins of the world. The benefits have not changed in that the glorious liberating work of salvation is still enjoyed by every believer.

I Corinthians 11: 24 and 25 both identify the phrase: "In remembrance of me." The table should accentuate no one or nothing but the Lord Jesus Christ. The 'me' is His right to be worshipped and venerated by His new creation, which He has purchased by His blood. "What can wash away my stain and sin, nothing but the blood of Jesus." Paul adds in Ephesians 3: 21, "Unto Him be glory in the church." Let Jesus be high and lifted up in every heart and every meditation of the table.

We have used throughout this work the background of many stories and settings to act as foil or show the beauty of the great pearl of great price. Jesus is that pearl and He is the centre attraction of the table. May He be high and lifted up.

In the freedom that we have received then appreciate this gift of salvation so we might live it before mankind. May the world see in us something they are missing and may it cause them to desire what we have. May they see that this glorious salvation is constantly refreshed by our realisation of the power of the table.

Study/Meditation 47

PAUL'S TABLE TEACHING – Part 2
The Proof Of The Table

I Corinthians 11: 26 centres our thoughts for this study/meditation. It states:

"For as often as you eat this bread and drink this cup, you proclaim the Lord's death till He comes."

The verse has many beautiful threads to it that can be woven into a beautiful tapestry portraying the vitality of the table. In my thinking the first and last phrases are linked together by the human element of time. On one hand the apostle Paul is saying as 'often as you share this table,' and on the other hand he puts forward the ending of all time, the coming of Jesus.

We are not about to dictate how often you or your church should celebrate communion. There are very good and valid reasons why certain churches celebrate it weekly, whilst others monthly, or whenever. We will not discuss the merits of one against the other, lest someone thinks we're an authority in this area. Hardly! That we are not. I have listened to churches, ministers and individuals put forward the reason for their frequency pattern of communion and come away convinced of each of the legitimacy of their logic.

But there should be some frequency pattern about celebrating communion. I would only suggest that if the frequency exceeds every six or eight weeks then perhaps the affect upon the congregation is diminished. It would be hard for them to keep it consciously in their thinking as an instituted feast of remembrance. Note the Scriptures say to celebrate it as 'often' not as 'infrequently' as you meet. There is definitely a note encouraging frequency.

Most of us would be aware that the early church met very frequently to remember the Lord's atoning work. In the church that was formed on the day of Pentecost, they met daily to boost fellowship, and prayer and to celebrate the Table of the

Lord (Acts 2: 42 and 46). The congregation would have been colossal to distribute the emblems amongst. It would seem that they broke up into smaller groups relating or aligning to houses. But it still reinforces the principle that frequency was more important to them than prolonged absence between communion.

I feel that coming to communion can become a habit that has both a positive and negative effect. Positive in that it brings regularity and expectation. Negative in that people can take it for granted, like how well do they listen to the announcements, which are weekly? Above all we need to keep the sacredness of the occasion paramount. When they gather around the table we want people to come with a fresh, eager expectation.

Frequency can breed familiarity if we allow it. Familiarity should never enter into the affairs of the table, and for this cause a change of timing, presentation, and where we place the celebration in the total service will all keep a vital freshness about the purpose of such a gathering. Those ministering the table must not create a rushed atmosphere around the communion feast as if we need to get this over with, as we have more important things to do. Time spent purposefully here may save many Christians much tension, worry, sickness and even premature death. These are very strong implications yet Paul specifically taught in this area (See Part 3; Meditation 48).

As we understand it, the timing has to do with frequency. Look at the timing at the end of the passage. It relates to the coming of the Lord. We will only gather at communion 'Till He Come.' The very coming of the Lord is tied up in the process as some Gordian knot with the remembrance of the table. Some day through the clear skies of this world, yet the darkened skies of humanity, the Lord will come.

Jesus is true to His Word. He is the Word of Truth. He said He will come and He will honour that. We may not keep our words but He 'always' does. Our words may pass away, His will not. Every time we meditate upon the table's potent symbols we sense the coming of the Lord is that much closer and the concept more alive in our hearts.

What is sad is that many Christians come to the table regularly and are unmoved as to the soon coming of the Lord. Even more tragic is that some seek their 'rights' to celebrate communion and yet do not even believe in His second coming. It seems incredible to believe that such is the case, but it is. Are they blind to what the Word says? They may be in the minority, but they do exist.

The table welds together the now, where we are right now, with the future in the coming of the Saviour. Keep alive this wonderful truth. Expect His coming and remember this powerful truth as we celebrate the Lord's Table. Jesus is coming back again.

Someone has aptly said: "The proof of the pudding is in the eating." Though we make the comparison in a reverent sense the same is true of the table. As we partake we: "Do show the Lord's death till He come." We 'show' it before the world. What does that mean to us? The word 'show/shew' are interchangeable. The word used by Paul in I Corinthians means as follows: "To allow to be seen, bring before sight, present to view, point out, display to advantage, make known, cause to understand, demonstrate and eventually to show."

Indeed this is a comprehensive listing that displays a much greater degree of participation in the redemptive work than we ever envisaged. The work of Calvary was, and is, so magnificent, so perfect, complete and so efficacious today that its effect can be visibly seen and demonstrated every day of our life. Indeed participation in communion should raise Christian expression so the entire world should know the wonder of Christ, because they see Him gloriously displayed in each of us.

Every Christian, because of their involvement at the table, should be living proof of the power of the efficacious work of Calvary and the power of the resurrection. In New Testament times some were so fanatical about communion that they claimed the emblems literally took on the form of the literal 'body' and 'blood' of Christ when partaken. This doctrine was later formalised as 'trans-substantiation,' by certain religions. Though we may disagree with it theologically, let us just catch for a moment the enthusiasm of those that hold this belief. They literally believe in a current encounter with the purpose of the cross. Let's not rubbish this reality though we may not believe the theology of the emblems literally transferring to the literal body and blood of Christ.

Let there be a quickening of our minds, like the early church, to fully appreciate the power and meaning of the emblems. Many lamely take the emblems as they pass and partake without the slightest thought of what they may have originally meant, or in fact presently mean.

As we thoughtfully partake let the emblems stimulate our consciousness in remembrance of what they stand for and what Christ has done for us. Let it create living proof of the working of Calvary. We can become demonstrative proof of what Jesus has done. Our lives should be proof that the world needs what we have – an encounter with life eternal.

As I enter into this precious relationship with Christ around His Table I am again applying the powerful blood, feeling its resurgent cleansing and being displayed to the world as living proof of the salvation of the Lord.

The word 'show/shew' challenges me. There is a searchlight within to see if indeed my life does amplify His atoning work before the world. Do I present to view His redemption? Do I point out to advantage Christ by my life? Am I displaying for all to see the way of salvation? These are weighty questions. This is the powerful challenge of 'show/shew.'

We are called to eat the bread and drink the cup. This very process speaks naturally of sustaining life. Indeed new life has come to us through Christ. But, that new life must be kept alive. It must be fed and nurtured. Prayer, Bible study, Fellowship with Evangelism are all ways of keeping that new life buoyant and enduring. Communion is also helpful in sustaining the new birth.

The words of Jesus in John 6: 31 to 59 are interesting in highlighting our eating of the Bread Of Life. Our English language unfortunately is rather limited in expressing deep shades of meaning. Jesus was very particular about His choice of words and the Holy Spirit preserved the same through the pen of John.

In reading the passage count the number of times 'eat' is actually used. But, consider that the passage used two different Greek words with two 'very different' meanings. The one word is: 'Phago' and the other is: 'Trogo.'

'Phago' simply means to eat, as we would all understand it. However, 'trago' means: "to eat, gnaw, chew, devour, to consume slowly with the purpose of sustenance." There is a very strong deliberation in the second meaning of the word. Jesus directly and deliberately uses this peculiar Greek word specifically in verses 54, 56, 57 and 58.

There is an overtone that to consume the flesh and blood of Christ is something far more meaningful than imply gulping it down and racing off to another or the next commitment. There is a slow devouring of the food so the fullness of the nourishment may satisfy the very depths of our being in the immediate and long term.

God is so concerned that we should extract the fullness out of the redemption that He has purchased. Why didn't Jesus use the word 'Phago' here right through the passage in John's Gospel? Simply because there was greater meaning, depth and relevance for us all to notice and enjoy. The 'Trogo' attitude applying to the body and blood of Christ, and hence the Lord's Table is a necessary part of our keeping alive its importance. Let us slowly consume and digest the merits of the redemptive work. Let's not be in a rush to get out of His presence.

We are in His presence and God is here to bless us. As we linger fully understanding the commodity of time in a 'frequency' of attending the table and we do so 'Till He Come' then our lives are empowered. But if we carelessly come to the table our lives may not reflect what we were born to mirror.

The table calls us deeper. Slow down in a hurried world and take time at His table to 'trogo.'

Study/Meditation 48

PAUL'S TABLE TEACHING – Pt.3
The Warning

It was an average congregation that the Jones' belonged to. They attended frequently in their church's mid-week program as well as Sunday services. Frank, their eldest son, was a nice enough young man, but inclined to be a little 'worldly' in the eyes of the pastor and others. He loved the Lord but trod a fine line when it came to worldly pleasures. Discos, clubing, wild parties and serious drinking were still very much on his agenda.

One night near midnight the pastor had picked Frank up from the local police station and with Frank's pleading had handled the matter without telling his parents. Jake was the police captain and he attended Frank's church. So he rang the pastor first, as it was a nuisance matter that affected Frank. The pastor was quickly at the police station and with Jake they dealt with Frank's misdemeanour. Frank was so grateful, that his parents were not informed. But, this kind action would come back to bite the pastor. For this reason of Frank's lifestyle, the pastor vetoed his nomination as Youth Leader for the coming year.

The youth group had experienced Frank's suggestions of social places they could go when he was on the youth committee. Most of the youth committee were horrified at some of his suggestions. The veto for Youth Leadership for the coming year struck a deep cord of hostility in the heart of Mrs Jones. She deeply resented the pastor's action and held it as a personal affront to her own position and spirituality in the church.

Frank had almost forgotten the incident of his brush with the law, but always understood the pastor knew more than his parents. But, with Betty Jones it was a different matter. Her husband Rob was on the board of the church and as such the pastor had spent a good deal of time discussing with him privately the reason for his position of not endorsing Frank as Youth Leader. He put forward the standards of the Word of God requiring us to be different from the world and the overall desire for a high standard for their young people.

Rob had appreciated the pastor's openness and confidentiality and accepted his direction and view. He sensed that it took courage for the pastor to take such a step, and although it involved his son, he stood behind the pastor's decision. When he learned of the incident at the police station he thanked the pastor for keeping it so private.

Rob fully understood but indicated he wouldn't be telling Betty. When she eventually found out, some weeks later, this further embittered his wife. Now she had an issue with Rob her husband as well as the pastor. She felt he didn't care about or support their son, or her. This difference often erupted in the now too frequent arguments always perpetuated by Betty.

Each Sunday the family was at church in force at the communion service with the rest of the church community. Frank's siblings had often also been drawn into Betty's tirade of criticism. More times than they cared to remember they had to deal with her acid tongue of criticism against the pastor and the church. But each of them shrugged it off as just adult differences.

Generally, as a family, they all sat together in church. Betty greeted the handshake of the pastor, in the porch, with the usual veneer of a smile. "May I speak with you pastor please," Frank asked as he shook hands. His mother watched as they strolled to the pastor's office. After a few minutes Frank returned very quiet and avoided all his mother's intrusive questions. The service continued and the pastor drew the congregation to a time of reflection around the Lord's Table.

He turned to a familiar passage that could almost be quoted from memory by a certain percentage of the congregation. "Would you read it for us this morning Brother Rob," asked the pastor looking over to Rob Jones. Rob stood and in a beautiful baritone voice that needed no microphone read:

"But let a man examine himself, and so let him eat of the bread and drink of the cup. For he who eats and drinks in an unworthy manner eats and drinks judgment to himself, not discerning the Lord's body. For this reason many *are* weak and sick among you, and many sleep. For if we would judge ourselves, we would not be judged. But when we are judged, we are chastened by the Lord, that we may not be condemned with the world." (I Corinthians 11: 28 to 32).

"Thank you, Rob," said the pastor. "Beautifully read I might say," as Mr Jones resumed his seat. Frank listened intently as the pastor outlined the importance of the table and the severity of the warning that was contained in the Corinthian passage. The words troubled him. He found himself reflecting on the implications of the passage and what he had just revealed to the pastor in private in his office.

Frank had reached an impasse. He knew that not one of his so-called friends knew he stood for Christ, or that he was a committed Christian. They had actually ridiculed him once when he even raised the topic of God, so he quickly dropped that topic and conversation. Something had happened to Frank a few days earlier when he was, on one rare occasion, reading his Bible privately at home.

The verses had stuck in his spirit. He had sought the pastor's advice this morning admitting he had been going the wrong way in life. He was genuinely concerned and committed to the fact that, from this point onwards, he was not going to follow the Lord at a distance, but make Him his very best friend.

He came back to the world of consciousness again as he heard the pastor say: "There's a price for coming to this table with bad attitudes, sin and anything wrong in your heart." The pastor went on to explain how that Paul was firm on this point that sin tolerated in the heart whilst partaking of the table caused one to eat unworthily and caused one to eat damnation to themself. Repentance was needed.

Three things are referred to as being the fruit of careless participation with unconfessed sin plaguing our hearts, when we come too casually to the table. The three things that can be harvested in our life are 'weakness,' 'sickness' and 'premature death.' We don't like the thought of any of these. We know that these are not part of the heritage in Christ that we all should enjoy. So we shun the fact that we can bring them on ourself as we partake carelessly of the table with wilful, unconfessed sin in our heart.

Before I became a Christian I attended a church where sin was divided up into types of sin, or degrees of sin. Each earned some degree or weight of punishment. Yet sin is sin. One unconfessed lie or unconfessed hatred in the heart will keep you out of the kingdom of God as much as murder or some other horrendous crime. Many fail to realise that if sin remains dormant, unrepentant, brooding and undetected beneath the surface it will eat into the very fibre of the soul and the three issues stated above may begin to take hold.

Hebrews 12: 1 says: "Therefore we also, since we are surrounded by so great a cloud of witnesses, let us lay aside every weight, and the sin which so easily ensnares *us*, and let us run with endurance the race that is set before us."

We tend to think of these 'sins' as huge aspects. They are big things in most of our estimation. We often don't give the word 'weights' in the text the slightest thought. The word 'weight' here is a unique word that is rendered 'tumour' or 'cancer' in the original Greek New Testament. It refers to the little things, the 'one-cell' sins that then multiply to become an insidious cancer ravaging the soul.

Song of Solomon 2: 15 talks of 'the little foxes' that spoil the vines as they nip the fruit that is growing. In our life there can be 'little foxes' nipping at the fruitfulness in our life. We need to deal with them. These are the areas we can bring to the table and surrender to constantly keep our heart right. We don't want sin to snare us. How wonderful God provides a process to keep our life clean.

Some might say that such a thought almost sounds like we are unsaved as we come to the table. No, a thousand times no! But don't allow anything to bring you into disharmony with Christ. Let the table settle it as you are reminded again of the cleansing nature of the blood. Self-judgement is far better than coming under the judgement of God for the respective sins that lie at the root of our heart.

Satan is so subtle. He knows just where to lay the finger of sin with its tiny seeds. He pats the soil of our heart so very gently as he plants it. Yet, he plants it. Small things can spoil the fellowship that we should have with the Lord.

Consider how I Peter 3: 7 shows us that the harmony between a husband and wife is so necessary to see their prayers answered and not hindered. Bitterness between either or both will hinder access to God in prayer. If such a thing is true in our prayer life as couples how we all need to pay attention to our attitudes to each other and the Lord as we come around His Table.

We want to be clean, sinless. Search out the very corner of your life that no trace of sin remains. I have heard of churches that announce a week or two ahead that communion will be on a particular Sunday. They do it so that individuals may put right any wrongs, straighten out any disharmony or misunderstandings. I think it is a worthy attitude. It is taking seriously the table's importance.

Paul was not implying that all 'weakness,' 'sickness' or 'premature death' was related directly to the incorrect state of the heart around the table. He was simply laying it open as being one of the causes. None of us wants weakness, sickness or a passing from this life prematurely. The implications could be catastrophic.

Yet the Corinthian passage demands our internal examination. The use of the word 'damnation' by the apostle Paul is an extremely strong one. We tend to use it when we refer to being cut off from God. There is nothing to imply that is the intended meaning here. But it is calling for great care. Judge yourself so you don't need to be judged by the great

Judge. Consider that Paul considered that this dire warning was so essential that he spends over fifty per cent of his passage about communion on this theme or aspect of truth.

Sin entertained within our life, whether a deed or thought, will have results that our human minds cannot comprehend. They may be short-term issues, but unconfessed sin can have long-term effect.

The pastor spoke on but Frank was already deeply moved. His face was tear-stained and his father had already put a loving arm around his shoulder as if to say: "That's all right son. You let it all go to Jesus."

Betty glared at Frank. "What had the pastor said to upset her son?" Her heart's attitudes were going from bad to worse. She was wounded by her own pride.

Frank let the emblems go by, but instead made his way quietly to the altar to kneel before the Lord. The pastor left him there to make his own peace with God before he spoke to him. Many other hearts were similarly stirred by Frank's openness, and like Frank were honest enough to make their way also to the altar. Soon some twenty folk were softly praying, some sobbing before the Lord. Rob and other church elders helped the pastor quietly pray for them. Frank's heart was not only clean that day, but he rejoiced to know Christ's cleansing had also come to so many others.

Betty sat fuming. She had partaken of the emblems of the table yet was unmoved in her attitudes. The service concluded and the Jones' went home quietly for different reasons. Frank sensed his cleanness that he had longed for. Rob drove home with a smile that came from deep within. Betty was quietened by conviction. Yet, she suppressed it and let her bad attitudes fester all afternoon into an ugly ulceration in her spirit. The other children chatted and giggled as usual in the back seat of the car.

Frank went on in his Christian walk from strength to strength. He met the challenges and temptations of life with a fresh vitality and commitment that he drew from his daily relationship with the Lord. He became an effective witness for

Christ to his friends. In subsequent years he did become Youth Leader and would lead the young people of the church down the paths of righteousness.

Betty took several months before she realised her body was bearing her soul. Frank sat one night and talked honestly with her of all his previous wayward ways and the gentle helpfulness of the pastor, not his criticism. Betty eventually broke and genuinely sought the forgiveness of the pastor for her godless attitudes and resentment. She said through intermittent sobs: "I've learned a great lesson pastor. You can't fool around with the message of the table. The emblems are not impotent symbols. They speak today and they can bring life or death."

So be careful as we approach the table. Open your heart to see the delight of salvation and the flooding presence of continual redemption.

Study/Meditation 49:

THE TABLE OF THE MARRIAGE SUPPER OF THE LAMB
Part 1 - The Table And Its Surroundings

Our minds are still mortal and cannot yet fully understand the eternal glories. When Christ returns and we are changed our entire body, inclusive of mental capacities, will undergo such incredible changes. It will be wonderful then to fully understand what now we can only wonder at. Yet, to us humans has been committed the Scriptures that reveal just a glimpse. Imagine how we will more perfectly understand the Scriptures when our minds are changed into what God originally designed them to be?

Revelation 19 is full of mystery. When we're fully changed into His likeness, at His coming, how we will fully understand the Scriptures then. Till then for the next two studies/meditations let us at least try. For a moment let's go into the colourful background of the 19th chapter of Revelations to see the surrounding and the magnificence of the table of the Marriage supper of The Lamb.

.o0o.

As far as the eye could see, which had been awakened to new dimensions and capacity, there was a kaleidoscope of colour. Tiered on every side were angelic and celestial beings that seemed to be mutely, reverently waiting with folded wings, for some major event. Then they were lost in worship and praise of the one true God.

Earthly eyes had never beheld such a sight, and were having trouble taking it in. The brilliance of those beings was stunning. The majesty of their stature and the glorious harmony, more unique than anything earth had heard, united their voices. The entire firmament of their habitation was aglow with their presence and charged with the throb of their worship.

Then a new song, in a renewed volume began and increased. It came as rumbling boom, discharging energy beyond measure, yet not assaulting to the ears, as millions upon millions of heavenly beings were all magnifying God and praising together. "Alleluia, salvation, glory, honour and power unto the Lord our God..." The singing continued with such rhythm and poetry, yet in a pattern free of necessary rhyme of earth. Other heavenly attendants were speechless.

Celestial beings folded their wings at such worship, and the one being worshipped. The song now came from what were once mortal lips. The angelic hosts were, and are programmed to worship. But this praise that was filling the entire limitless ends of heaven and the infinity of glory, was coming from the throats of humanity. It came from the depths of the hearts of those that were once flesh and blood. Angels quivered with emotion and anticipation, awestruck that such praise was being given to their God by humanity voluntarily, not because they were programmed to do so.

Back on earth, there was burning and destruction. Desolation and defeat etched their mark over the earth. Literally, certain parts of the earth were dead or dying as those last horrific days, before the coming of the Son of God, were ringing out in human blood. Cities were burning. Souls were burning. The earth was burning under the smarting wrath of judgement. Antichrist's reign was almost over. The harlot had seduced her last earthly king. The day of reckoning was at hand

Whilst the earth died the glories of heaven throbbed with the praise of the vast, great infinite multitude. Only God Himself knew the entire number. Only the eternal one could call them all personally by name. Angels blushed to see the wonder of men and women arrayed in so fine a garment of the purest white. Man has always thought that angels exceed them in glory and majesty. Now it was these celestial creatures that bowed low in adoration of the work that the atoning blood of the Lamb had wrought in every man and woman before them. They stood in awe of mankind who chose willingly to worship.

Crescendo after crescendo of the praises of this multitude rose up till the twenty-four elders and the four beasts, of description unbelievable, fell down and worshipped God with loud cries of: "Amen. Alleluia." Heaven has no walls but it seemed that the intertwined praise and worship of the elders, beasts and the vast multitude bounced and resounded throughout the very limitless length and breadth of heaven. How was it possible that the cry of adoration and praise of the twenty-four elders and four beasts was in complete harmony, symmetry and audio-balance of the multiplied millions of the redeemed? But this is heaven. It doesn't operate by earthly restraints.

In a dimension of sound, not yet known to mortals, the volume of the praise and worship seemed to reverberate and lift in waves of accentuated majesty for hour after hour in a place where time was no more, nor ever had been. In the centre of this indescribable majesty was God Himself. Seated upon His throne our God glistened in a way that mere human words seem irreverent to describe. Flawed human attempt to describe is impossible.

John's best effort in Revelations is as follows. His appearance was the exquisite beauty and lustre of jasper and sardine stone. Light shimmered from His presence like lightening. A rainbow completely circled the throne above. Yet the rainbow was not of the colours of earthly rainbows. It was deep emerald, with such richness and beauty as never seen before. The throne was surrounded with majesty. Revelations 4: 1 to 6 attempts to describe it.

There are no words adequate or with sufficient creative genius enough to detail the glory of our God and the majesty of His throne. He is the very centre of the scene. He is the centre of all existence.

Then another vibration began to announce the coming of other voices. They sounded like the crashing, pounding waves of the ocean. It swelled, it ebbed, getting louder and louder till the entire heavens were filled with the heralding announcement of the Marriage Supper of the Lamb of God. It announced the Son of God and it glorified the Bride of the Lamb.

We do not know, we cannot tell how long these manifestations of praise, worship and honour went on for before the Marriage Supper of the Lamb was commenced. For eternity does not live in the dimension of time. A thousand years is but a day in the presence of Almighty God.

Ceaseless praise and worship will seem but seconds in fellowship with our eternal Father. Men ask will they recognise this one or that? Let us be assured whether we will or not will be secondary to the outflow of praise, honour and glory that will flow from our lives and lips. Then thousands of years will slip past in eternity and it seems as mere days. For time will be no more and the glory of our God and the majesty of His might and that of His Son will rule, reign and captivate totally everybody.

We have taken time to present something of the backdrop of, or to the Marriage Supper Of The Lamb, because so often we get the impression that it will be just another wedding breakfast or celebration, similar to what we have attended in the past here on earth.

The manna of the Old Testament was called 'Angel's food.' So if that is the name given to heavenly provided food imagine the rare delicacies that this Marriage Supper of the Lamb will hold. Food will probably be in a different form and state, totally different from anything known to man today.

Three things are central to this event. These are:
1. The presence of God upon His throne.
2. The presence of the Son of God as the Bridegroom.
3. The presence of the Body of Christ as the Bride.

We will be there in that great crowd, not as some idle spectator, grand though that might be, but there as an active participator. Will our minds be able to fully comprehend the full majesty and glory of that moment? Certainly it will be difficult with our minds in their present state. Such glories are indescribable and only fully understood by the changed mind of the resurrected body.

Note we're called 'blessed' for being called to the Marriage Supper of the Lamb. The table of feasting will be spread in such a fashion that we cannot humanly envisage. The finest the earth has to offer will look as nothing in the sight of this royal celebration. It is almost beyond belief that we have been called to this sovereign, eternally planned occasion. The wedding table feast is our right only by His love. In actual fact the only people who should be celebrating the Table of the Lord down here on earth are the same as the ones that will be celebrating the table of the Marriage Supper of the Lamb in the eternals.

Men and women can partake of the table here on earth that have no relationship with Christ, and therefore no right to partake of it. But, no one will be at the heavenly celebration that has either not deliberately made themselves ready or not have their name in the Lamb's Book of Life.

What a celebration it will be. What glories will surround that sacred and hallowed moment when the Bride of Christ will be with its Lord. What a table. What a salvation. Indeed our hearts should be earnestly looking forward to that day when we be united with our Lord forever. But, let us not only look forward, but also reach forward to that day. May each of our hearts be clean and stay clean as we sense His preparation of us coming to the Lord.

It is hard to imagine what we will look like. It is equally hard to imagine what those heavenly realms will look like. Tiers of angelic hosts, towering above the natural vision of the eye will be singing rapturous heavenly melodies of worship whilst the Bride and the Lamb of God unite at the Marriage Supper of the Lamb.

Never is it possible here, with human abilities, to describe the scenes of heaven, but ever should we desire it. Central to it all will be the Lord and the table. It will not be small and human as our tables in our church services, whilst we are here on earth. This will surpass the possible widest comprehension of our minds.

So, let every Christian so fellowship, so eat and drink of the emblems of an earthly table, with such a heart of purity and passion for the things of God, that it reflects our anticipation in the Marriage Supper of the Lamb to come. Here on earth is a table of remembrance. In glory it will be the table of marriage, that consummating union of the Bride and the Lamb. May it charge our hearts with purity.

Study/Meditation 50

THE TABLE OF THE MARRIAGE SUPPER OF THE LAMB
Part 2 - The Bride Of The Table

Revelations 19: 7 to 9 says: "'Let us be glad and rejoice and give Him glory, for the marriage of the Lamb has come, and His wife has made herself ready.' And to her it was granted to be arrayed in fine linen, clean and bright, for the fine linen is the righteous acts of the saints. Then he said to me, Write: 'Blessed *are* those who are called to the marriage supper of the Lamb!' And he said to me, 'These are the true sayings of God,'"

What a spectacle. The Bride and The Son of God joined in the Marriage Supper of the Lamb. If the glory that attends God is not enough to put us in awe, then the magnificence of this celebration will in the words of one of old leave no spirit left in us. Our human minds cannot contain all that is involved. We don't know the precise details. But, we would be awestruck for an eternity in being called not to spectate, but to participate.

Whether the Bride of Christ will be one fusion or identity, or keep its multiplicity of membership we have no understanding. Don't be dogmatic about those heavenly glories. Stay flexible. We read in Scripture that we're 'one,' and Lord make us so. But, on that day 'oneness' will reign.

Early in Revelation, from the midst of the arena of eternal attention will rise the Lamb of God, slain from the foundation of the world. Now we see Him in this passage as the Bridegroom coming for His Bride. The Bride bows low for she senses her once, mortal and inferior state. Yet, she bows with the grace of the finest of royalty.

Was it one that bowed, or a countless multitude of untold millions? You could not tell. The Bride moves and acts as one and from the angel most removed from the display centre to those in close it seems that there is just one person as the Bride. Folded wings of celestial beings, shield their faces as they attempt to gaze on the beauty of the Lamb and His Bride.

I personally feel that the Son of God will have on the pre-earthly glory of His divinity. Revelations 1: 12 to 17 and Daniel 10: 5 and 6 attempt to share its magnificence. Not that the Bride could ever outshine the Bridegroom, but she will ever be stunning, glorious, beautiful, fully redeemed.

The Bride moves with grace and dignity. Her garments were whiter than any thorough washing or dry-cleaning could ever make them, or any human eye had ever seen. The fabric of her garment was the softest, yet the simplest of linens. But those folds, the exquisite draping of it, made like no other garment on earth or heaven is glorious to behold. It was clean and white beyond the earth's understanding or ability to produce. It was spotless and not a wrinkle or mark was found on its entire beautiful form.

All of heaven breathed sighs of admiration as the Lamb of God moved throughout the sea of glass with His Bride at His arm and presented her before the throne of God. Standing alongside His Father the Lord smiled down at the Bride that had been purchased by the merit of His wondrous blood. God spoke and all heaven was electrified at the vibrations of His voice. None but the Bride could understand it. As she heard she bowed low before the throne and ten thousands upon ten thousands of angels rose to unite their voices in harmony unheard, the Hallelujah's of praise and worship.

Minutes, or was it hours or days passed with that crescendo of worship and praise ascending. No one sensed the time in the realms where time is no more. The Bride rose united with the Son of God. She moved to the table of the Marriage Supper of the Lamb. The entire fellowship of that feast will be something that will only be understood in glory. The length of time, if such terms can ever be used of heaven, that the Marriage Supper of the Lamb lasted we do not know. But the romance of the moment, the majesty and glory of the moment will have to wait till we get there to be fully understood.

Many truths can be extracted from this moment of the Marriage Supper of the Lamb. I think that each of us can understand the central reference and centrality in the passage is 'The Lamb.' Twice in verses 7 and 9 the stress is on 'The Lamb.' It is the consummation of His desire, His redemption and His salvation towards the entire world. The Son stands with His spotless Bride and it is His day. The Bride is there because she made herself ready, not because it was her day. Indeed it will be a day, like none before, for the Bride, but the day is the 'Lambs.'

The Bride has made herself ready. What Bride does not make herself ready to meet her groom when being joined in marriage? Long hours of preparation go into those few short moments at the altar. The Bride is determined to be and look her best on the wedding day. As we sit around the Table of the Lord is this the aspiration of our heart? Do we really desire to be the very best when He comes? Are we consistently making ourselves ready for the Lamb? Do we sense every day, and as we draw around the table, how much we need to keep our lives straight and pure unto the coming of the Lord?

The Table of the Lord, which we partake of, is indeed a table of purity and the fullness of righteousness. Let us draw near to see God's eternal righteousness woven into our hearts so skillfully like a golden thread. I John 3: 2 says: "Beloved, now we are children of God; and it has not yet been revealed what we shall be, but we know that when He is revealed, we shall be like Him, for we shall see Him as He is."

We rejoice and glorify God knowing that we shall be changed and will be like Him when He appears. This will indeed be true for our mortality, as we will put on immortality etc. Yet, this is not the burden of this text for our attention. The phrase: "We shall be like Him" is *not* in the future tense. It is the present tense, the now existing form. This verse strongly implies and unfolds the truth that we 'should' be reflecting Him when He comes. It is not totally or significantly saying the changes will occur after (or in the eternal realm), but we will already be reflecting Christ when He comes.

No, I'm not reading anything into this verse. You read it very carefully. It says we shall be like Him when (at the moment of His coming) He comes. This then is the purifying hope that the apostle John suggests in verse 3 - "And every man that has this hope in Him purifies him/herself, even as He is pure."

This is definitely the Bride making herself ready, and not some whimsy 'Lord make me pure' attitude when we're really not taking our responsibility seriously to prepare ourself. To me verse 2 demands that I take responsibility to be like Him, as much as humanly possible, when He appears. It should preoccupy our life, that it becomes the purifying factor Till He Come. It is the responsibility of the Bride to make herself ready. We have everything provided by our Lord. We need to take it and do it. Let us therefore step courageously into a life of holiness of life and deed, so we may be ready when He comes.

The Lord is working in His church to prepare His Bride for His coming. Paul captures this in Ephesians 5: 25 to 27 when he says by the Spirit: "Husbands, love your wives, just as Christ also loved the church and gave Himself for her, that He might sanctify and cleanse her with the washing of water by the word, that He might present her to Himself a glorious church, not having spot or wrinkle or any such thing, but that she should be holy and without blemish."

How Christ works on the church to produce purity. How patient He is. How lovingly He works in each of our lives. The power of the Word of God lays claim to my life time after time, as the Lord, through the agency of the Holy Spirit causes change to affect that Christ-likeness and His righteousness deep within us. He prepares His own Bride.

As we gather around the Table of the Lord, there should be an administration of the Holy Spirit in each of us, deep in our hearts. Do we turn away or are we soft to the divine intervention of the Spirit in our life?

Often the issue of 'predestination' is raised as a vexing question. Some feel very strongly one way, others very strongly another. I'm not going to even list those ways lest it cause contention. When people ask me my opinion I have a stock answer. I'm not so concerned as to 'how' I am predestined, but 'what I was predestined to.' Far too often people argue about predestination as theological experts – and after all who of us really knows? I think eternity will bring many surprises as to our theological accuracy.

Romans 8: 29 says: "For whom He foreknew, He also predestined *to be* conformed to the image of His Son, that He might be the firstborn among many brethren." The verse is not dealing with 'how' we're predestined. That causes conflict. It majors on 'why' we're predestined. That causes conviction and purpose in life.

The fact that predestination concerns itself with becoming like Jesus interests me a whole lot more than the 'how' argument. A man/woman can be lost in severe debate on 'how' we're predestined; convinced they have the truth, yet be personally unchanged in His presence. Some can even argue as experts and not even be saved. They sadly can even evidence rudeness, hostility and lack of tolerance in presenting their 'how we are predestined' view. How godless and soulish is that? That to me is predestination hypocrisy. Catch hold of the eternal plan and predestined purpose to be made into His image. That is the Bride 'preparing herself.'

The Bride of Christ does not put on her wedding gown till after the 'Bema Seat' or 'Judgment Seat of Christ.' At this judgment all falseness and works of none-effect will be swept away, or burned away. I Corinthians 3: 11 to 15 deals with this. Peter tells us in I Peter 1: 7, "That the genuineness of your faith, *being* much more precious than gold that perishes, though it is tested by fire, may be found to praise, honor, and glory *at the revelation of Jesus Christ*." (Emphasis ours).

Catch hold of the concept. We are being prepared here and now to be part of the Bride of Christ. Better to have those trials of fire in our life, that will prepare us unto His coming, than to be judged and found wanting after His coming. Better to let things burn away now in this life, that will prepare for His coming, than to be judged and found wanting at the Judgment Seat of Christ.

The Lord is indeed preparing His Bride and she 'will' be stunning, breathlessly beautiful. Revelations 19 mentions the 'righteousness' of the saints. That word is actually plural and should be translated 'multiple righteousness.' But, that doesn't fit our strict English grammar code. However, it is simply implying multiple acts of righteous behaviour in the life of the believer. Keep clean and let our cleanliness shine before a decadent world.

The Lord says: "I am jealous over you with a godly jealousy, for I have espoused you to one husband, that I may present you as a chaste virgin to Christ," (II Corinthians 11: 2). Chaste, pure virgin quality. These are serious qualities in a world that ignore the need for purity. Can it be that because the earth now thinks nothing of virginity and purity its meaning in the spiritual has also been grossly demeaned? Paul introduces these qualities in a world that was corrupt to the core – such was Corinth. He emphasizes this by saying: "Not having spot, or wrinkle, or any such thing; but that it should be holy and without blemish."

The more one searches the purity of the Bride's preparation, the greater we stand in need of change, day by day. The Lord desires to say of the church, as allured to in Song of Solomon 4: 7, "Thou art fair, my love, there is no spot in thee." Purity processed through our relationship with Him. It is not a second work of grace. It is an outworking of His salvation. We walk in a finished work, let's live in the same.

The table is a finished work. Redemption is finished. Let's walk in the fullness of it. As we draw around the table may we sense that it should be a daily expression of our life. May we reflect on the finished work. May we be sanctified as the table is sanctified. May we hear, whilst here on earth, the voice of God saying to us, as we sup around the table:

"The king's daughter is all glorious within; her clothing is of wrought gold" (Psalm 45: 13).

Because – she has deliberately made herself ready.

Study/Meditation 51

THE GREAT TABLE OF GOD'S WRATH

If we could literally behold and absorb with our senses the horror of the sight I'm about to refer to, I'm sure we would turn ill as we seek to hide from the Great Table of God's Wrath. Only from Scripture can we glean any insight of the soul-damming sight of the final slaughter.

Birds without number swarmed across the plain. On occasions with senseless noise as their stimulant, they rose as a thick black cloud, blocking the sun and shadowing the earth with their sinister presence. When they settled again they tenaciously fought over the smallest of morsels of flesh, whilst large portions of animal carcasses and human corpses lay rotting for their feeding.

Some birds were literally so full of carrion flesh that amongst their vast numbers they could not get a long enough run to lift off into the air and so flopped awkwardly, squawking into a patch of ravenously feeding birds. This confusion commenced another vicious squabble, as if the intruder was going to take their overabundant spoils.

The carcasses were days old. Every conceivable form of life lay rotting throughout the valley. So great was the slaughter that the corpses of mankind lay in heaps and the process of decay was clearly underway. Here and there piles of the dead were crowned by huge birds of prey, bolder and more savage than the rest. They seemed to be protecting their newfound eyrie as if it was personal territory.

Guns that had once filled the earth with their noise and menace lay mutely still, often still gripped by a mere bone of a finger with an occasional bird indolently and disrespectfully making it their perch. An eagle disrespectfully pulled at the shining medallion that mocked the chest of a dead solider and officer. What had been a crisp uniform now lay in tatters with hardly the presence of the human form inside. It is hard to imagine the depravity of the slaughtered.

Animals of the field and horses that had belonged to their military mounts lay stagnant and still, bloating, rotting with equal purification. Here and there could be seen the remains of an officer of rank. In one corner a king lay faceless and motionless, half immersed in a pool of blood. Horses lay fully bridled, covered over the head with rotting congealed remnants of blood.

With every hour the field that extended beyond vision filled with even more birds of prey. Called, as if by a superhuman voice, they had risen to the air from what seemed to be the four corners of the earth. They made their way by direct invitation to Israel. Their focus eventually narrowed towards the great valley of Esdraelon. Armageddon was over and man's violence filled the cup of wrath. They had drunk their own bitter brew.

Now by prophetic ordination the birds of the air swooped in to take their fill of the dead and sin-ridden rotting. The passage in Ezekiel seem to imply not only were birds of prey present. There's an inference that every type of feathered fowl of the air was there. Could it be that nature itself turned full fury, with even none flesh-eating birds now gorging themselves on flesh, in one last act of depraved hostility against humanity that had caused the earth and creation itself so much pain and concern?

Note that amongst this squalid array of flesh-eating parasites of birds, stray animals wandered here and there feeding also on the seething mass. The carnivorous guests are no longer concerned to catch their prey live and feed on the warmth of fresh blood pulsating from still-kicking life. Nature had turned strange circles of justice till many animals, that had never touched or fed on carrion, were gorging themselves as if it was earth's last meal,

Perhaps the presentation of the above could justifiably be in the minds of some less than spiritually edifying. We agree. Yet, there needs to be a clear warning in this day and age of what impending judgement awaits the earth. This day will come.

Jesus is coming soon. It is only 'Till He Come' that we celebrate the Table of the Lord. World sin and sinning cannot go on unchecked and unnoticed. A log of record is being kept. And man will pay in full one day. The account will be settled.

How strange is the indifference of man to God's provision. He rejects the power of the Blood of Christ, to meet his need and yet will pay with his own blood in the final hour of need. He scorns the power and preciousness of the Table of the Lord, yet will one day be part of the Great Table of God's Wrath.

Those that seek not to be separated to a holy walk in the Christian life, fail to realise that he or she one day will be separated to eternal judgement. Strange creature is man.

The two primary passages that deal with the Great Table of God's Wrath are found in Ezekiel 39: 17 to 22 and Revelation 19: 17 to 18. Here in graphic detail in both the Old and New Testament the ancient seers reach into the future and draw awesome horrific sketches of what will unfold in panoramic detail at the end of time.

Here today we celebrate the Table of the Lord whilst here on earth. Then the earth will be the table where divine judgement will be spread for those who can bear to look. The great collection of the military and their armies will lose their lives. But, they will also lose their distinctiveness and their marks of allegiance. They will all be a blended mass that rose against the Son of God. They will be guests at the dreadful table. Death is their invitation.

Reading of Ezekiel 39 verses 4 and 11; along with Matthew 24: 40 to 42 will be helpful in our understanding. Before us we see the armies and nations of Gog and Magog. Some suggest that this includes Russia. I'll leave exact identification to brighter minds than mine. Gog and Magog were mingled in death with the unsuspecting world. Understanding the titles used of some of the dead we are seeing a wider representation of nations. Let's not get lost in the detail to miss the overall truth. See the broader picture, rather than getting lost in the argument about minor issues.

Some countries today would say they would never be involved in such an uprising. But hold it. Didn't you know that the United Nations itself has actual representation already in the Valley of Esdraelon? Already world representation sit as 'early mourners' on what will one day be the largest field of battle the world has ever known.

We do not suggest that this is the first as well as the last battle at the end of the age. Years have dragged on, three and a half at least, with such horror, bloodshed, and loss of life. The earth has known the fullness of what some call the Great Tribulation. Thermonuclear warfare will have ripped the sky and the world open like a bleeding sore. Vegetation will be so scarce as the Biblical vials are poured out throughout the earth. Water will be so polluted that men will fight over the last drops of clean, uncontaminated water and thousands of others will die whilst drinking the rest.

Death, famine and pestilence accompanied by great fear will stalk humanity in the earth. It will lay rude, crude hands on all at will without respect to person or title. Commerce will lie in devastated ruin and men of wealth will be like paupers within minutes as world financial markets totally collapse.

Demonic forces will seem to have sway for a short time. Possibly the only recognised, accepted worship will be Satanic and demonic aligned. It will attempt to reign on the earth. 'Morals,' no the word cannot be used without making its meaning blush ... the world will be amoral! Truth will not exist. It will crawl in drunken form in the streets, reeling from bitter blows of all, till dead.

All of this will occur to those who will not, in fact actually who will refuse, to come under the shadow of the redemptive purpose of Calvary. Sinners and saints alike do not take lightly the dreadful days ahead as mere passing of fantasy. There are real days of dread to come.

Kings, captains, mighty men, cavalry and all men both bond and free as well as horses are listed amongst the rotting carrion on whom the birds of prey, and nature-revolted carnivores, are feeding. Men, women and children had turned in one last bitter rage against the coming of the Son of God Himself.

When we read the passages that deal with this gruesome episode in man's history we are paralysed with awe. Revelation 19 seems to clearly indicate the armies of the world will attempt to turn their weak munitions, capable of destroying mankind but not God, against the very Son of God Himself, as He descends in glory.

Imagine their fantasy in thinking that they could fight against the Lord's Christ. Demon-duped hordes grovelling for cover will be slain by the might and majesty of His coming. Revelation 19: 19 so clearly shows the useless futility of their battling against the Lord and against His army that descends with Him.

Every fowl was filled with the stinking decay of man's flesh (Revelation 19: 21). The Great Table of God's Wrath has not only been spread, but the 'feast' has been consumed. The world reeks of its own end product of sin. "Thus you will be filled at my table," thunders the words of the prophet in Ezekiel 39: 20. My description of this table may to you be graphic and offend some. But, dear friend, it is nothing compared to the horror it will be.

We are privileged to sit around the Table of the Lord. We have/will be spared the violence and horror of that Great Table of God's Wrath. We sit and remember how the power of the blood of Christ has covered mankind and freed us from sin. All that will accept Christ's cleansing power will be safe.

In that day, indeed right now, we are privileged to be redeemed, creatures. May the terror of that awesome day to come to fill us with a holy fire to speak out, live out and go out to warn all mankind of the dread of the Great Table of God's Wrath. Let's tell them about the glorious covering in the Blood of Jesus, and the preciousness of the Lord's Table remembrance.

Study/Meditation 52

THE MILLENNIAL TABLE

I am fully aware of the broad spectrum of belief of any possible reader, especially about matters relating to the second coming of Christ. And, I do not wish to start any controversy on all issues eschatological. I'll leave your great minds to figure out the details. I only want to use the passage we shall consider as a springboard to our meditation. Many take this passage to be relative to the period called the Millennium. You can figure out its exact timing yourself.

Even if the reader would disagree on the timing or existence of the Millennium, it is not the dogmatism of the setting that is my major theme here, rather, let that be minor to the central theme of the working of Calvary and the remembrance of the same around the Table of the Lord. We also do not wish to relegate the table to merely an act of remembrance, but a living expression within the life of every believer.

The passage we shall use, merely as a foil to our study/meditation, to show off the lustre of the gem of salvation, is in Ezekiel. Ezekiel 40: 39 to 43 and 41: 22 and 44: 16 is the centre of our focus. It discusses a table in the temple of what is termed the 'Millennial Period' and the millennial land. What a magnificent temple is described. The building itself is colossal. It holds many magnificent rooms and porches designated for specific religious purposes. As you move from one area to another, from outside to inside you would eventually come to the main entry hall.

A door leads from the entry hall into a side room where the flesh of the sacrifices is washed before being taken to the altar. On each side of the entry hall adjacent to the passageways there are two tables where the animals for sacrifice are slaughtered for the burnt offerings, sin offerings and guilt offerings, to be presented in the temple. Outside of the entry hall, on each side of the stairs going up to the north entrance there are two more tables per side. So there are eight tables in all. Four are inside and four outside where the sacrifices were cut up and prepared.

Inside and outside the tables stood ready to hold the sacrifices still, as it died in a reinstituted sacrificial order. Inside and outside sacrifices were offered. Many Christians today want to be totally inclusive with their Christianity, deeming salvation to be an internal church rite just for their denomination. But salvation should be seen inside and outside the church, and its physical structures, which we somehow have amassed to represent Christianity. Not many 'sinners' feel too comfortable coming into churches. Let us take the message out, through our lives, to them living our Christianity and the power of a redeemed life, so they will not only just see it, but also desire it.

Outside the sanctuary are countless thousands upon thousands that urgently need the message of salvation that the Table of the Lord, so ably speaks. Remember that Jesus Himself was crucified and slaughtered outside the city walls. If these internal and external tables speak of anything it is not to institutionalise the message of the church.

The readings show there were four stone tables where the butchering knives and other implements were laid. There were tables for the sacrifices and tables for the instruments of sacrifice.

Calvary became the table, the table of the world when the Lamb of God was slain upon its rugged stone-crown top. He was spread out for all to see. Access to the Father's great plan was complete through Christ's offering of Himself.

Stone tables held the instruments of sacrifice. Christ is the Rock of Ages. He has become this table from which all mankind can feast.

But, we could view the stone another way. The stone-hard tables can prefigure the stone-hard hearts of mankind. Indeed our sin was the instrument of His death. But His sacrifice liberates mankind. The death of Christ will continue to be the pivotal centre of God's love. Calvary made His great mission complete.

The tables of the Millennium were around the gate. Gates speaks of access. Calvary has given access to every man. Indeed Christ is the door, the gateway and the glory of the access. The tables discussed in the passage are around the north gate. North is a cardinal point of direction. Certainly, Calvary has given mankind the greatest sense of direction in life. "This is the way, walk ye in it," are encouraging words relating to our salvation. The Lord's Table is meant to reinforce that experience. This is a day and age of restlessness. Many lack direction, yet they seek it in the wrong places. Calvary is our direction, compass and clarity. The tables by the north gate speak of this.

As we move from the north gate with its tables associated with the entry hall, we move through a succession of areas, till we stand before the table of Ezekiel 41: 22. We are now in: "The separate place" (Ezekiel 41: 13). When we are considering this temple we are aware of its drastic difference from the wilderness table of Moses, or even the tables of Solomon's Temple. There are no ark or mercy seat, veil, or cherubs above the mercy seat. They are missing. The only article of furniture described is the table or the altar of wood cited in the reading that corresponds to the table of shewbread, which mirrors communion with God.

Here in front of the holy place stands an altar of wood approximately three and a half feet square (just over a metre square). Its height was five and a quarter feet high (nearly two metres). "This is the table that is before the Lord." From the context of the passage, we get the opinion that this table stands alone before the holy place. Reading the last reference shows the importance the Lord places on this table. Wood is an altar, not stone. How symbolic is this of the greatest wooden artefact from the past?

Is there anything more important symbolically than the wooden cross of Calvary? It was raised with sin's evil yet innocent sacrifice hanging from its cruel form. You can almost hear heaven's comment, the same as Ezekiel's when considering the cross. "This is the table that is before the Lord." Never was there a grander provision for mankind.

Previous demonstrations of God's love for humanity have generally been an expression between God and a select group of people, generally speaking, the Jews. But in the consummating hours of Calvary, the veil was rent. Then the world at large, inclusive of all races was for the first time embraced by redemption, and love, and brought into the right relationship with God. So the table of God's provision was spread in His Son and that provision was acceptable. When we gather around the Table of the Lord we are in fact partaking of the acceptable provision.

Within the Old Testament there were occasions where desperate men had laid hold of the horns of the altar to plead for forgiveness. Sometimes it worked, on other occasions it didn't. But there is no altar that mankind can take hold of like Calvary. Though man may try everything he can, to rid his soul of sin, nothing will avail except salvation provided through Jesus. It alone brings right relationship with God. We have to grasp the altar of His love and lie prostrate before His presence, knowing the great redemption that is ours, is only ours through the Father's acceptance of the offering of sin provided by His Son.

Come within the temple and stand quietly around the priests as they move about in their meditation and quiet service. Hear the words of Ezekiel 44: 16 binding their every activity. "They shall enter into my sanctuary, and they shall come near my table, to minister unto me, and they shall keep my charge."

We see a reinstitution of the priestly order, with some changes from the Aaronic order. How and when it may occur we don't exactly know. Yet, what we can be assured of is their attention to sacred duty was similar to priests of old. Take time to review the Old Testament comment on how the priests prepared themselves for service. If every Christian would approach the table with the same sense of preparation, that these priests gave to their coming to the table, then what a difference it would make in the lives of many.

The Lord still requires His priesthood pure and clean. We are now a priesthood of believers. We should all know how to come into His sanctuary. As ordinary people, we need to know whose presence we are coming into. God is there to meet with His people. The priests were told to come near and serve on the table. Too many want to worship Him afar. They came around the table in conformity expecting a blessing from God. But, they didn't live close to redemptive principles or let them course through their being on a daily basis.

Coming close requires determination. "To minister unto Me," was the calling of the priests referred to. Do we feel called to 'minister unto Him,' and therefore drawn close to the table? The instruction was solemn. The priests were to keep His charge. When we gather at the table does it fill us with holy zeal and fire that it invigorates us again to keep the faith that has been committed unto us?

Despite trying to figure out the exact placement of the Millennium, in relation to the coming of Christ, the message of its table is inspiring. It calls for a holy people to continue to serve before God making the world aware, by our lifestyles, that Jesus is the answer.

CONCLUSION TO THE STUDIES & MEDITATIONS

No matter what denomination we represent, there is with each of us a desire that our people will become more like Christ. Attitudes around the Table of the Lord are often only a reflection of other attitudes in a person's life as a whole. If life is casual and indifferent to the demands of full consecration, then no doubt that will be reflected in their attitudes around:

- Reading the Word of God.
- Praying
- Fellowship.
- The Lord's Table.

These essential criteria for personal and church growth are best developed in or by Church attendance. Rapt attention at communion may often be at the eyeball level, not at the heart level. Different people emphasise different aspects of worship as important as being possibly more important than other aspects. We over-emphasise none. The Word of God, Fellowship, Breaking of Bread (communion) and Prayer are all to me co-equally important (Acts 2: 42). They should be held in unified complementation, not a competition with each other.

We trust these studies/meditations contained in this collection will bring lasting blessings to those to whom they are exposed. May Christ be central to every one of our hearts. There is nothing complicated about the Christian life. Although many have made it so.

Perhaps one of the most sublime portions of Scripture I could use in conclusion, expressing the simplicity of what the Lord desires in each and every one of us, is found in Micah 6: verses 7 and 8. It says:

> "Will the Lord be pleased with
> thousands of rams,
> Ten thousand rivers of oil?
> Shall I give my firstborn *for* my transgression,
> The fruit of my body *for* the sin of my soul?
> He has shown you, O man, what *is* good;

And what does the Lord require of you
But to do justly, To love mercy,
And to walk humbly with your God?"
[Emphasis ours]

The utter simplicity of fellowship with our God and creator, through our Lord Jesus Christ, is clearly seen. This fellowship can be enriched, deepened and constantly renewed around the Table of the Lord.

It is our desire that every Christian would find a new dimension of fellowship, and a new purpose for living the 'Christ-Filled Life' as they gather around His Table. May each of us become more like Christ daily, as we desire to come into His fullness. Let these simple studies/meditations be an inspiration and blessing to the household of faith - *Till He Come!*

Ivan Herald
Sydney
© 2023

(Australian Family And Marriage Education)

www.ingramcontent.com/pod-product-compliance
Lightning Source LLC
Chambersburg PA
CBHW051037160426
43193CB00010B/971